The Singing Voice in Contemporary Cinema

Genre, Music and Sound

Edited by Mark Evans, University of Technology Sydney

Over the last decade Screen Soundtrack Studies has emerged as a lively area of research and analysis mediating between the fields of Cinema Studies, Musicology and Cultural Studies. It has deployed a variety of cross-disciplinary approaches illuminating an area of film's audio-visual operation that was neglected for much of the mid- to late 1900s. Equinox's *Genre, Music and Sound* series extends the emergent field by addressing a series of popular international film genres as they have developed in the post-War era (1945–present); analyzing the variety and shared patterns of music and sound use that characterize each genre.

Published

Drawn to Sound: Animation Film Music and Sonicity
Edited by Rebecca Coyle

Earogenous Zones: Sound, Sexuality and Cinema
Edited by Bruce Johnson

Ludomusicology: Approaches to Video Game Music
Edited by Michiel Kamp, Tim Summers and Mark Sweeney

Movies, Moves and Music: The Sonic World of Dance Films
Edited by Mark Evans and Mary Fogarty

Sounding Funny: Sound and Comedy Cinema
Edited by Mark Evans and Philip Hayward

Terror Tracks: Music, Sound and Horror Cinema
Edited by Philip Hayward

The Music of Fantasy Cinema
Edited by Janet K. Halfyard

The Singing Voice in Contemporary Cinema

Edited by
Diane Hughes and Mark Evans

SHEFFIELD UK   BRISTOL CT

Published by Equinox Publishing Ltd.

UK: Office 415, The Workstation, 15 Paternoster Row, Sheffield, South Yorkshire S1 2BX
USA: ISD, 70 Enterprise Drive, Bristol, CT 06010

www.equinoxpub.com

First published 2020

Diane Hughes, Mark Evans and contributors 2020.

All rights reserved. No part of this publication may be reproduced or transmitted in any form or by any means, electronic or mechanical, including photocopying, recording or any information storage or retrieval system, without prior permission in writing from the publishers.

British Library Cataloguing-in-Publication Data
A catalogue record for this book is available from the British Library.

ISBN: 978 1 78179 445 6 (hardback)
      978 1 78179 112 7 (paperback)
      978 1 78179 738 9 (ePDF)

Library of Congress Cataloging-in-Publication Data
Names: Hughes, Diane, (Music teacher) editor. | Evans, Mark, 1973- editor.
Title: The singing voice in contemporary cinema / edited by Diane Hughes and Mark Evans.
Description: Bristol : Equinox Publishing Ltd, 2020. | Series: Genre, music and sound | Includes bibliographical references and index. | Summary: "This volume focuses on the singing voice in contemporary cinema from 1945 to the present day, and rather than being restricted to one particular genre, considers how the singing voice has helped define and/or confuse genre classification"-- Provided by publisher.
Identifiers: LCCN 2020019348 (print) | LCCN 2020019349 (ebook) | ISBN 9781781794456 (hardback) | ISBN 9781781791127 (paperback) | ISBN 9781781797389 (ebook)
Subjects: LCSH: Motion picture music--History and criticism. | Singing in motion pictures.
Classification: LCC ML2075 .S625 2020 (print) | LCC ML2075 (ebook) | DDC 781.5/42--dc23
LC record available at https://lccn.loc.gov/2020019348
LC ebook record available at https://lccn.loc.gov/2020019349

Typeset by CA Typesetting Ltd.

Contents

1	The Singing Voice in Contemporary Cinema *Diane Hughes and Mark Evans*	1
2	Singing, Sonic Authenticity and Stardom in *Dancer in the Dark* *Nessa Johnston*	20
3	Find Your Voice: Narratives of Women's Voice Loss in American Cinema *Katherine Meizel*	38
4	Singing a Life in Bondage: Black Vocality and Subjectivity in *12 Years a Slave* *Gianpaolo Chiriacò*	52
5	Ghost Singers: The Singing Voice in Korean Pop Cinema *Sarah Keith and Alex Mesker*	73
6	Voices of Sheila: Resignification in Filmic and Non-filmic Contexts *Nina Menezes*	89
7	Before #MeToo: Hearing Vulnerability *Diane Hughes and Mark Evans*	112
8	Trailer Trash or Inspired Vocalization? Song as Promotion and Aesthetic Object in Cinematic Previews *James Deaville and Agnes Malkinson*	132
9	'You've Got a Friend in Me': Singing Voices in the *Toy Story* Films *Natalie Lewandowski and Penny Spirou*	150

10 The Singing Voice and its Use to Evoke Unease, Discomfort
    and Violence   168
    Liz Giuffre and Mark Thorley

11 The Female Singing Voice:
    Gospel, Blues, Epic Stories and Animation   183
    Anne Power

12 From Despicable to Happy:
    Animated Vocality in the Evolution of Felonius Gru   196
    Veronica Stewart and Diane Hughes

    Index   213

1 The Singing Voice in Contemporary Cinema

Diane Hughes and Mark Evans

Cinematic Singing Traditions

While the function of spoken voice in cinema has been explored by theorists such as Chion (1999), the role of singing in cinema has received less discussion and theorization. Where examination has taken place, it has focused on particular singing contexts, vocal techniques, gender concepts or vocal/repertoire types.[1] This volume offers a diverse and inclusive discussion of the use of singing in cinema. Singing is a highly effective form of verbal and non-verbal[2] communication and can instantaneously convey narrative, context and emotion. Singing therefore involves a range of expressive capabilities. Research identifies that vocal parameters (such as loudness and dynamics) expressed through singing may correlate with emotional states including sadness, tenderness, anger and joy (see Scherer et al., 2017). Expressive singing may also be revered for its commemorative, transcendent and/or musical capabilities, or even scorned for a lack of technical prowess. Either way, singing almost invariably elicits attention, reaction and, sometimes, empathy. As such, the deliberate inclusion of singing provides a range of creative possibilities in film.

Songs and their performance by singers are core elements of Western and international music cultures and have been prominent in cinema (see Dyer, 2012) since the introduction of synchsound recording and playback technologies. Inducted into the American National Film Registry for its significance,[3] *The Jazz Singer* (Alan Crosland, 1927) marked Hollywood's entrée into the synchronous sounding[4] of voice and song.[5] Described as "less [of] a talking picture than a singing picture" (Taylor, 2009: 8), this adaptation of a Broadway play[6] featured one of the leading entertainers of the time, Al Jolson. Containing several of Jolson's well-known songs,[7] the film provided a compilation of his then familiar and popular 1920s melodies in a "proto-jukebox" format (Goldmark, 2017: 768). While the most striking and negative aspect of the film for contemporary audiences is no doubt Jolson's performance in "blackface" (wearing theatrical "blackface" make-up), *The Jazz Singer* signalled the naissance of cinematic singing and the screen musical, as well as Hollywood's growing reliance on celebrity capital.

The combination of celebrity and singing in cinema is not without some problematic tensions. The casting of celebrities in film generally increases the likelihood of audience interest and financial reward. Actors, unknown for their singing, may therefore be cast in roles that actually require "singing". Similarly, singers hired for their celebrity status may also be required to "act". Historically, the fledgling era of cinematic singing segued into the Golden Age of Hollywood and the development of studio-produced screen musicals. As the expressive and musical capabilities of singing in cinema became more apparent, the process of dubbing the singing voice was made possible by advances in screen sound technology and voice synchronization capability (Cooper, 2016; Dyer, 2012: 16). Soprano Marni Nixon once explained that vocal dubbing was "part of the working singer's job in Hollywood".[8] Describing dubbing as a way of funding her own "coachings" (Nixon as quoted in Jones, 2008), Nixon's vocal ghosting reportedly covered some of Hollywood's biggest movie stars, including Deborah Kerr in *The King and I* (Walter Lang, 1956), Natalie Wood in *West Side Story* (Jerome Robbins and Robert Wise, 1961) and Audrey Hepburn in *My Fair Lady* (George Cukor, 1964). Indeed, according to Nixon, vocal dubbing was sometimes shrouded in secrecy.[9]

Vocal dubbing was also notable as an uncredited role. While ostensibly no more contentious than the use of stunt doubles in film, vocal dubbing speaks to how the uniqueness and individuality of the acoustic voice may be emulated with calculated intent. While technological treatment and/or enhancement of vocals may assist the dubbing process, a level of actually impersonating the vocal qualities of others may also be required, as Nixon explained: "I took great pride in having nobody notice that there was any difference in the accent, in the speech pattern, and the sound... the timbre of the voice. I tried to colour my voice so that it became them."[10]

Rather enigmatically then, vocal dubbing queries the common assumption that each voice is unique and capable of highly individualized vocal and musical expression (see Hughes, 2014, 2017a; Dyer, 2012: 7). Similarly, the screen musical traditions of singing to track and lip-synching (to support or construct diegetic elements) would ostensibly constrain individual and in-the-moment expression. It was films such as *Les Misérables* (Tom Hooper, 2012) that challenged this notion by enabling, and indeed requiring, the cast to actually perform songs as they were filmed. Hugh Jackman, who played the lead character of Jean Valjean, explained that "[while] the idea of singing live is daunting... what it gives you is this freedom".[11] Such expressive autonomy was achieved in *Les Misérables* by using concealed earpieces that relayed piano accompaniment[12] to the actors and allowed the actors to determine their vocal tone, song tempo and musical realism. As Eddie Redmayne, who played the role of Marius, recalls: "What comes with this way of working is you get the fragility of a voice which matches with the emotions of what a character's saying".[13]

While Hooper's production of *Les Misérables* was innovative in its scope and breadth of capturing live singing, previous direction has also preferred to record live vocals. As director Peter Bogdanovich explained in a 2013 interview with reporter, Kim Masters, on the use of singing in his film *At Long Last Love* (1975):

> [Burt Reynolds and Cybill Shepherd] could carry a tune and put a song over actingwise. It was shot the way they did *Les Mis* [sic]. I loved the spontaneity of live singing. I asked [20th Century] Fox to invent for me some kind of tiny speaker that would fit inside the actor's ear. They had earpieces, and there was an electronic keyboard attached to a camera car, and they sang to that. Subsequently we put the orchestra in. I was doing something they used to do in the very early days of sound, 1929, 1930.[14]

Cinematic singing traditions also include those that may be perceived to be "live" or those that provide an "internally" narrated character perspective. Certainly, as cinematography and associated technologies evolved, the use of singing in cinema shifted from the classic Hollywood musical (with spontaneous outbursts of character song) towards singing in narrative film. Berliner and Furia (2002) explained:

> Crippled by economic difficulties, changing film and music styles, and the loss of the convention that allowed movies to present songs as spontaneous expressions of characters' feelings, contemporary cinema had to develop new conventions in order to incorporate musical entertainment into film narrative... The conventions of cinematic realism seemed to preclude the stage practice of spontaneously breaking into song to express one's feelings (19–20).

The spontaneous song was essentially eclipsed in contemporary cinema by the concept of the "internal song" (Berliner and Furia, 2002: 24–27). By portraying "the psychological interiority of a character" (2002: 25), the internal song can provide a musical monologue or function as a "musical soliloquy" (2002: 24) that may actually be independent of the actor. In this way, the singing of others can symbolically represent a character's "voice". In films where actors are not expected to sing, internal songs may largely determine the cinematic convention of singing and song.

Singing Proficiency, Vocal Production and Vocality

The conventions outlined above mark the distinctive capabilities of singing and the singing voice in cinema. This volume surveys the various ways by which singing is incorporated into contemporary cinema. It is, however, not a book about musicals *per se*; nor is it a volume specifically about the biopic with its potential for specific proclivities and traits. Rather, it considers how singing may be used more broadly, and explores how the voice is both represented and integrated into filmic events. The use of singing and song, within a clever interplay of diegetic and non-diegetic components, extends beyond personified characterization and interiority. It can, in other words, inform narrative. As such, there are myriad motivations for the inclusion of song and singing in cinema (Dyer, 2012: 9–15). Gorbman (2011) writes:

> A character can sing from happiness or sadness, as a response to love or companionship, as an expression of aloneness or group solidarity. Singing can act rhetorically to elicit a reaction from others… Increasingly, in the age of digital music formats and platforms, characters sing to make allusions, often in ironic parody or recontextualisation of song performances; and singing with other characters forges bonds, identities, rivalries (158).

Unlike most discussions on vocal performances, Gorbman theorizes what she terms "artless singing" (157–59). Here, Gorbman extends our understanding of cinematic singing by considering those inclusions not intended to be professional musical performances (159). Artless singing, she argues, tends to be portrayed diegetically, both spontaneous and authentically aligned to the character and/or narrative. Moreover, while there may be variations or imperfections in vocal delivery, such depictions are not necessarily "bad" singing. Rather, it is singing that reflects the everyday, or "real life" (157).

If there is indeed "artless" singing in cinema, it follows that technically impressive singing is, by default, "artful". In turn, Gorbman's notion of the "artless" is problematized; in cinema, even artless singing is "a musical number, a scene scripted, rehearsed, polished, shot, recorded, and edited" (159). As such, all singing in cinema is intended as being musically performed irrespective of whether the execution is "perfect" or otherwise. We therefore extend Gorbman's notion to recognize the plurality of singing inclusions in cinema, rather than its being an implicit dichotomy. We also sidestep subjective terms like artful and artless to show how singing in cinema is complex and multi-dimensional. Cinematic singing is thereby approached in three main ways: intent (principal associations); context (types); and vocal production encompassing proficient through to naïve singing (including vocal technique). Pertinent here then is how singing is physically embodied to produce an acoustic sung sound (vocal production). This requires some unpacking.

The singing voice is a physical method of communication and expression. The production of vocal sound, including vocal technique for singing, requires a coordinated interaction of the breath, airflow and vocal cords/folds, together with resonating spaces and articulatory function (Hughes, 2017b: 15). Singing is also dependent on neural connectivity (Zarate, 2013) with the brain being "uppermost in the systems of singing" (Leigh-Post, 2014: 2); singing aligns with emotive states and lived experiences (Hughes, 2014). The connection and interplay in and for vocal sound is thus anchored in the self (Hughes, 2013) and in individual vocal tract morphology (Fitch and Giedd, 1999). Indeed, singing, as an extension of spoken voice, is inextricably tethered to the individual, as Johar (2016) explains: "Speech is a highly complex interaction of communicative as well as informative characteristics that convey information about the speaker's identity, his emotional state and the situational context" (14).

Singing intent and emotion may be synchronous in their audibility; vulnerability or expressive determination may also be marked. Singing therefore has the capacity to heighten and expose the distinctiveness of the self and of acquired characterization. The physicality of voice, coupled with various socio-cultural contexts, experiences and influences (Hughes, 2014), forms a singer's *vocality* (Tongson, 2011; Meizel, 2011). In these ways, through its communicative, expressive and personalized attributes, vocality defines what it means to be human.

A Taxonomy of Cinematic Singing

To help map how singing is used in film, and to chart the various cinematic uses of the singing voice, we propose the following taxonomy. In doing so, we have analysed a varied mix of iconic and lesser known examples to reveal the depth of contemporary cinematic singing and to avoid a reliance on symbolic or well-known singing inclusions.[15] To exemplify the ubiquity of cinematic singing, we purposely encompass films for wide-ranging audiences. Our discussion concentrates on synchsound in live action cinematography. This is primarily because other aspects of synchsound such as animated anthropomorphized singing is also encompassed in the types and contexts identified below.

Singing as Narrative and Agency

Singing may provide a significant narrative construct for film. Here, the singing forms a focus of the film through which sub-plots develop and emerge. Because the act of singing is featured in such films, methods of vocal production, proficiency and technique are brought to the fore. In these three films, for instance, singing features as the protagonist and/or as the pursuit of the lead role: *Boychoir* (François Girard, 2014), *Florence Foster Jenkins* (Stephen Frears, 2016) and *Teen Spirit* (Max Minghella, 2018).

In *Boychoir*, singing (as musical expression) leads the fictional narrative, as the film's director, François Girard, explains:

> [Music is] a very powerful language to connect with an audience… The words are encumbered in so many different ways… The music speaks freely about emotions and in the film context, I think it's such an incredible vehicle.[16]

The plot is centred on a talented but abandoned and unsettled boy who is accepted into a prestigious choral school. The film features singing instruction and vocal technique in ways that are seamless within the narrative. The boys are instructed in proficient singing and vocal technique (including articulation, vocal tone, breathing and musicality). It is through the acquisition of vocal technique that the true talent of Stet Tate (Garrett Wareing) becomes evident. Initially, Stet is encouraged not to force or overload the singing voice.[17] Once Stet engages with the appropriate technique and musicality, his ability in singing is clearly evident. It is also through his diegetic singing that the sound of the breath for singing is audible. What is more, and despite the long tradition of boys' choral singing,[18] the film obviously challenges practices that frame school choral singing as distinctly "feminine" alongside associated negative male labelling or name-calling which "almost exclusively applied in school choral contexts" (Harrison, Welch and Adler, 2012: 7). These sentiments are echoed by Plum (2015), who notes how *Boychoir* may encourage "boys to sing in all forms of choral performance [which] is a continual challenge for music educators and choral directors" (66).[19]

Where *Boychoir* shows a narrative depiction of proficient singing, other films focus on naïve singing, or a singing style conspicuously bereft of strong vocal technique. One example here is *Florence Foster Jenkins*. This biographical film traces Florence Foster Jenkins's passionate yet amateurish style of singing, shown with warmth and humour, under the banner of "every voice deserves to be heard".[20] In turn, the singing provides a catalyst by which themes of eccentricity, vulnerability, courage and acceptance are explored. The film takes heiress Florence Foster Jenkins (Meryl Streep)[21] into a world of singing lessons, commercial studios and radio broadcasting, as she ultimately prepares for a performance at Carnegie Hall. Unkind reviews from critics aside, Jenkins nonetheless charms others and garners support as a philanthropist and patron of the arts. Throughout the film, Streep masterfully appropriates Jenkins's naïve singing.[22] Streep's on-screen accompanist, Cosmé McMoon (Simon Helberg), describes Jenkins' singing in a comedic scene thus: "a little flat… her vocal cords, they don't phonate freely, her phrasing is haphazard and as for her sub-glottal pressure, it defies medical science". However, and as Frears described, such naïve singing is often difficult to emulate: "You can only sing badly if you are a good singer, and Meryl is a very good singer, she has a head start."[23]

Similar to both *Florence Foster Jenkins* and *Boychoir*, *Teen Spirit* also focuses on singing aspirations. The film traces teenager, Violet Valenski (Elle Fanning), and her quest to be a professional singer. Opportunities for singing on the Isle of Wight, where Violet lives, are limited. She sings in the church choir and in a local bar. Violet's mother, Maria (Agnieszka Grochowska), believes that singing in the choir should suffice as it is where Violet "sings for God". For Violet, though, it is far from enough. She longs to escape the rural and stifling environment imposed on her by her impoverished mother and their strained circumstances. When talent scouts for a television singing competition, "Teen Spirit", schedule a local audition, Violet enters, unbeknownst to her mother. Instead, she enlists the aid of former opera singer Vlad (Zlatko Buric), who poses as her uncle/manager. The audition process is gruelling. Although she makes it through to the local finals, Violet is told that she should have chosen a song better suited to her vocal range. Vlad is subsequently tasked with both improving Violet's singing and convincing her mother that she should compete. Then, when the winner of the local finals is shown to have fraudulently applied for the competition, Violet makes it to the televised finals instead – and wins.

While the film's narrative veers towards being somewhat stereotypical of triumph over adversity, *Teen Spirit* provides an interesting exposé of television shows that seek to exploit their contestants. It is also a subtle comment on what actually renders a "singer". This is evident throughout the film. Violet's friends refer to her as "a singer"; and when Violet tells "Teen Spirit" producer Jules (Rebecca Hall) that one of her goals is "to sing", Jules replies that "a lot of people like to sing, you can sing". The film includes many examples of diegetic and non-diegetic singing. The diegetic inclusions relate mostly to Violet's respective performances but also include Violet dancing to the music she "hears" through headphones and Vlad playing records of his opera singing. Non-diegetic examples of interiority include those where there is character reflection or narrative ideation.

In each of these films – *Florence Foster Jenkins*, *Boychoir* and *Teen Spirit* – the dichotomy of proficient versus naïve singing, or singer versus non-singer, is evident. These ambiguities mirror entrenched societal perceptions, as Pascale (2005) explains:

> The Western perspective of singing is wedded to a multitude of assumptions and beliefs and, over a period of time, has taken on complex meaning. It is associated with subtle nuances, such as valuing the high, lilting soprano voice over the alto. It is connected to various philosophies and strongly held convictions, such as improving vocal performance through the mastery of musical literacy, and even exclusionary practices, such as selecting out the "better singers" [sic] and suggesting that others refrain from singing at all (166).

Due to such divergent abilities and experiences, then, singing may be relatable or aspirational, scorned or revered; it may provide social and cultural commentary, or provoke attention. In all three filmic examples considered above, it is the actual singing that provides individual agency.

Singing as Bonding or Healing

Regardless of whether a person identifies as a singer or not, singing can still help with both socialization and human bonding. Reflecting on their research, Pearce, Launay and Dunbar (2015) wrote:

> the distinguishing feature of singing was that it bonded groups more quickly than the other activities... in the singing classes, shared musical activity initially facilitated group bonding by bypassing the need to get to know everyone in the class individually, creating general feelings of positivity towards everyone present (7).

As a universal capability that requires embodied experience and a level of personal vulnerability, singing creates immediacy and evokes response. In turn, several films are noteworthy for their portrayals of group singing as a meaningful route to human connection.

Almost Famous (Cameron Crowe, 2000) celebrates rock music through its inclusion of numerous, often iconic classics, in ways that ensure a rock and roll sensibility permeates the film's narrative. *Almost Famous* captures the nomadic "life on the road" as the somewhat fractured members of the band, Stillwater, tour and interact with fans and groupies. A bus scene that features 'Tiny Dancer' (Elton John and Bernie Taupin, 1972) proves a key bonding moment for those on the tour. As the song starts, diegetic elements come into play: heads nodding in time, drumsticks beating, and individuals gradually join in singing to create a unison chorus effect. Similar bonding is seen in *Beautiful Girls* (Ted Demme, 1996) when piano player Willie Conway (Timothy Hutton) leads his friends in a rendition of 'Sweet Caroline' (Neil Diamond, 1969). Here, unrealized potential, dreams and relationships are supplanted by raucous singing that appears natural and spontaneous. In *Wayne's World* (Penelope Spheeris, 1992), singing as bonding is heard in several scenes and is used to underscore developing relationships and friendships. In one particular scene, bonding is achieved through the collective singing of 'Bohemian Rhapsody' (Freddie Mercury, 1975). The scene depicts five male friends driving together in a car as they head for a night out. As the characters join in raucously singing over various lines of the original track, they culminate with collective singing and energetically "head bang" to a rousing guitar section. In this case, the synchronization of 'Bohemian Rhapsody' actually reignited the song's off-screen popularity.[24] Clearly then, the influence and impact of filmic singing and song can extend well beyond the film alone.

The healing connection afforded through communal singing appears to be heightened when its inclusion is motivated by spirituality and/or hope.[25] This is evident in *Breakthrough* (Roxann Dawson, 2019) in a scene that follows the decision to remove the life support of teenager, John Smith (Marcel Ruiz). As his medically induced coma treatment is halted, John's friends gather outside his hospital room and collectively unite in singing. The diegetic singing of 'Oceans (Where Feet May Fail)' (Matt Crocker, Joel Houston and Salomon Ligthelm, 2013) is reminiscent of a prayer vigil; candles flicker as the crowd builds and the communal singing becomes more prominent.

Singing as Manifestation of Chemistry or Romance

Singing has long been associated with romance in Western culture. No matter the genre or style, love has been a perennial theme of arias and songs, some of which are practically mandatory at events like weddings. In the two examples considered here though, karaoke scenes serve to show how singing can convey not just romantic love but a profound and almost palpable "chemistry" as well. The use of karaoke singing in film also serves to depict vulnerability and openness which is conducive to furthering a sense of emotional connectivity. In *Lost In Translation* (Sofia Coppola, 2003), a party-like karaoke scene works towards the film's two leads Charlotte (Scarlett Johansson) and Bob (Bill Murray) naïvely singing to each other. The focus here is on their growing intimacy afforded by their singing, albeit that there are others in the scene and that the attraction between the two leads remains unrealized. While the singing strengthens an unlikely and developing bond between the two, it also enables the characters to appear vulnerable and deeply expressive to each other. Similarly, in *My Best Friend's Wedding* (P. J. Hogan, 1997), karaoke again sets the stage for expressive singing with a more comedic intent. Kimberly Wallace (Cameron Diaz) sings her version of 'I Just Don't Know What To Do With Myself' (Burt Bacharach and Hal David, 1964) to her devoted fiancé Michael O'Neal (Dermot Mulroney), naïvely and painfully out of key. While fellow bar patrons start to heckle and jeer, Michael looks on lovingly; Kimberly perseveres – and wins over the bar crowd as well with her (ultimately) spirited performance.

Singing as Character Revelation, Motivation and/or Realization

The use of singing as motivation and to aid in the realization of self-identity is clearly evident in *Dumplin'* (Anne Fletcher, 2018). Set in the world of teenage beauty pageants, pageant convenor and former pageant winner Rosie Dickson (Jennifer Aniston) clashes with her teenage daughter, Willowdean Dickson (Danielle Macdonald). Willowdean does not share her mother's love of beauty competitions, has low self-esteem, and desperately needs someone to believe in her. Her one adult confidant, Aunt Lucy (Hillary Begley), has died, but passed on to her niece a love of Dolly Parton. Willowdean thus finds solace and guidance from impersonators who regularly perform Parton's hits at a local club. The singing in *Dumplin'* is therefore mostly lip-synched save for a striking "live" vocal performance by an "unlikely" runner-up in the pageant, Millie Michalchuk (Maddie Baillio). However, both the lip-synching and Millie's almost gospel rendition provide poignant inspiration for character self-realization and motivation.

Another example of singing as motivation occurs in the satirical comedy, *The Secret Life of Walter Mitty* (Ben Stiller, 2013). The diegetic singing of 'Space Oddity' (David Bowie, 1969) by Cheryl Melhoff (Kristen Wiig) precedes and underscores a helicopter scene in which magazine employee, Walter Mitty (Ben Stiller), becomes increasingly confident. This is despite Mitty's usual cautious approach to life and his reservations about the seemingly intoxicated helicopter pilot. He is, however, inspired to board the flight by imagining his co-worker Cheryl, with whom he is infatuated, singing to him. The singing starts with simple acoustic guitar accompaniment where Cheryl assumes a "piedpiperesque" role that sees her lead Mitty outside towards the helicopter. The diegetic components are masterfully and gradually interwoven with the Bowie track; by the time Mitty jumps into the helicopter, only Bowie's track is audible.

Less humorous are filmic depictions of singing which hinge on ridicule and humiliation. One such scene appears in *Nashville* (Robert Altman, 1975), through the character of Sueleen Gay (Gwen Welles) (see also Chapter 7, this volume). Here, the somewhat deceived Sueleen naïvely sings to a room full of men who expected her to perform a striptease and who ridicule her singing efforts. Sueleen, however, is utterly confused as she just wants to sing. She is bullied into finishing the show and, crestfallen, she reluctantly undresses.

Singing as Uplifting and Comedic Components
There are many examples where singing is used in film for comedic effect, as comic relief, or as "feel good" celebration/distraction. All these devices are evident in *Isn't It Romantic* (Todd Strauss-Schulson, 2019). After being mugged, architect and love cynic Natalie (Rebel Wilson) regains consciousness and finds herself in a romantic parallel universe. The narrative focuses on Natalie's efforts to escape this altered reality in which her co-worker Josh (Adam DeVine) is set to marry. At a pre-wedding function, Josh's fiancée Isabella (Priyanka Chopra) coerces Natalie into singing. The subsequent and reluctant karaoke performance of 'I Wanna Dance with Somebody' (George Merrill and Shannon Rubicam, 1987) is both comic and subversive. As Natalie taps the microphone, feedback is audible and a waitress accidently pulls out a power cord as Natalie starts singing. Natalie continues and a gradual diegetic accompaniment is heard as a waiter shakes a cocktail in time. The percussive accompaniment continues with elements of food and beverage being served and tapped, and darts being thrown onto a dartboard. A group of female "backing vocalists" emerge from the audience to sing the chorus along with Natalie, and in her efforts to divert Josh's focus away from Natalie, Isabella steps in between Natalie and Josh to lead a call and response "duelling" section. The inclusion of 'I Wanna Dance with Somebody' contemporaneously serves as both comedy and comic relief. However, celebratory singing led by a now in-love Natalie back in the normal world closes the film as the cast collectively sing/perform 'Express Yourself' (Madonna and Stephen Bray, 1989).

A similar sensibility is provided in *Little* (Tina Gordon, 2019). An often discourteous but successful business mogul, Jordan Sanders (Regina Hall), is transformed into a 13-year-old version of herself (Marsai Martin) and has to negotiate the world as a school student under the guardianship of her former personal assistant, April

Williams (Issa Rae). In a key bonding scene the teenage Jordan and adult April spontaneously start performing 'I'm Going Down' (Norman Whitfield, 1976) in a crowded restaurant; while some patrons look on bemused or bewildered, others clearly enjoy the performance. Two elderly patrons join in the singing with April and the song ends to appreciative applause. Jordan and April sing using elements of soul/rhythm and blues and pop vocals that include hard onsets and soft releases of sound, call and response, and melisma. Here, the vocals are strong and purposeful in delivery. The comedic elements extend the narrative by revealing that the teenage Jordan is not going to be dictated to by her adult assistant.

Comedic singing often has a specific and isolated role in films and in these contexts, the singing is neither central to the plot nor is it comprehensively featured. The following examples are where the comedic singing is largely inconsequential to the narrative development. In *Superbad* (Greg Mattola, 2007), the singing of 'These Eyes' (Randy Bachman and Burton Cummings, 1968) by Evan (Michael Cera) is far from perfect or even proficient. Evan's singing displays insecure vocal register flips, breaks and musicality issues in both pitch and rhythm. This entertaining performance provides comic relief that diffuses a scene in which Evan is surrounded by drug users. Similarly, in *Easy A* (Will Gluck, 2010), Olive Penderghast (Emma Stone) sings 'Pocketful of Sunshine' (Natasha Bedingfield, Danielle Brisebois and John Shanks, 2008) to an imaginary track after opening a card from her grandmother that "plays" the song. Over the course of the next two days, Olive is seen singing while painting her toenails, singing to her dog, and even singing in the shower while washing her hair. Again, the singing is comic with varying dynamics and an alliterative word play when at one point Olive repeatedly opens and closes the card to repetitively sing. The singing of 'Afternoon Delight' (Bill Danoff, 1976) appears in a scene in *Anchorman: The Legend of Ron Burgundy* (Adam McKay, 2004) in which Ron Burgundy (Will Ferrell) discusses the meaning of "love" with male colleagues. Ron bursts into song and is gradually joined by his male colleagues who provide harmonic interest through a chorus of different vocal qualities including falsetto. Their singing is interrupted by phrases of spoken dialogue in an almost call and response pattern. Here, the comedic singing serves to "camouflage" underlying sexist behaviours and gendered stereotypes.

Singing as Performance
In films that feature singing performances within the narrative, the act of singing may be evident as a showcase for the featured performer. Films such as *The Rose* (Mark Rydell, 1979) featuring Bette Midler, *The Bodyguard* (Mick Jackson, 1992) featuring Whitney Houston, and *A Star is Born* (Bradley Cooper, 2018) featuring Lady Gaga reveal a breadth of cinematic singing as performance. Showcasing singing as performance is also explored in the film *Inside Llewyn Davis* (Joel Cohen and Ethan Cohen, 2013) in which the narrative traces the story of fictional folk singer, Llewyn

Davis (Oscar Isaac). With his personal life in turmoil, Davis also continually grapples with life as a folk singer; the year is 1961. Nothing Davis plans or undertakes is ideal either in process or realization. Davis is hired to play guitar and sing backing vocals for the recording of a song with comedic elements,[26] 'Please Mr Kennedy' (Ed Rush, George Cromarty, T Bone Burnett, Justin Timberlake, Joel Coen and Ethan Coen, 2013). While there are numerous "live" folk singing performances throughout the film, the recording of this particular song is vocally striking. Although Davis is "happy for the gig", he seems unimpressed with the song. The song appears as an on-screen live performance of a studio recording where Davis sings alongside the song's on-screen writer (and off-screen co-writer) Jim Berkey (Justin Timberlake) and fellow singer Al Cody (Adam Driver). Following the song's studio rehearsal, the recording of the singing is interactive with unison singing, harmonies, answering phrases and personalized vocal nuances. The contrast between the singing voices adds to the vocal integrity of the song's performance.

Singing as performance in cinema also allows for the narrative of audience participation/response to be foregrounded. In *High Fidelity* (Stephen Frears, 2000), record store salesman and lead singer in a band, Barry Judd (Jack Black), gives an energetic performance of 'Let's Get It On' (Marvin Gaye and Ed Townsend, 1973). In the audience are Rob Gordon (John Cusack) and his recently reunited girlfriend, Laura (Iben Hjejle). Rob is not convinced that the band will be well received. He is pleasantly relieved when Barry starts to sing and is seen to happily dance with Laura. By featuring the audience response, the performance serves to simultaneously extend the narratives of Barry, Rob and Laura. A different, almost voyeuristic, audience perspective is offered in the film, *Emma* (Douglas McGrath, 1996). Here, the performance begins with Emma Woodhouse (Gwyneth Paltrow) playing a period piano (a pianoforte) in a recital context. The camera pans from behind the audience as Emma begins to sing. As Emma is about to segue into a second verse, Frank Churchill (Ewan McGregor) stands and begins to sing. He joins Emma at the piano and they continue the song as a duet. Frank's clear vocal tone provides a contrast to Emma's gentle and breathy singing. The song, 'Silent Worship' (Arthur Somervell, 1928),[27] is performed in a historical context. The singing features meticulous pronunciation and somewhat predictable phrasing. As Frank sings the melody, Emma sings a lower harmony which is slightly at odds with a "classical" aesthetic. The recital continues with a more rounded classical resonance evident in Jane Fairfax's (Polly Walker) subsequent performance. In contrast to the structured performance, the impromptu singing of Violet Sanford (Piper Perabo) on top of the bar in *Coyote Ugly* (David McNally, 2000) is seen to temper the crowd's aggression and allows the audience to join in singing 'One Way Or Another' (Debbie Harry and Nigel Harrison, 1979). Later, Violet features singing as structured performance with 'Can't Fight The Moonlight' (Diane Warren, 2000) and the film concludes with a cameo appearance of LeAnn Rimes singing with Violet.

Singing as Interiority
Songs are significant in a film's soundtrack and when featured as interiority in film, they often represent emotional and reflective moments. For example, 'Each Coming Night' (Sam Beam, 2004, performing as Iron & Wine) in *The Last Song* (Julie Anne Robinson, 2010) provides a subtle underscore of scenes in which a father, Steve Miller (Greg Kinnear), is dying. As Steve reflects on his children, the soft and breathy vocal tone of Beam's voice is reminiscent of Steve's vulnerability and sadness. The song is heard over images and diegetic non-verbal sounds as the children are seen supporting their father. Vocal underscoring as interiority does not preclude the inclusion of sounds relating to the diegetic action. In such instances, the audibility of the singing may vary in and across scenes. In *Honey* (Bille Woodruff, 2003), Honey Daniels (Jessica Alba) reflects on not prioritizing her friendship with Gina (Joy Bryant). The song 'Know Your Way' (Ebony Alleyne and Richard Taylor; performed by Ebony Alleyne and later released in 2007) underscores Honey's introspection and is heard throughout Honey's subsequent discussion with Gina although at a much softer level. In both examples, singing provides an interior monologue and represents the "vocal sound" and inner voice of the respective characters.

Overview of Singing in Contemporary Cinema

The functional taxonomy outlined above highlights several of the many intents and contexts in which singing may be situated in film. The respective contributors to this volume expand our taxonomy with a range of key associations discussed below. While singing inclusions may encompass one or more principal associations, this volume is largely focused on cinematic singing as female vocality (Chapters 2 and 3), as cultural expression (Chapters 4 to 6), as industry signifiers (Chapters 7 and 8), and as variations of character revelation (Chapters 9 to 12).

The first two chapters of this volume consider deployments of the female singing voice with varying narrative intents and levels of agency. Nessa Johnston (Chapter 2) explores singing as performance through the lens of "singer as actor". Here, Johnston analyses Björk's appearance in *Dancer in the Dark* (Lars von Trier, 2000) and argues that Björk's singing simultaneously carries "embodied life" and a recognizable "sonic signature". Johnston argues that despite the contrast between Björk's characterization of Selma and her singing in rehearsal versus her singing in performance, the singing is "always distinctively Björk's voice". Interestingly, and as Johnston attests, it is the appearance of Björk as Selma that collapses the delineation of film and pop star. Katherine Meizel (Chapter 3) further extrapolates female singing in film by exploring voices in relation to sociocultural themes including individual agency and voicing difference. She investigates the ways that young women's voices may be "manipulated, appropriated, silenced, suppressed, and ultimately regained". By exploring female singing and a key association of agency, Meizel examines a chronology of voicelessness in cinema. She identifies an ideological shift that restores female cinematic singing from "symbolizing the vulnerability of identity" including its "susceptibility to manipulation" to that of affirming individual agency through the context of "found" voice.

In the next three chapters, consideration is given to cinematic singing and cultural expression through which narrative and/or agency are explored. Here, associations relating to heritage and culture are key. Gianpaolo Chiriacò (Chapter 4) leads with a poignant discussion on the significance of singing within the American slave culture. He does so by exploring black vocality in *12 Years A Slave* (Steve McQueen, 2013) and argues that McQueen makes a filmic contribution to the "contemporary conceptualization of a traditional African-American singing voice". Furthermore, Chiriacò positions the way that sound in the film is polarized and how this differentiation reflects narrative polarities including "slavery versus freedom". Sarah Keith and Alex Mesker (Chapter 5) examine the "tensions and ambiguities related to the singing voice in K-pop" through their exploration of two South Korean films. By focusing largely on female singers and singing in these films, Keith and Mesker discuss the impact of modernity/contemporary culture that reveals tension between expectations of vocal ownership as opposed to the negation of vocal identity. Nina Menezes (Chapter 6) discusses Bollywood singing in both filmic and non-filmic contexts. She does so by examining a song and dance sequence from the film, *Tees Maar Khan* (Farah Khan, 2010) and by considering the inherent use of singing and elements of parody. She posits that these and other elements contribute to a "highly-gendered, musical, textual, visual pastiche", and concludes with discussion around resignification.

The following two chapters focus on different aspects of cinematic singing as depicted in the music and film industries. As such, key associations aligned to aspects of performance, expectations and individual agency are evident. Hughes and Evans (Chapter 7) provide an analysis of singers and songs in the context of the music industries and, in doing so, examine a number of salient and topical issues. Their chapter traverses key associations of singing in cinema as narrative and agency together with singing as performance. In some examples, singing as comedy and/or romance is used to mask industry challenges and concerns. In their discussion on singing and songs as heard in film trailers, James Deaville and Agnes Malkinson (Chapter 8) position song in film trailers as being both aesthetically and commercially significant. They argue that trailers provide audience engagement largely through the allure created by "the sung song" and conclude that the uses of singing in film and in trailers are different, and that the latter expressively serves as an enticement for the associated film.

The final four chapters of this volume highlight the power of cinematic singing in relation to the principal association and capabilities of cinematic singing for character realization and performed intent in animated and non-animated contexts. Natalie Lewandowski and Penny Spirou (Chapter 9) canvas appropriations of the song, 'You've Got a Friend in Me' (Randy Newman, 1995), in the *Toy Story* film series. They argue that the "re-use and re-versioning of the song through the use of several different character voices and genre manipulations illustrates the importance of song in representing a continuing voice for otherwise 'lifeless' animated characters". Liz Giuffre and Mark Thorley (Chapter 10) examine the use of cinematic singing that extends beyond "performances of pleasantness" to "evoke feelings of unease or violence". In this chapter, Giuffre and Thorley explore singing and communal singing, and its impact, in specific filmic contexts. While their discussion demonstrates how "the central characters use singing… to administer control or intimidation", Giuffre and Thorley conclude that these uses of singing cannot be divorced from the film's overall sonic context. By primarily exploring the key association of singing as character revelation, Anne Power (Chapter 11) considers the ways that "female voices command attention" in film. Choosing not to enter potential debates surrounding the two animated films – *Hercules* (Ron Clements and John Musker, 1997) and *Sita Sings the Blues* (Nina Paley, 2008) – Power instead explores cinematic singing largely through the advancement of narrative and characterization. She discusses vocal tone, along with associated visual and musical factors, that influence the resultant synchronization of singing and concludes that the impact of singing in film occurs through a juxtaposition of vocal and musical elements. In the final chapter, Veronica Stewart and Diane Hughes (Chapter 12) consider the term "vocality" and its related contexts so as to generate theoretical frameworks for both singer-songwriter vocality and animated vocality. They explore animated vocality through the progressive evolution of the character, Felonius Gru, in the *Despicable Me* films.

Conclusion

The prevalence of singing in cinema is notable and under-analysed. And yet, cinematic inclusions may aid both realism and fantasy in film as the human attraction to singing with its expressive capabilities is profound. Singing is therefore a significant expressive technique in cinema through which the axiom of "finding one's (singing) voice" in all its manifestations – metaphorical, literal, discovered, veiled, ghosted, cultural, celebrated – may be explored. In this volume, we seek to inclusively position singing in film, music and sound studies. Our volume serves to provide comprehensive discourse on filmic singing, on singing as and for elements of narrative, on vocality more broadly, and on singing (re)signification in cinema.

We sincerely thank the respective contributors to this volume, together with the reviewers,[28] whose collective interest and efforts enabled the realization of this volume, *The Singing Voice in Contemporary Cinema*.

About the Authors

Diane Hughes is an Associate Professor in Vocal Studies and Music at Macquarie University. Vocal health and wellbeing are a focus of her work; her research interests include singing contexts such as industries and recording, vocal artistry, emotion in song, the singer-songwriter and vocal pedagogy. She co-authored *The New Music Industries: Disruption and Discovery* (2016) with Evans, Morrow and Keith, published by Palgrave Macmillan. She is an advocate for music education and for multidisciplinary voice studies more broadly.

Professor Mark Evans is Head of the School of Communication at the University of Technology Sydney. He is series editor for the Genre, Music and Sound book series published by Equinox Publishing. Recent books include *Sounding Funny: Comedy, Cinema and Music* (with Phillip Hayward), *Moves, Movies and Music: The Sound of Dance Films* (with Mary Fogarty), and *The New Music Industries: Disruption and Discovery* (co-authored with Hughes, Morrow and Keith), published by Palgrave Macmillan.

Notes

1. Examples of particularized discussions of singing in film include Banfield (2000), Fleeger (2008), Greene (2009) and Dyer (2012).
2. Frith (1998) posits the non-verbal sounds of emotion as "inarticulate articulacy" (192).
3. *The Jazz Singer* was inducted into the National Film Registry in 1996. See https://www.loc.gov/programs/national-film-preservation-board/film-registry/complete-national-film-registry-listing/ (accessed September 18, 2018).
4. Synchronous sound was achieved utilizing Vitaphone technology. This enabled "one motor to drive both the projector and the turntable holding the 16" soundtrack disk", according to Ron Hutchinson, *The Jazz Singer*, Library of Congress (n.d.), https://www.loc.gov/programs/static/national-film-preservation-board/documents/jazz_singer.pdf (accessed September 18, 2018).
5. The Vitaphone system utilized a sound-on-disc format that was then amplified throughout picture theatres (Koszarski, 1989: 16).
6. The short story "A Day of Atonement" (Raphaelson, 1922) and a subsequent play *The Jazz Singer* (Raphaelson, 1925) led to the development of the movie (Goldmark, 2017: 767–68).
7. This is listed in the trailer to *The Jazz Singer (1927) - Trailer*, Warner Bros. Entertainment, https://www.youtube.com/watch?v=mW6GfJ5Tvms (accessed January 8, 2019).
8. Nixon's quotation is reported in an interview with Roger Catlin in 2013 the source of which is "Stand-in for the Stars – the Art of the Dubbing Singer", *The Guardian*. The article was published in *Guardian Weekly* which *"incorporates material from the Washington Post"*. See https://www.theguardian.com/film/2013/jun/25/marni-nixon-hepburn-musicals-monroe (accessed September 19, 2018).
9. See Chris Jones (2008), "A Visit with Legendary Hollywood 'Ghost Voice' Marni Nixon" [Interview]. *Chicago Tribune*, https://www.youtube.com/watch?v=dIS7xnE4nNA (accessed September 19, 2018).
10. Ibid.
11. This quotation by Hugh Jackman is featured in Universal Pictures (2012), *Les Misérables Singing Live Featurette - Official HD* [Featurette], https://www.youtube.com/watch?v=0Su_n0PAuXk (accessed September 20, 2018).

12. The piano accompaniment was ultimately replaced with full orchestration according to production sound mixer, Simon Hayes, the source of which is Universal Pictures (2012), *Les Misérables Singing Live Featurette - Official HD* [Featurette], https://www.youtube.com/watch?v=0Su_n0PAuXk (accessed September 20, 2018).
13. This quotation by Eddie Radmayne is featured in Universal Pictures (2012), *Les Misérables Singing Live Featurette - Official HD* [Featurette], https://www.youtube.com/watch?v=0Su_n0PAuXk (accessed September 20, 2018).
14. Bogdanovich's quotation is featured in a 2013 interview "Peter Bogdanovich on the Making of 'At Long Last Love' (QandA)" with Kim Masters, *The Hollywood Reporter*, https://www.hollywoodreporter.com/news/peter-bogdanovich-making-at-long-562198 (accessed September 20, 2018). An edited version of the interview is also available in *The Hollywood Reporter* 419(21): 84. Both versions are based on an interview conducted by Masters for the Californian radio station KCRW; see https://www.kcrw.com/about (accessed May 27, 2020).
15. Symbolic singing inclusions often appear in "listoid" type compilations in popular culture media. Examples of these include *The Best Movies About Singing* available at https://www.ranker.com/list/best-movies-about-singing/ranker-film and *Top 10 Unexpected Singing Moments in Non-Musical Movies* available at https://www.youtube.com/watch?v=P_NdwVi4k0k (accessed May 28, 2020).
16. This is from an interview with Bonnie Laufer Krebs (2014), *BOYCHOIR - Garrett Wareing and Francois Girard Interview*, https://www.youtube.com/watch?v=eunqp5a1OgM (accessed September 24, 2018).
17. Vocal overload has the potential to damage the voice (see Hughes 2017b).
18. This is an established tradition in the United Kingdom where boys are selected "purely on musical and vocal aptitude" (Williams, 2012: 125).
19. Two additional examples of cinematic representations that feature and "promote" children's choral singing, along with aspects of vocal technique and musicality in song, are *The Chorus/Les Choristes* (Christophe Barratier, 2004) and the documentary, *Wide Open Sky: Little Voices, Big Dreams* (Lisa Nicol, 2015).
20. This is featured in the film trailer by Paramount Pictures (2016), *Florence Foster Jenkins Trailer (2016) - Paramount Pictures*, https://www.youtube.com/watch?v=qth6y8SrXNY (accessed October 15, 2018).
21. Additional depictions of Streep's filmic singing are outlined by Gorbman (2011: 159–70).
22. Florence Foster Jenkins, as a performer, is described as being somewhat deluded in believing that she was indeed "a great coloratura soprano" (Sjoerdsma, 2008: 131).
23. This was reported by Anne Thompson for IndieWire on August 12, 2016, in "How Meryl Streep Embraced Being Awful in 'Florence Foster Jenkins' – Video", https://www.indiewire.com/2016/08/meryl-streep-florence-foster-jenkins-stephen-frears-interview-hugh-grant-1201715740/ (accessed May 29, 2020). The full YouTube interview is available at https://www.youtube.com/watch?time_continue=241&v=QLjohHjA7AQ&feature=emb_logo. Similar reporting includes an interview with Stephen Frears by Iain Blair in 2016 the source of which is "Stephen Frears: Florence Foster Jenkins: Telling the Story of the World's Worst Singer", *Post*, September 2016, p. 14, *Gale Academic Onefile*.
24. Elahe Izardi, in 2018, reported that the inclusion of 'Bohemian Rhapsody' in *Wayne's World* resulted in the song charting at No. 2 in the Billboard Hot 100 some twenty years after the song's original release. Source: "Scaramouche! The Story of How 'Bohemian Rhapsody' Ended up in *Wayne's World* and Became a Phenomenon Again", *The Washington Post*, https://www.washingtonpost.com/arts-entertainment/2018/11/02/scaramouche

-story-how-bohemian-rhapsody-ended-up-waynes-world-became-phenomenon-again/ (accessed September 27, 2019). This is supported by the Billboard Hot 100 listing that followed the film's release in February 1992 as the song is charted as peaking at No. 2 on May 9, 1992. See https://www.billboard.com/music/queen/chart-history (accessed September 27, 2019).
25. Singing in religious contexts is usually communal and can be aligned to prayer (for example, Smith, 2010).
26. The comedic elements are particularly evident in the answering phrases when a bass/baritone voice provides a stark contrast to the higher male voices.
27. The song version is an appropriation of an aria, 'Non lo dirò col labbro', which was written two hundred years earlier by George Frideric Handel for his *Tolomeo* opera. A *Grove Music Online* entry by Anthony Hicks on "Tolomeo [Tolomeo re di Egitto ('Ptolemy, King of Egypt')]" lists the English text ("Did you not see my lady") attribution to Arthur Somervell, under the 'Silent Worship' title. See also The LeiderNet Archive and notes by Paul Fontenoy, at https://www.lieder.net/lieder/get_text.html?TextId=18711 and https://www.lieder.net/lieder/get_text.html?TextId=18713 (accessed September 27, 2019).
28. The reviewers encompassed singing voice researchers and media/film researchers. We are grateful for the diligence they employed during the review process.

References

Banfield, S. (2000) "Stage and Screen Entertainers in the Twentieth Century". In *The Cambridge Companion to Singing*, edited by J. Potter, 61–82. Cambridge: Cambridge University Press.

Berliner, T. and P. Furia (2002) "The Sounds of Silence: Songs in Hollywood Films since the 1960s". *Style: Time, Music, and Textuality* 36/1: 19–35.

Chion, M. (1999) *The Voice in Cinema*, trans. Claudia Gorbman. New York: Columbia University Press.

Cooper, D. (2016) "'Pictures That Talk and Sing': Sound History and Technology". In *The Cambridge Companion to Film Music*, edited by M. Cooke and F. Ford, 29–50. Cambridge: Cambridge University Press.

Dyer, R. (2012) *In the Space of a Song: The Uses of Song in Film*. Abingdon, Oxon: Routledge.

Fitch, W. T. and J. Giedd (1999) "Morphology and Development of the Human Vocal Tract: A Study Using Magnetic Resonance Imaging". *Journal of the Acoustical Society of America* 106/3: 1511–522.

Fleeger, J. (2008) "Protecting an Aria, Singing the Cinema: In Search of a Shared Vocabulary for Opera and Film Studies". *Music, Sound and Moving Image* 2/2: 121–25.

Frith, S. (1998) *Performing Rites: Evaluating Popular Music*. Oxford: Oxford University Press.

Goldmark, D. (2017) "Adapting *The Jazz Singer* from Short Story to Screen: A Musical Profile". *Journal of the American Musicological Society* 70/3: 767–817.

Gorbman, C. (2011) "Artless Singing". *Music, Sound, and the Moving Image* 5/2: 157–71.

Greene, L. (2009) "Speaking, Singing, Screaming: Controlling the Female Voice in American Cinema". *The Soundtrack* 2/1: 63–76.

Harrison, S., G. Welch and A. Adler (2012) "Men, Boys and Singing". In *Perspectives on Males and Singing*, Landscapes: The Arts, Aesthetics, and Education, 10, edited by S. Harrison, G. Welch, and A. Adler, 3–12. Dordrecht: Springer Netherlands.

Hughes, D. (2013) "An Encultured Identity: Individuality, Expressivity and the Singing-self". *Australian Voice* 15: 13–19.

Hughes, D. (2014) "Contemporary Vocal Artistry in Popular Culture Musics: Perceptions, Observations and Lived Experiences". In *Teaching Singing in the 21st Century*, Landscapes: The Arts, Aesthetics, and Education, 14, edited by S. Harrison and J. O'Bryan, 287–301. Dordrecht: Springer Netherlands.

Hughes, D. (2017a) "'Art' to Artistry: A Contemporary Approach to Vocal Pedagogy". In *The Routledge Research Companion to Popular Music Education*, edited by G. D. Smith, Z. Moir, M. Brennan, S. Rambarran and P. Kirkman, 177–89. London and New York: Routledge, Taylor and Francis Group.

Hughes, D. (2017b) "Vocal Health Challenges and Contemporary Singing: Implications and Advocacy". *Australian Voice* 18: 14–22.

Johar, S. (2016) *Emotion, Affect and Personality in Speech: The Bias of Language and Paralanguage*. Switzerland: Springer International Publishing, SpringerBriefs in Speech Technology.

Jones, C. (2008) "A Visit with Legendary Hollywood 'Ghost Voice' Marni Nixon" [Interview]. *Chicago Tribune*. https://www.youtube.com/watch?v=dIS7xnE4nNA (accessed September 19, 2018).

Koszarski, R. (1989) "Vitaphone's First Night". *MoMA* 2/2: 16–17.

Leigh-Post, K. (2014) *Mind-body Awareness for Singers: Unleashing Optimal Performance*. San Diego: Plural Publishing.

Meizel, K. (2011) "A Powerful Voice: Investigating Vocality and Identity". *Voice and Speech Review* 7/1: 267–74.

Pascale, L. M. (2005) "Dispelling the Myth of the Non-singer: Embracing Two Aesthetics for Singing". *Philosophy of Music Education Review* 13/2: 165–75.

Pearce, E., J. Launay and R. I. M. Dunbar (2015) "The Ice-breaker Effect: Singing Mediates Fast Social Bonding". *Royal Society Open Science* 2/150221: 1–9. http://dx.doi.org/10.1098/rsos.150221 (accessed October 15, 2019).

Plum, N. (2015) "The Inspiration of Music and Film: *Boychoir* Brings Singing to the Big Screen". *The Choral Journal* 55/9: 65–66.

Scherer, K. R., J. Sundberg, B. Fantini, S. Trznadel and F. Eyben (2017) "The Expression of Emotion in the Singing Voice: Acoustic Patterns in Vocal Performance". *Journal of the Acoustical Society of America* 142: 1805–15.

Sjoerdsma, R. D. (2008) "Editor's Commentary". *Journal of Singing* 65/2: 131–32.

Smith, K. (2010) "The Singing Assembly: How Does Music Affect the Faith Life of a Worshipping Community?" *Australasian Catholic Record* 87/3: 284–95.

Taylor, J. (2009) "Speaking Shadows: A History of the Voice in Transition from Silent to Sound Film in the United States". *Journal of Linguistic Anthropology* 19/1: 1–20.

Tongson, P. (2011) "Choral Vocality and Pop Fantasies of Collaboration". *Journal of Popular Music Studies* 23/2: 229–34.

Williams, J. (2012) "Cathedral Choirs in the United Kingdom: The Professional Boy Chorister". In *Perspectives on Males and Singing*, Landscapes: The Arts, Aesthetics, and Education, 10, edited by S. Harrison, G. Welch and A. Adler, 123–47. Dordrecht: Springer Netherlands.

Zarate, J. M. (2013) "The Neural Control of Singing". *Frontiers in Human Neuroscience* 7: 237. Available at https://www.ncbi.nlm.nih.gov/pmc/articles/PMC3669747/ (accessed October 15, 2019).

2 Singing, Sonic Authenticity and Stardom in *Dancer in the Dark*

Nessa Johnston

Following his provocative founding of the Dogma 95 movement and his own addition to its oeuvre with *The Idiots* (1999), the Danish filmmaker Lars von Trier appeared to abruptly reject the austerity regime of Dogma's "Vow of Chastity" by shooting *Dancer in the Dark* (2000), a relatively big-budget musical entertainment. The commercial success of the first wave of Dogma 95 films ensured that the release of *Dancer in the Dark* was a major event not only for European arthouse cinema generally, but also for the rising star of Danish cinema as the only film from that country screening in competition at the 2000 Cannes Film Festival (Stevenson, 2002: 150). Central to the film's marketing and reception was the unusual star appeal of its lead actress, the Icelandic singer Björk Guðmundsdóttir, usually known as Björk. Along with the film's Palme D'Or win, her Best Actress award at Cannes consolidated her performance as central to the film. Björk's singing voice is pivotal, with her unusual "indie" stardom encapsulated by her voice when considered as both sound element and performance element. Furthermore, her existing star persona crossing over between the indie and pop music worlds channels perceptions of her performance as *Dancer in the Dark*'s protagonist Selma.

Despite the apparent lavishness and star appeal of the film, I will begin by illustrating its post-Dogma 95 self-reflexivity, as a discernible "response" to Hollywood. Having set this as the context, I will follow two interlocking lines of argument. Firstly, that Björk's star persona channels perceptions of her performance as Selma. Although the narrative references within the lyrics are in Selma's voice, the singing voice we hear is unmistakably Björk's, and the companion album of songs from the film is part of Björk's oeuvre, marketed as a Björk album, collapsing distinctions between actor, singer, film star and pop star. Hence the tantalizing "recurring pop question" of the voice's sincerity or authenticity (Frith, 1996: 210) is mapped onto Björk's emotional performance as the fictitious Selma. Secondly, the musical numbers are presented as fantasies within Selma's mind, with "fantasy" and "reality" worlds delineated by two contrasting approaches to the sound mix (Kerins, 2010: 71). However, the distinction between the two sound worlds collapses during the final scene of Selma's execution mid-song, the only original Björk-authored song in the film audibly sung on location rather than lip-synced. Thus, the use of location-recorded sound frames the performance as offering a new level of "access" via the singing voice that seems to promise a glimpse of the inner emotional life of Björk the pop star.

Background

Stevenson describes *Dancer in the Dark* as "a contradiction in terms: a social-realist musical" – apparently an entertainment film paradoxically "not intended to entertain people" (Stevenson, 2002: 149). Set in small-town USA in the 1960s, the plot concerns Selma, a young Czechoslovakian immigrant who works in a factory and saves all her meagre earnings, ostensibly to send to her father back home. Unbeknownst to all but her friend Kathy who works at the factory, Selma is actually going blind, with a congenital condition she has passed on to her young son Gene, and the purpose of her savings is actually to pay for an operation that will save his sight. While her life is hard, she takes comfort in Hollywood musicals, a world in which "nothing dreadful ever happens", and as such the film is punctuated by musical numbers that are depicted as escapist fantasies in Selma's mind. Her apparently kindly neighbour and landlord Bill, who has secret debt problems, steals her money. When she confronts him, a struggle ensues, and Bill begs her to kill him. She murders Bill, takes the money and goes straight to the clinic to pay for Gene's operation. She is then apprehended by the police and prosecuted for Bill's murder. Kathy attempts to appeal the prosecution, but wants to use the money for Gene's operation to pay for it. Selma refuses, preferring to sacrifice her life for the sake of Gene's sight, and is put to death by hanging. The film's downbeat ending in particular puts it at odds with the musical genre's traditional "feel-good" tendencies.

Taking production lore into account, the film can be viewed as hinging upon contested authorship or authorial conflict. Initially, von Trier employed Björk to write the music for *Dancer in the Dark*, on her understanding that a "real" actress would play Selma; however Björk was eventually persuaded to take on the role, despite her reluctance to appear in the film (Stevenson, 2002: 148–49). Indeed, according to Stevenson's account, von Trier threatened to abandon the project entirely if Björk would not take the role, which would have meant abandoning two year's work on the composition of the music. Björk's emotional involvement in the project is further underlined in this account by "psychological battles" between her and von Trier over their attachment to the Selma character – with Björk coming to feel that "she knew Selma better than he did" (Stevenson, 2002: 149).

These questions of authorship become especially intriguing if *Dancer in the Dark* is located within the context of von Trier's and Björk's respective bodies of work. Nicola Dibben's book-length study of Björk repeatedly situates the music of *Dancer in the Dark* alongside Björk's 2001 album *Vespertine*, in terms of their shared studio sound and vocal performances, and notes that the song 'Unison' on *Vespertine* expresses sentiments regarding her authorial battles with von Trier (Dibben, 2009: 68). Meanwhile, for von Trier, *Dancer in the Dark* can be situated in relation to the Dogma 95 Manifesto and *The Idiots*, with a stripped-down filmmaking approach that focuses upon eliciting spontaneous, improvisational performances from actors, posited as a reaction to cinema's "elevation of cosmetics to God". To be certified as a Dogma 95 film, its director must adhere to a list of rules (mainly technical restrictions) entitled "The Vow of Chastity", forbidding particular technical and stylistic practices, in an effort to reign in artificiality in pursuit of a more "truth"-ful cinema.[1] Peter Schepelern has observed that, while *Dancer in the Dark* is not a Dogma 95 feature, following on as it does from the Dogma 95 certified *The Idiots*, the influence of the Manifesto is stylistically palpable: "It breaks nearly all the Dogma rules but it manages to keep two of Dogma's most effective means of expression: the intense acting and the hand-held camera" (Schepelern, 2003: 68). Schepelern does not mention sound, but the approach taken to sound in *Dancer in the Dark*, outside of its musical numbers, is similarly influenced by the Manifesto, in particular the employment of Rule #2: "The sound must never be produced apart from the images, or vice versa. (Music must not be used unless it occurs where the scene is being shot)". These intersections of Björk's work and von Trier's approach frame Björk's performance as Selma therefore as being somehow more than a performance – Björk "being" or "becoming" Selma "too completely, without the professional distance an actor brings to the task" (Stevenson, 2002: 149), with von Trier "forcing the truth" out of the Selma character.

This peculiarly troubled, emotional context is further brought to bear upon spectatorial appraisal and connection with Björk's performance. In essence, if Björk "became" Selma rather than "merely" acting the part, to what extent does a fan of Björk watching *Dancer in the Dark* feel engaged by the emotional trauma of Selma or of Björk? In his seminal work on cinema stardom, Richard Dyer argues that: "The fact that [stars] are also real people is an important aspect of how they signify, but we never know them directly as real people, only as they are to be found in media texts" (Dyer, 1998: 2). The register of Björk's performance as Selma further adds to the peculiar conflation of performer and character. Barry King posits screen acting as a question of impersonation versus personification (King, 1985: 42). With professional actors, impersonation is regarded as "good acting" and personification as "poor acting" (King, 1985: 30), yet paradoxically "impersonation... suppresses what in non-actors would be regarded as the authenticating markers of their personality" (King, 1985: 31). Björk's status as "non-actor" means that on screen, though she may have "become" Selma in a manner that is true to the emotional life of the character, her physical and vocal mannerisms are uniquely identifiable as Björk's, mapping upon the seemingly authentic Björk communicated through her music and her indie stardom. Tellingly, one review described Selma's performance as "radiant in her childlike – and Björk-like – passion" and praises her performance's "powerful artlessness" as well as "the originality of her musicianship" (Gleiberman and Schwarzbaum, 2000). The peculiarity of Björk's performance of Selma then is the conflation of her "becoming" Selma rather than playing the part of Selma with her distinctly non-actorly "Björk-ness", rendering Björk and Selma apparently one and the same.

Genre and Audiovisual Style

Dancer in the Dark separates its musical numbers from the rest of its pro-filmic reality, delineating them as Selma's daydreams. The soundtrack in the "reality" sequences eschews non-diegetic sound, and has a very screen-centred, generally monophonic-sounding 2.0 stereo sound mix. Visually, "reality" is characterized by the use of shaky hand-held digital video camera and a desaturated colour scheme reminiscent of amateur home video or fly-on-the-wall documentary. The connotations of this convey a sense of spontaneity and authentically captured (as opposed to carefully staged) performance. In contrast, the "fantasy" musical sequences use a dynamic, three-dimensional, 5.1 surround sound mix, incorporating non-diegetic sound (most notably orchestral sounds), looped samples of initially diegetic location sounds, and studio-recorded vocals, along with a rekeying of the original vocal register. Visually, the musical numbers use more saturated colours and are shot with an array of one hundred stationary digital video cameras instead of hand-held cameras, with rapid edits between shots producing a uniquely digital stylistic effect.[2] This elaborate multi-camera shooting method evokes a different kind of spontaneity more reminiscent of live television, but it is in the collision of these two styles that the effects of their contrasting approaches to sound are most readily apparent.

This leads to abrupt shifts in tone and audiovisual register when the film switches from the "Dogma-style" of the naturalistic "reality" scenes to the non-naturalistic musical number scenes and back again. Director Lars von Trier has expressed this desire for abrupt shifts in tone, describing the core idea of *Dancer in the Dark* as being "a collision between man and abstraction, or... The human and the artificial, truth and untruth" (Björkman, 2003: 232); hence, a collision of two contrasting styles. Their respective sounds are essentially "Dogma-eque", designating the "reality" sequences, versus what can be crudely categorized as its excessive "opposite", defining Selma's "fantasy". Over the course of the film, there are moments where the two styles overlap, which form a trajectory moving towards an eventual triumph of "reality" over "fantasy" in the final scene, the implications of which are discussed in more detail in the final sections of this chapter.

Dancer in the Dark explicitly foregrounds its relationship to Hollywood musicals in a number of ways. The first scene shows Selma and her friend Kathy at a rehearsal of an amateur production of *The Sound of Music* (based on the 1965 film of the same name). Kathy is played by Catherine Deneuve who has starred in the well-known French musical *The Umbrellas of Cherbourg* (Jacques Demy, 1964), and whose casting was regarded by critics as incongruous (Stevenson, 2002: 161–62; Travers, 2000), suggesting that association with her past role and its intertextual referencing was a more important factor in her casting than any bid towards realism. In the scene, Selma rehearses the number 'My Favourite Things' (Richard Rodgers and Oscar Hammerstein II, 1959) on stage, with the director and chorus singing along. However, this scene is not staged as a "fantasy" musical number but in the Dogma-esque "documentary" style, shot using very shaky hand-held camera, frequently panning and zooming, and a washed-out colour palate that is visibly digital video rather than film (with its flatness and deep focus). The sound is similarly "Dogma-eque" location-recorded sound – the music is a diegetic piano accompaniment and the dialogue has an improvisatory quality (hesitations and overlap). Overall, the sound has a "rough" or "live" material quality, which sounds less "clean" than the studio-recorded sound of the "fantasy" musical number sequences later.[3] So, as Schepelern and also Alessandro Ago have observed, *Dancer in the Dark* breaks every rule in the Dogma 95 Manifesto (Ago, 2003), and despite the glaring extratextual references, through the use of hand-held camera and sync location-recorded sound, along with the performances of the actors, the "reality" sections of the film evoke Dogma 95 stylistically to the point of appearing to have been shot in that manner. Hence, this opening scene positions the film as a Dogma-esque "response" to the Hollywood musical, as well as setting the register of "reality" to be later juxtaposed with "fantasy".

In these "reality" sequences the sound seems to conform to the Manifesto's Rule #2, as well as using close miking to give us a very intimate perspective on dialogue, and on Selma's voice in particular. Maasø's (2008) "Proxemics of the Mediated Voice" can help classify how Björk's voice is perceived in these scenes. Maasø uses terms normally used to describe camera shot size/perspective, from extreme close-up to extreme long shot, to categorize the mediated voice's acoustic aspects as determined by microphone perspective. Because of typical sound recording practice in film and television, in which actors tend to be tightly miked in order to obtain intelligible dialogue on location, microphone perspective in film sound varies merely between extreme close-up and medium close-up, whereas intended earshot (that of the audience/spectator) tends to be uniformly in medium shot. The most variation is in vocal distance – and in sum, this means that we can hear a full range of vocal distances in any one film, from the softest whisper to the loudest shout, but always at a uniform volume because of practices in post-production sound mixing (Maasø, 2008). Selma's singing in the rehearsal scene, with its trademark noisy, mid-phase breathing at odds with conventional vocal control, sounds distinctly Björk-like (Dibben, 2009: 102), but its hesitant, nervous delivery also suggests a lack of performer confidence, appropriate to a nervous amateur, and her voice is almost drowned out when the chorus sing. However, we hear a more close-up intimate perspective on her voice. The reflected sound of the room is not as noticeable on her voice as on the voices of the other singers, including the director, so even though Selma's voice is not any louder, it still stands out from the others, suggesting a close-up microphone perspective. As the scene unfolds, more and more close-up headshots of Selma and Kathy are used, inviting the viewer into a visually intimate place, amplifying the intensity of the actors' performances, and encouraging identification with the characters depicted. Therefore, the close-up of microphone perspective and vocal distance on Selma's voice anticipates already the importance of visual zooms and close-ups to the audiovisual style of *Dancer in the Dark*, with the sound working in support of the intimate perspective communicated by the camera style – the Dogma 95 style of "intense acting and handheld camera" as identified by Schepelern (2003).

With their rehearsals of well-known musical numbers in this scene and others, *Dancer in the Dark* evokes comparison with the conventions of Hollywood musicals as discussed by Jane Feuer, who argues that scenes of "'improvisation' in a rehearsal atmosphere" in the backstage musical compound and amplify the sense of "spontaneity" inherent in any film (Feuer, 1993: 12). However, Selma quickly abandons her commitment to the musical rehearsals and for much of the film the musical numbers are staged as fantasies in her imagination instead. While Feuer points out that there are many examples in Hollywood musicals of professionals playing the role of amateurs, the narrative significance of Björk's performance as Selma is particularly interesting because it presents a schism between the amateur rehearsals, the musicals Selma watches in the cinema, and the fully formed musical numbers depicted. This first scene establishes the dominant style of the "reality" sequences. The screenplay describes it as follows:

> SELMA and KATHY rehearse an amateur theater production. SELMA sings and dances to an upbeat piano accompaniment. She performs with naiveté and abandon, but with little talent. She is radiantly happy (Von Trier, 2000: 1).

This performance of a musical number is a rehearsal, with diegetic sound performed amateurishly, without finesse, and shot in a rough-and-ready documentary style. The next time we encounter a musical number is when Selma and Kathy watch a Busby Berkeley musical at a cinema; this time, the musical is well-crafted and polished, but perceived through a second order of mediation, with the characters observing its fantasy from a more "real" perspective. But both these presentations of musical numbers foreshadow the first metadiegetic "fantasy" musical number, 'Cvalda', performed in the factory, setting up the narrative for Selma's flight of fancy, also delineating it from "reality" as well as from the Hollywood numbers projected at the cinema. The approach to the sound in all three of these iterations of music is similarly delineated (in the cinema scene, we hear the film's sound as though transmitted through speakers in the cinema, inflected with reverb from the room in which Selma and Kathy sit), with the sound in 'Cvalda' shifting to a widely spatialized 5.1 mix in sharp contrast to the narrower, more screen-centred sound mix up to that point.

I will discuss the sound of the "fantasy" musical numbers in more detail below; however, it is telling that the wider spatialization of the 5.1 mix is the aesthetic approach taken for the Björk-authored songs performed in the film, because as Richard Dyer observes:

> Songs in films take up literal but also temporal and sometimes metaphorical space. They impose musical time and length on spoken and acted narration. They allow voices to fill or carry over space and, in dance, permit – even incite – bodies to do the same. This can be lovely, but it may also be disruptive, threatening, subversive. If a song may expand on the narrative moment it may also interrupt its drive (Dyer, 2012: 30).

Hence the lusher, wider 5.1 mix takes up sonic space alongside the temporal and metaphorical space, immersing the audioviewer in a literalized sonic rendition of the "disruption" of space Dyer identifies. Sonically, the "fantasy" musical numbers disrupt the space mapped out by the Dogma-esque audiovisual style, temporarily expanding the spatio-temporal world of the film.

Bjork's Voice

By casting a well-known musician without formal actor training, the film is distinguished from musicals of recent years such as *Moulin Rouge* (2001), *Everyone Says I Love You* (1996), *Mamma Mia* (2008), *Sunshine on Leith* (2013) and *Les Misérables* (2013), which use performers primarily known as actors (albeit with some exceptions) trying a hand at singing (with varying levels of success). At the same time, Björk the singer has been widely praised for the seemingly authentic emotional expression of her voice (Dibben, 2009: 131). Similarly her musical work is promoted as springing from a uniquely authored creative vision and a perceived sincere commitment to artistic integrity:

> In promotional material Björk is represented as a musician who is able to release the music she wants, supported by a record company which is free from the taint of commerce; an innovative artist who constantly strives for the new; making music as an involuntary and spontaneous act – a way of life rather than work, and one with therapeutic, self-expressive value; connected to nature; and a prodigy who was "born singing" (Dibben, 2009: 132).

2 Singing, Sonic Authenticity and Stardom in *Dancer in the Dark*

Regarding sound generally and voice in particular, the notion of authenticity, as understood in the context of recorded media encompassing both film sound and musical recordings, is further clarified by Jacob Smith's work. Smith describes mediated sonic authenticity as a system used by performers and technicians that utilizes a particular set of effects to create a sense of "immediate presence" (Smith, 2008: 6), which reconciles the seemingly contradictory notion that sound recordings can have a "live" feel. Although I have earlier emphasized the "live" and intimate quality of location-recorded sound in the Dogma-esque "reality" sequences of *Dancer in the Dark*, I do not wish to downplay Björk's authentically emotional vocal presence during the fantasy sequences. Though the two audiovisual registers within the film are firmly delineated as "rougher" location-recorded sound versus "cleaner" studio-recorded sound, they are not strictly dichotomous. In an article questioning the dichotomy between "liveness" and recordings posited by Philip Auslander (1999) and others, Jessica Teague asserts that: "Although recording technology has the power to separate the voice from the body, it cannot erase the presence of the embodied life in the voice" (Teague, 2012: 124). So though Björk's lip-syncing of the songs might re-key our reception of her performance during the fantasy sequences (along with other non-sonic factors such as staging, choreography and colour-saturation), her voice still carries an unmistakable sense of "embodied life" and personal "Björk-like" sonic signature.

Some reviews (good and bad) implicitly remark upon Björk's voice when assessing her performance as a whole; for example one critic dismisses her portrayal of Selma as "a squeaking, chirruping diva turn" (Bradshaw, 2000), with Björk's voice described in a synecdochic relationship to her screen performance. Dibben discusses in detail the much remarked-upon "'alternative' character" of Björk's voice, with its unusual variety of different contrasting timbres (Dibben, 2009: 102):

> a "belting" vocal style typical in music theatre and pop ballads (in which the chest voice is carried high into the upper register), a head voice, shouting, whispering, and a sound between singing and speaking which often has a child-like quality... Moreover, she uses a wide range of vocal noises (extended vocal techniques): guttural throat growls, shrieks, squeaks and noisy inhalations and expirations. Rapid changes in her vocal tone within and between songs suggest a mercurial shift between emotional extremes (Dibben, 2009: 102).

These distinctive "mercurial shifts" can be traced, compared and contrasted between songs, within songs, and between "fantasy" and "reality" sequences of *Dancer in the Dark*.

Selma's singing in the rehearsal scene which opens the film, discussed above, lacks confidence, appropriate to the character's timidity, and her dialogue delivery is soft-spoken, shy and almost child-like. It is not until the first "fantasy" musical number, 'Cvalda', that we hear her sing in the confident "belting" vocal style appropriate to the boisterous, upbeat tone of the song and its lavish orchestral accompaniment. Though her voice starts the song with a fricative semi-whisper of "Clatter, crash, clack!", by the line "Look at me, entrancer!" we hear her singing voice at full pelt for the first time, and she continues to sing exuberantly and confidently for the rest of the song. Hence, Björk's varied palate of vocal styles are implemented to convey the differing "fantasy" and "reality" versions of Selma.

The material qualities of Björk's voice are important to note in analysis, but they cannot be discussed separately from the wider signifying system of the Björk star persona: "In the modern era, all celebrities, especially singers, are not just faces or bodies, but are understood as faces, bodies, voices, and stories all at the same time" (Duffett, 2011: 175). A selection of the songs from *Dancer in the Dark* was released simultaneously with the film as a Björk album entitled *Selmasongs* (2000). Although the narrative references within the lyrics are in Selma's voice, the voice that sings on the album is recognizably Björk, and the album of songs is part of Björk's oeuvre, marketed as a Björk album. Within the film, there is a contrast between Björk's vocal performance in the "fantasy" and "reality" sequences. While in both, she is recognizably and distinctively Björk the star, in the "reality" sequences her voice is hesitant and halting, tentative and childlike, sometimes verging on a mumble. However, during the fantasy musical sequences, her voice sounds like a studio recording and her performance is characterized by confident abandon – she becomes more Björk than Selma. But more importantly, despite this contrast, her voice is always distinctively Björk's voice. Hence, the two distinct audiovisual styles delineate not only "fantasy" and "reality" Selma, but also "pop star" and "private" Björk – the "reality" sequences functioning as backstage sequences allowing access to a naturalistic, seemingly non-staged version of Björk. Jacob Smith highlights the reciprocal relationship between twentieth-century covert sound recordings of "real" people being "themselves" and the development of contemporaneous realist acting styles (Smith 2008: 188). Hence, realism is measured in relation to how much it resembles the contemporary mediation of the non-acting "real" person.

Because of her status as a popular music star (albeit one with indie credibility) and the distinctiveness of her singing voice (Björk can never be mistaken for another singer and vice versa), Smith's theorization of the mediated voice needs to be supplemented with theory specific to popular music. Though *Dancer in the Dark* has been described as more operatic in tone than a classic Hollywood musical (Grimley, 2005; Wolfe, 2001), with its grandiose orchestral overture prologue providing a gilt-edge to the Dogma-esque action, Björk's singing is not operatic. As Simon Frith explains, in opera the sound of the voice is determined by the score, whereas in pop the singer is "her self" (Frith, 1996: 186–88). Writing about pop singers and performance, Frith describes how we "hear a multiplicity of voices" in a pop song:

the character presented as the protagonist of the song, its singer and narrator, the implied person controlling the plot, with an attitude and tone of voice; but there may also be a "quoted" character, the person whom the song is about (Frith, 1996: 198).

This is true of all pop songs, but situating these songs within the cinematic world and narrative of *Dancer in the Dark* has the effect of multiplying and even confusing our perceptions of whether we are watching/hearing Selma and/or Björk singing about her inner emotional life. Frith goes on to explain that:

On top of this there is the character of the singer as star, what we know about them, or are led to believe about them through their packaging and publicity, and then, further, an understanding of the singer as a person, what we like to imagine they are really like, what is revealed, *in the end*, by their voice (Frith, 1996: 199; original emphasis).

This is analogous to our perception of any star in any film; however, when the star of the film is a pop star, a particular allure surrounds their performance:

In one respect, then, a pop star is like a film star... For the pop star the "real me" is a promise that lies in the way we hear the voice, just as for the film star the "real" person is to be found in the secret of their look (Frith, 1996: 199).

What we get with *Dancer in the Dark* then, with its "Dogma-esque" audiovisual style, "forcing the truth out of its characters and settings" is the enticing idea of gaining access to the emotional life of Björk herself, previously promised by the singing voice heard in her music releases.

It is worth re-emphasizing at this point that other analyses of Björk's songs in *Dancer in the Dark* cite them musically within Björk's wider oeuvre, and thematic concerns that run through all her music, beyond the thematic concerns of the film. In particular, Dibben links the use of sampled rhythms, especially of the factory machines in 'Cvalda' and of the skipping vinyl crackle in the later number 'Scatterheart' as a reiteration of Björk's desire to reconcile art and technology, a theme articulated repeatedly in her work. Dibben argues that making these machine sounds the basis of the two songs imbues technology with a "magical" quality, in contradistinction to pervasive notions of technologies of the modern era as oppressive and alienating. By triggering the fantasy sequences, these machine sounds also bridge the gap between fantasy and reality (Dibben, 2009: 87). Dibben's analysis is interesting in light of my discussion above because it is more concerned with considering the songs to be Björk's songs rather than elements of the fictional world of *Dancer in the Dark*, thus even at the scholarly level, the performance of the character of Selma is cited as an iteration of the "authentic" Björk – Björk the artist.

Digital Sound, Location Sound, and Affect

The "fantasy" musical sequences in *Dancer in the Dark* are particularly striking because of how much their overall sound contrasts with the "Dogma-esque" sound of the rest of the film. This is marked by their use of sound space, as well as a musical aesthetic created by the use of digital sampling and quantization. Every song in *Dancer in the Dark* starts with a loop of a rhythmical sound Selma initially perceives within the diegesis, which then becomes the basis of the song. As we move from a wash of ambient sound, to the quantized rhythm of the sample, and Björk's studio-recorded singing voice, the silences in between the sounds become more apparent – silences that can be considered characteristic of music in the digital era. Danielsen and Maasø's analysis of Madonna's 'Don't Tell Me' (a song which came out the same year as *Dancer in the Dark*) shows that while it is a conventionally written country-style pop song, it uses mediation and digital silence (reminiscent of skipping CD players) in a manner that is not associated with singer songwriters or folk/country music, marking it aesthetically as a product of its time (2009: 132). In the same manner, the use of samples of location sound to build rhythm in *Dancer in the Dark* is highly aesthetically "digital" and impossible to reproduce live. The rhythms in *Dancer in the Dark* could not be played by a musician, whereas they can be copied and pasted in a digital audio computer programme. In addition, the spatial qualities of the 5.1 surround sound mix separate competing sonic elements in a manner that exaggerates the digital silences between beats. While there is sincerity in Björk's vocal performance in these songs, the digital aesthetic foregrounds the "artificiality", or rather, the impossibility, or incompatibility with "reality", of the music that accompanies her.

What is notable is that the types of sounds sampled (the "raw material" of the samples) can be framed discursively through von Trier's commentary as a quest for sonic authenticity. Von Trier has explained that he would have liked to have used more "real" sound in the musical numbers but could not because of technical issues, although he does not go into any detail about this (Björkman, 2003: 231). In the "Selma Manifesto", which he wrote prior to filming, von Trier lays a blueprint for how Selma's fantasy musical numbers will sound:

> She loves the simple sounds of living expression... hands, feet, voices, and so on... (the sighs caused by hard work?)... the noise from machines and other mechanical things... the sounds of nature... and above all the little sounds caused by chance... the creak of a floor when a floorboard develops a defect (Björkman, 2003: 238–39).

The raw materials of the sounds used as the basis of the songs are "real" or "natural" (even if their looping and quantization is not). Each song starts off with a rhythmic sound that occurs in the diegesis – for example 'Cvalda' begins with the sound of machines, some of which are heavily panned, drawing attention to the shift in the spatialization of the sound mix, and 'I've Seen It All' begins with the sound of the passing train. However, as this sound becomes partly unstuck from its visual referent through its digital sampling, and its digital looping turns it into the rhythm of the song, the representational role of the sound becomes less important than its role as part of the song and the inherent material quality of the sound. This demonstrates a unique instance of the phenomenon observed by Andy Birtwistle, that reappropriation of location sound can "collapse the representational into the material" (Birtwistle, 2010: 58–59), in this instance by becoming the underlying "groove" of the musical number.

As well as the use of sampling and quantization in the musical numbers, which marks them as distinct from the "reality" sequences, another distinctive feature is the spatial playfulness of the 5.1 surround sound mix during these sequences. While Björk's voice stays for the most part in the centre channel, centred upon the screen, all other elements (the rhythm, the strings, the backing voices) float freely and dynamically around the audioviewer. For example, during 'Scatterheart', sung after Selma has killed Bill, the chorus includes a vocal by Selma's son Gene, who cycles in circles on his bicycle singing, "You just did what you had to do". This scene is depicted visually through a long shot of Gene, followed by a close-up of Björk watching him, followed by a shot of him taken from a camera attached underneath his bicycle, a close-up of his face, then an extreme close-up of his spokes. Simultaneously, the sound of the bicycle spokes clicking moves in a wide, regular, circular motion around the spectator, completely free of its onscreen referent with no clear relation to image scale. Visual movement in space and sonic movement operate independently of one another. In the "fantasy" depicted in *Dancer in the Dark*, sound and image can float freely of one another, whereas in "reality", sound and image are synchronized and irrevocably fused.

On the use of surround sound in the musical sequences in *Dancer in the Dark*, Mark Kerins writes that:

> In the context of the movie, this binary approach creates a sharp contrast between the monotonous real life of its heroine Selma… and her exciting, life-affirming fantasy world, in which the musical sequences occur. But it also suggests the inability of monophonic-based sound and its "rules" to accommodate Selma's creativity and imagination, which can only be rendered in multi-channel (Kerins, 2010: 71).

What is important to highlight here is the contrast between the two worlds, and the jarring effect of moving from one to another when the two are so audiovisually delineated. The jarring effect caused by the contrast between the two audiovisual worlds is used more and more frequently as the narrative progresses. In 'Scatterheart', for the first time the film introduces an interruption midway through the musical number as "reality" intrudes into the fantasy. Selma goes outside and the colours of the world suddenly become desaturated, accompanied by low-level ambient noise, but she then hears the "ping" of a flagpole moving in the breeze, which starts up a new rhythmic accompaniment and brings the "fantasy" song world back. This highlights the fragility of Selma's fantasy world, which breaks down more easily as the narrative progresses towards its heart-breaking conclusion. The ending of 'Scatterheart' incorporates bolder juxtapositions than previous numbers. Towards the end, a very artificial-sounding studio reverb is added to Björk's vocal, magnifying and enlarging the sound world of her fantasy, but then an abrupt visual change to "reality" occurs with a cut from a happy, dancing Selma to a dazed, unhappy Selma, while strings continue to play. This works as a visual "flash" of reality intruding, which is followed by the rhythmic sound and image of a pipe with water flowing out of it (which accompanies the rhythm of the song), cutting to a shot of it flowing arhythmically and indifferent to Selma's emotional state. It is in moments like these where the contrast between the two audiovisual worlds becomes almost unbearably poignant.

Extratextual information regarding this scene further adds to the emotional intensity of it. It was reported that Björk suffered a nervous breakdown following the filming of the murder scene, which itself is excruciatingly prolonged and messy. Furthermore, Dibben has remarked that the albums *Vespertine* and *Selmasongs* include greater use of her voice's upper register and less vocal projection. While it is true that the songs in *Dancer in the Dark* sound more like conventional show tunes, such as 'Cvalda' and 'In the Musicals', as well as the chorus of 'I've Seen It All', which use more of the "belting" singing style, the verses of 'I've Seen It All' and most of 'Scatterheart' use this more intimate upper register, which Dibben connects with themes of "internalization" that crop up in both albums (Dibben, 2009: 106). Sonically, 'Scatterheart' sounds less like a show tune and more like a song from *Vespertine*, in which her collaboration with the electronic duo Matmos further developed her experimentation with microsampling – very much evident in the sounds and rhythms of *Dancer in the Dark/Selmasongs* (Dibben, 2009: 20). Hence, the more personal emotional and introspective tone of the song, following on from the traumatic event in the narrative of the film, with its extratextual traumatic event of emotional breakdown and conflict with von Trier, once again lead to a conflation of performer and character, and arguably a manifestation of a battle for authorial control in the juxtapositions between the von Trier Dogma-esque "reality" location-recorded sound and the Björk "fantasy" studio-recorded sound.

Further ruptures of the two audiovisual worlds take place later on, and these culminate in the execution scene, subjecting the viewer to the emotionalism engendered by the gap between the "fantasy" of the musical sequences and the grim "reality" of the non-musical sequences. Paul Thèberge argues that for Selma, it is silence that oppresses her. He describes how *Dancer in the Dark* "uses music and sound to bridge the gap between the utopian tendencies of the Hollywood musical and the inevitable suffering and victimization of melodrama" (Thèberge, 2008: 61). In the first half of the narrative, Selma is seen to be able to escape into a musical fantasy no matter how grim her circumstances, simply by drawing upon the chance rhythms of background noises, but later as her circumstances become more dire, she becomes increasingly oppressed by silence and the escape of the musical sequences come less easily to her.

Davina Quinlivan emphasizes the effect of Rules #2 and #3 of the Dogma 95 Manifesto on the mediation of corporeal performance – "the limitations of sound-recording devices and the restriction of sound editing enable an uninterrupted, unrefined quality of live sync sound that captures the lived, breathing body of the performer" with hand-held camera "encourage[ing] actors to pay less attention to camera set-ups and to concentrate on each other's performance" (Quinlivan, 2012: 130). In an earlier work on the role of breath in Emily Watson's performance in von Trier's 1996 film *Breaking the Waves*, Quinlivan argued that the sound of her breathing, though evocative of the hyperreal and symbolic, is simultaneously unexceptional and mundane, and "cannot fully articulate artifice, because it marks her body's relationship with reality, that is, the immediate reality or 'truth' of that moment within which it occurs" (Quinlivan, 2009: 159). Similarly, in *Dancer in the Dark*, the breathing and sobbing of Björk that characterize her vocal performance during the scene of Bill's murder and the execution scene is an example of how synchronized location-recorded sound can simultaneously authenticate the reality of the moment, as well as initiate a felt emotional response: "the specific act of *hearing* breath... draws attention to an embodied encounter between film and spectator that might relate to a kind of aural form of haptics" (Quinlivan, 2009: 159).

The final scene of Selma's execution is both the culmination of Selma's story and the culmination of the repeated rupturing of the two audiovisual worlds. Björk's harrowing performance in this scene includes her screaming and struggling against attempts to put a hood over her head. Gradually she becomes aware of the sound of her own heartbeat, is reassured by it, and this sparse rhythmic accompaniment provides the backing to her final musical number. Thèberge comments upon the sparseness of this musical arrangement, describing it as a "structural silence": "Selma's voice alone echoes in the reverberant space of the execution room (all other voices and sounds in the room are muted – a diegetic silence reigns except for the voice of Selma)" (Thèberge, 2008: 61). Her singing is defiant of this oppressive silence. Considering the two sound worlds discussed above, most notably it is the only instance of Selma/Björk performing one of her own songs (as opposed to a number from *The Sound of Music*) audibly on location in "reality" rather than using a lip-synced studio recording in the "fantasy" audiovisual world. Her voice reverberates around the room with a natural reverb that Thèberge argues puts the audience "within the same acoustic space as the victim"

(Thèberge, 2008: 62). In addition, the prison guards react with perplexed astonishment to her performance, signalling that this song is taking place in "reality" rather than in Selma's imagination. Hence, to use von Trier's notion that *Dancer in the Dark* is about "the collision between... the human and the artificial, truth and untruth" (Björkman, 2003: 232), we find in this scene a triumph of the "truth" of location sound over the "untruth" of post-synchronized post-production sound.

The execution scene makes for uncomfortable viewing, which Caroline Bainbridge attributes to this final collision of the film's two registers:

> a heart-wrenching sequence which involves a great deal of mobile camera-work and frequent close-ups of Selma's anguished facial expression, von Trier ties together the emotional and pseudo-realist traits of the film... [the] movement between registers is eventually collapsed (Bainbridge, 2007: 114).

But as well as the connotations of truth and intimacy associated with hand-held camera and close-ups, the contrast between the location-recorded vocal performance and the earlier post-synchronized "fantasy" performances also communicate emotional rawness and forced intimacy. The material quality of the recording of the song not only signals Selma's character's final "live", "authentic" expression, but also rekeys Björk's singing voice in a way that suggests an unmasking of the studio-produced singing voice heard previously during the musical numbers (and indeed, across Björk's musical oeuvre) to reveal a raw, emotional "truth" underneath – the culmination of the promise and potential of the Dogma 95 style to "force the truth" out of "characters and settings". It is impossible to separate Selma's song in the execution scene from Björk's performance oeuvre; Frith argues that in pop music culture, it is the star that matters more than the performance event – "a performance in a history of performances" (Frith, 1996: 211). Furthermore, all voice recordings by pop singers promise sincerity and authenticity by virtue of the intimacy conveyed by studio recording:

> technology, electrical recording, has exaggerated this effect by making vocal performance more intimate, more self-revealing, and more (technologically) determined. The authenticity or "sincerity" of the voice becomes the recurring pop question: does she really *mean* it? (Frith, 1996: 210).

So even though the fantasy musical numbers in *Dancer in the Dark* can be understood as further iterations of Björk's own work, regardless of whether or not she writes in the fictitious voice of Selma, the song sung during the execution scene and its particular material quality suggests a whole new level of "sincerity".

What makes the use of location sound in the execution scene peculiarly disturbing, coupled with the "home video" aesthetics of digital video throughout it, is that it creates the apparent sense of accessing the inner emotional life of Björk. This can be further contextualized by the publicity surrounding *Dancer in the Dark*'s production. As mentioned earlier, allegations of emotional conflicts between Björk and Lars von Trier were heavily publicized up to and around the time of its release (Stevenson, 2002: 152–54). Simultaneously, Deneuve described her approach to creating the role of Selma as "play[ing] on her feelings" rather than acting (Stevenson, 2002: 152). One reviewer described the film as a "psychological snuff film" and as "emotional pornography" (Stevenson, 2002: 159). Somewhat perversely, von Trier describes the on-set conflict between him and Björk as "an enrichment for the film but not for me personally" (as cited in Stevenson, 2002: 152); elsewhere Björk's falling out with von Trier has been widely noted and she has stated she will never speak to von Trier again (Bainbridge, 2007: 13). It is as if the film's "Dogma-esque" aesthetic approach invades the emotional privacy of the singer Björk, whose voice, through its Barthian "grain", invites "physical sympathy" (Frith, 1996: 192) from the audioviewer. More recent revelations of alleged sexual harassment and abuse perpetrated by von Trier upon Bjork (Scharf, 2017) have since shed light upon the graveness of previously reported on-set conflict during the film's production, providing a deeply discomforting layer of knowledge that informs any subsequent revisiting of *Dancer in the Dark*.

About the Author

Dr Nessa Johnston is Senior Lecturer in Media, Film and Television at Edge Hill University, UK. Her research and teaching interests include sound in screen media, critical production studies, and production/sound aesthetics in low-budget and art cinema, encompassing independent, experimental and cult cinema. She has published on film sound in several edited collections and journals including *Music, Sound and the Moving Image*, *The Soundtrack*, *The Velvet Light Trap*, *Alphaville*, *Popular Music* and *The Palgrave Handbook of Sound Design and Music in Screen Media*.

Notes

1. The text of the Manifesto is available online at: http://pov.imv.au.dk/Issue_10/section_1/artc1A.html (accessed February 28, 2014), as well as in print in Hjort and MacKenzie (2003: 199–200), Roman (2001: 40–41) and Kelly (2000: 226–28).
2. Lars von Trier details this method in interview in the documentary *Von Trier's 100 Eyes* (2000): "The principle is to aim one hundred cameras at the dance scenes and then we just go for it and see what happens. The cameras are unmanned so we'll get loads of random effects. Lots of badly framed shots etc. Actually it's similar to the hand-held camera I am using for the acted scenes. It allows the dancers and actors complete freedom because the entire space should be covered. It isn't, of course. We'd need one thousand or ten thousand cameras. But it's fun to try."
3. Michel Chion asserts that: "there is no link in a sound film between the filmmaking process and the finished product. One can create the impression of direct sound in a postsynchronized film… conversely, a film can seem postsynchronized… when in fact

it has been recorded with direct sound" (Chion, 2009: 221). Though this is technically correct, for the purposes of identifying the stylistic distinction between sound worlds in *Dancer in the Dark*, the method with which this "rough" or "live" sound was achieved is not as important as the fact that it sounds less "clean" relative to the sound of the musical numbers.

References

Ago, A. (2003) "Once Upon a Time in Amerika: *Dancer in the Dark* and Contemporary European Cinema". *Spectator* 23/2: 32–43. http://cinema.usc.edu/archivedassets/059/11482.pdf (accessed May 1, 2012).

Auslander, P. (1999) *Liveness: Performance in a Mediatized Culture*. London: Routledge.

Bainbridge, C. (2007) *The Cinema of Lars von Trier: Authenticity and Artifice*. London: Wallflower Press.

Birtwistle, A. (2010) *Cinesonica: Sounding Film and Video*. Manchester: Manchester University Press.

Björkman, S. (2003) *Trier on von Trier*. London: Faber and Faber.

Bradshaw, P. (2000) "Dancer in the Dark". *The Guardian*, September 15. http://www.theguardian.com/film/2000/sep/15/1 (accessed February 23, 2014).

Chion, M. (2009) *Film: A Sound Art*. New York: Columbia University Press.

Danielsen, A. and A. Maasø (2009) "Mediating Music: Materiality and Silence in Madonna's 'Don't Tell Me'". *Popular Music* 28/2: 127–42.

Dibben, N. (2009) *Björk*. London: Equinox Press.

Duffett, M. (2011) "Elvis Presley and Susan Boyle: Bodies of Controversy". *Journal of Popular Music Studies* 22/2: 166–89.

Dyer, R. (1998) *Stars* (new edition). London: British Film Institute.

Dyer, R. (2012) *In the Space of a Song: The Uses of Song in Film*. Abingdon, Oxon: Routledge.

Feuer, J. (1993) *The Hollywood Musical* (2nd edn). London: British Film Institute.

Frith, S. (1996) *Performing Rites: Evaluating Popular Music*. Oxford: Oxford University Press.

Gleiberman, O. and L. Schwarzbaum (2000) "Movie Review: *Dancer in the Dark*". *Entertainment Weekly*, September 22. http://www.ew.com/ew/article/0,,277661,00.html (accessed March 1, 2014).

Grimley, D. M. (2005) "Hidden Places: Hyper-realism in Björk's *Vespertine* and *Dancer in the Dark*". *Twentieth-Century Music* 2/1: 37–51.

Hjort, M. and S. MacKenzie, eds (2003) *Purity and Provocation: Dogma 95*. London: British Film Institute.

Kelly, Richard (2000) *The Name of This Book is Dogme95*. London: Faber and Faber.

Kerins, Mark (2010) *Beyond Dolby (Stereo) Cinema in the Digital Sound Age*. Bloomington, IN: Indiana University Press.

King, Barry (1985) "Articulating Stardom". *Screen* 26/5: 27–51.

Maasø, A. (2008) "The Proxemics of the Mediated Voice". In *Lowering the Boom*, edited by J. Beck and T. Grajeda, 36–50. Urbana, IL and Chicago: University of Illinois Press.

Quinlivan, D. (2009) "Von Trier's Breath Control: The Sound and Sight of Respiration as Hyper-realist Corporeality in Breaking the Waves". In *Realism and the Audiovisual Media*, edited by L. Nagib and C. Mello, 152–63. Basingstoke: Palgrave Macmillan.

Quinlivan, D. (2012) *The Place of Breath in Cinema*. Edinburgh: Edinburgh University Press.

Roman, S. (2001) *Digital Babylon: Hollywood, Indiewood and Dogme 95*. Hollywood, CA: iFilm Publishing.

Scharf, Z. (2017) "Björk Stands by Sexual Harassment Claims after Lars von Trier Denial, Reveals More 'Paralyzing' Abuse". *Indiewire*, October 17. https://www.indiewire.com/2017/10/bjork-sexual-harassment-lars-von-trier-denial-1201888174/ (accessed May 29, 2020).

Schepelern, P. (2003) "'Kill Your Darlings': Lars von Trier and the Origins of Dogma 95". In *Purity and Provocation: Dogma 95*, edited by Mette Hjort and Scott MacKenzie, 58–69. London: British Film Institute.

Smith, J. (2008) *Vocal Tracks: Performance and Sound Media*. Berkeley: University of California Press.

Stevenson, J. (2002) *Lars von Trier*. London: British Film Institute.

Teague, J. E. (2012) "Liveness in *Ma Rainey's Black Bottom*". In *Sound Clash: Listening to American Studies*, edited by K. Keeling and J. Kun, 111–27. Baltimore: Johns Hopkins University Press.

Thèberge, P. (2008) "Almost Silent: The Interplay of Sound and Silence in Contemporary Cinema and Television". In *Lowering the Boom*, edited by J. Beck and T. Grajeda, 51–67. Urbana, IL and Chicago: University of Illinois Press.

Travers, P. (2000) "Dancer in the Dark". *Rolling Stone*, October 6. http://www.rollingstone.com/movies/reviews/dancer-in-the-dark-20001006 (accessed February 23, 2014).

Von Trier, L. (2000) *Dancer in the Dark (FilmFour screenplay)*. London: FilmFour Books.

Wolfe, C. (2001) "When You Can't Believe Your Eyes: Voice, Vision, and the Prosthetic Subject in *Dancer in the Dark*". *Electronic Book Review*, September 1. http://www.electronicbookreview.com/thread/musicsoundnoise/operatic (accessed February 22, 2012).

Filmography

Breaking the Waves (1996) Denmark/Sweden/France/Netherlands/Norway/Iceland/Spain, dir. Lars von Trier.

Everyone Says I Love You (1996) USA, dir. Woody Allen.

Idiots, The / Idioterne (1998) Denmark/Spain/Sweden/France/Netherlands/Italy, dir. Lars von Trier.

Les Miserables (2012) UK, dir. Tom Hooper.

Mamma Mia (2008) USA/UK/Germany, dir. Phyllida Lloyd.

Moulin Rouge (2001) USA, dir. Baz Luhrmann.

Sound of Music, The (1965) USA, dir. Robert Wise.

Sunshine on Leith (2013) UK, dir. Dexter Fletcher.

Umbrellas of Cherbourg, The / Les parapluies de Cherbourg (1964) France/GDR, dir. Jacques Demy.

Von Trier's 100 Eyes / Von Trier's 100 øjne (2000) Denmark, dir. Katia Forbert.

3 Find Your Voice:
Narratives of Women's Voice Loss in American Cinema

Katherine Meizel

In August 2013, the Walt Disney Company held an online singing competition called "Find Your Voice". Fans registered as members of the website Disney.com were invited to upload a personal video cover of a song from the 1989 animated musical *The Little Mermaid* (Ron Clements and John Musker). The contest was hosted on the site's "Disney Princess" page, and out of the ten submissions awarded prizes, eight were from girls and women between the ages of 4 and 21. The Disney film, based on Hans Christian Andersen's 1837 tale, is equally girl-centric, following a teenaged (mer-)girl's struggle toward social and sexual maturity and self-worth, as she gives up her voice to a nefarious sea-witch in a Faustian exchange for the magical opportunity to leave the water in search of a prince's love. In the Find Your Voice contest, three song choices were offered, and six of the winning entries covered 'Part of Your World', a ballad proclaiming the mermaid Ariel's yearning for new horizons, knowledge, belonging and self-expression – desires in pursuit of which Ariel yields and then reclaims her voice, and which certainly represent intimately familiar concerns for contemporary American girls.

The continuing success of *The Little Mermaid* at its quarter-century mark is owed not simply to a universality of adolescent longings, but also to deep-rooted and fluid discourses about the singing voice and identity in Western culture. The idea of *finding one's voice*, in particular, is a desire linked to intertwined feminist and literary and moralizing trends in the late twentieth century. It implies the attainment of a quasi-mystical key to agency and self-knowledge, but the process of finding also denotes, even requires, a precedent loss. It is this lost-and-found narrative that I examine here, in the film histories that converged in and emerged from *The Little Mermaid*. In this chapter, I seek to show how late twentieth-century cinematic projects like Disney's *Mermaid* are grounded in a long tradition of lost women's voices in film and literature.

Losing a Voice: Stories of Singers on the Verge of Womanhood

The cinematic narrative of voice loss traced in Disney's *The Little Mermaid* is a tried and true one, though the order of the components may vary: a young singer on the verge of womanhood leaves her home for a chance at a better life; she loses her voice due to some physical or psychological trauma, and must find it again through enacting love, self-esteem, faith, and/or a restoration of her personal values. Recent movies have built upon this trope over and over; for example:

- Terri is a young singer with dreams of stardom, but after her brother's death she feels unable to sing, until her mother and aunt convince her to find her voice at a Los Angeles summer program for talented youth (*Raise Your Voice*, Sean McNamara, 2004).
- In a grittier formulation of the tale – Lewellen is a young white girl in the 1950s who finds an emotional escape from her abusive home life through Elvis Presley's songs. After she is raped by a local teenager, it takes the guidance of her friend Charles, an African American religious snake-handler, to help her find her voice and sing again (*Hounddog*, Deborah Kampmeier, 2007).
- Bobbie is an aspiring young singer whose voice came from angels in Heaven, but after leaving her bandmates behind and furiously confronting the father who had abandoned her, thus breaking the moral conditions of her gift, she loses her voice and can only find it again by changing her ways (*Pure Country 2: The Gift*, Christopher Cain, 2010).

Some of these stories, for example Terri's in *Raise Your Voice*, draw on the American Dream myths of Hollywood's golden age, when ingénues like *A Star Is Born*'s (William A. Wellman, 1937) Esther Blodgett took flight from the heartlands to follow their hearts toward California and the silver screen. Some, such as *Pure Country 2*, more transparently evoke the Christian morality of Andersen's original "Little Mermaid", in which it is not only love the girl seeks, but also the immortal soul that accompanies it. The mermaid's ensoulment, which happens beyond the story's temporal framework, is ultimately the result of a deus ex machina rescue by sky spirits after she has failed in her quest, after she has experienced the agonizing loss of her voice, the growing pains of walking on her own two feet, and finally, sacrifice and worldly death. She thus must pay in flesh and blood and voice for the privilege of becoming a woman, as Lewellen must, and like Lewellen is harassed by serpents (those biblical pushers of feminine knowledge). But she is also special, like Terri and Bobbie; the sea-witch asks for her voice in payment for the commodity of humanity because she sings the most beautifully. In the Disney film, the villainess actually sings using the appropriated voice, transforming herself into a paragon of human beauty and effectively controlling her rival's identity. At the end of Andersen's story, the little mermaid not only regains a sounding voice, but she has earned a better one than she had before, one that matches those of the daughters of the air: "so lovely and so melodious that no human music could reproduce it" (Andersen, 1983: 75).[1]

The little mermaid, though, is only one thread in the tapestry; today's tales of girls' voices weave together several crucial cultural themes, particularly:

1. the metaphorical/metaphysical location of individuality and agency in the voice;
2. the related idea that the voicing of difference can serve as an affirmative utterance of individuality;
3. the idea that a voice is at once the central locus of identity but though *in* the body, is not quite *of* the body – spiritual enough, separate enough to be stolen, replaced, or even transplanted into another body.

This chapter investigates these themes as sociocultural meanings with which young women's voices have been inscribed onscreen, and the ways in which voice is seen as something to be manipulated, appropriated, silenced, suppressed, and ultimately regained.

Finding a Voice: A Late Twentieth-century Notion

The exhortation to "find your voice", to recognize one's individuality and self-worth, is at this point so deeply embedded in North American culture that it seems to be timeless, without history. But though individuality is a key element in the mythologies of Americanness, and though the equation of voice with agency is in itself not new, the more specific articulation of the metaphor has roots traceable both to trends in writing analysis and pedagogy, and to the pivotal identity movements that shaped the nation's social, economic, political, philosophical and cultural climate in the late twentieth and early twenty-first centuries. It is only a short distance between a narrative concept of voice (as in an author's voice) and an agentive one (voice as a way of authoring one's own life); both trends have dialectically contributed to the discourse of finding a voice. The 1970s social movements inspired by the preceding struggle for African American civil rights, including second-wave feminism, were largely driven by a rhetoric of "speaking out" and of "gaining a voice" (Bauman, 2008: 10). Examining writing textbooks of this time, Darsie Bowden (1995) pinpoints Donald Stewart's 1972 *The Authentic Voice*, as a seminal document. Stewart advised students: "Your authentic voice is that authorial voice which sets you apart from every living human being despite the common or shared experiences you have with many others" (Stewart, cited in Bowden, 1995: 175). Other "voicist" (Bowden, 1995: 178) scholars turned to a more social, intersubjective view of language and of voice, where "all discourse is inhabited by meaning from other contexts and uses" (Bowden, 1995: 186). This is an idea perhaps most extensively theorized in Mikhail Bakhtin's *The Dialogic Imagination*, first published in its entirety in 1975 (the year of his death), in which Bakhtin introduces the concept of *multivocality* as a "multiplicity of social voices"

(1981: 263) which, though they do not blend together to make a cohesive whole, may be "orchestrated" by an author to create his novel's narrative text (Mey, 1998: 153). Bakhtin understands that among the heteroglot voices in this text, the writer's "own voice must also sound; these voices create the background necessary" (1981: 278) for this to happen, and the writer's voice cannot be truly heard without them. In their 1997 analysis of *Femininity and Shame: Women, Men, and Giving Voice to the Feminine*, Barbara L. Eurich-Rascoe and Hendrika Vande Kemp offer a (third-wave) feminist perspective, defining literary voice as *"self-declaration in an interpersonal context that has the primary goal of maintaining interpersonal connection"* (1997: 7, emphasis in original).

By the late 1980s, journalists were asking writers and performing artists the question "when did you find your voice?" as in a 1989 *Time* interview with Ann Landers (Taylor and Landers, 1989), and a 1990 interview in *Guitar Player* with the Kinks' Dave Davies (Resnicoff, 1990). And by 2000 the Surgeon General's report on women and smoking called out the Virginia Slims company for exploiting the language of the women's movement in its global "Find Your Voice" advertising campaign, begun the previous year (Koplan, 2000). That campaign also painstakingly targeted women of colour, emphasizing themes of liberation and enfranchisement and infuriating many who saw the project as an effort to globalize addiction in women (Kim and Chung, 2011).

The phrase also flourished in vocal pedagogy, though extant evidence on the internet appears to date only from the early 2000s, and around the same time the *Idols* franchise was encouraging young singers to make music "their own" – it is worth noting that in 2007, Season 5 *American Idol* winner Taylor Hicks published *Heart Full of Soul: An Inspirational Memoir about Finding Your Voice and Finding Your Way* (Hicks, 2007). I have elsewhere written about the *Idol* process of creating individualized performances, and I invoke the work of philosopher Charles Taylor (1989) as he connects the concepts of expressive individualism and the search for an authentic, "inner voice". Both are, he suggests, rooted in an entanglement of the Calvinist shift toward the establishment of a personal covenant with God, and the impact of naturalist philosophy in the Western history of thought. This convergence led to thinking in which "what is primary is the voice within, or according to other variants, the élan running through nature which emerges inter alia in the voice within", and God "is to be interpreted in terms of what we see striving in nature and finding voice within ourselves" (Taylor, cited in Meizel, 2011: 122–23).

Lose Your Voice: A History of Voicelessness in Film

The cinematic painting of voice as a locus of identity is far older than Disney's musical, older even than the Disney brand. The early film industry, filled with technologically silenced voices, was fascinated with their substance and insubstantiality. Despite silent film's inherent unvoicing of singers, opera – what Paul Fryer calls "the semaphore art form" (Fryer, 2005: 3) – and its purveyors were seen as ideal cinematic fare. With the development of the new medium, entertainment in the first years of the twentieth century involved a great deal of nearly lightning interplay between literature, theatre and the silent screen. *The Girl of the Golden West*, for example, emerged as a play (1905), an opera (1910), a novel (1911) and then a film (1915). Cecil B. DeMille adapted the sources of several operas; in addition to *The Girl of The Golden West*, in the same year DeMille produced *Carmen*, starring Geraldine Farrar. Opera performers like Farrar, trained in the precise and passionate externalization of emotion, supplied some significant early silent acting. And the lack of recorded voice, Michel Chion suggests, not only failed to faze the audiences who watched silent singers onscreen, but actually enhanced the cinematic experience in its encouragement of "dreaming" (Chion, 1999: 9). Because of these trends, silent stories about singers, when they came, were not at all an outlandish phenomenon. And in a genre where all voices were equally silenced (and therefore also equally heard), dramas of voice loss were perhaps inevitable.

Trilby

Two films in 1915 helped to popularize the theme of voice loss, Maurice Tourneur's adaptation of George du Maurier's 1894 novel *Trilby* and Frank Crane's *The Stolen Voice*. In the former the character Svengali, a nefarious Jewish musician and hypnotist, finds a young half-Irish grisette's voice utterly captivating – exhibiting all the expressive capabilities desired of an artist, despite her utter inability to sing in tune – and through something akin to mesmerism turns her into the most skilled, celebrated touring singer of her time. A girl of mixed class and heritage, at the beginnings of the novel and the film, Trilby works as a (sometimes nude – though she is covered up from head to toe when the film begins) model, not realizing, until it is pointed out to her, that what she is doing is morally dubious. Trilby is first overpowered by Svengali when he hypnotically cures her terrible headache, and she trades the loss of control brought on by her illness for another, more insidious variety. After he has taken her under his wing, when she sings she is unaware of her actions, and fully controlled by Svengali. When he dies, enfeebled by the abuse of his powers, she loses her glorious voice, and only finds it again at the moment of her own demise shortly after. Though her story, on the surface, appears to involve a voice that is given, not stolen, it is really one in which a woman's authentic voice is replaced – a wild and out-of-control singing that must be transformed to conform more closely to a popular aesthetic of beauty, that must be carefully controlled by a man. The bestowing of a beautiful voice, though, does constitute a kind of upside-down *Little Mermaid* tale. The other part of Trilby that is fetishized in du Maurier's novel is her foot, rendered in ink again and again by her admirer and love interest Billee. The concept of her foot is linked to her risqué modeling career (Fleeger, 2014: 31), and as she moves from one social world to another, she metaphorically exchanges that foot for a voice (while the mermaid exchanges her voice for feet). In *Mismatched Women: The Siren's Song through the Machine*, Jennifer Fleeger (2014) connects Trilby to the Odyssean sirens who lured sailors to their deaths and set the stage for a fear of women's voices.

After Trilby: Stolen Voices and Morality

In *The Stolen Voice*, a sort of reverse-*Trilby* (and co-written by an actor in Tourneur's film), it is a man who is the victim of Svengali, his voice and sweetheart taken from him in jealousy, and he is unable to sing again until the hypnotist's sudden death. Several subsequent versions of the *Trilby* story followed these, and since then imposed and silenced voices have never stopped sounding onscreen: the ensuing list includes *The Goose Woman* (Clarence Brown, 1925), a late silent film in which an opera singer loses her voice following the birth of her illegitimate child; *A Lady's Morals* (Sidney Franklin, 1930), in which a fictionalized Jenny Lind sings to excess; Al Jolson's *The Singing Kid* (William Keighley) in 1936; *A Little Bit of Heaven* (Andrew Marton) with Gloria Jean in 1940; the thriller *A Woman's Secret* (Nicholas Ray) in 1949; *Singin' In the Rain* (Stanley Donen and Gene Kelly, 1952), a much lighter discourse on the voice as an object unstuck in the body, removable and transferrable through the miracles of technology (see Silverman, 1988); Elvis's beloved *Jailhouse Rock* (Richard Thorpe) in 1957, in which his throat is injured in a fight; the Pavarotti vehicle *Yes, Giorgio* (Franklin J. Schaffner) in 1982; the mermaid reworking *Splash* (Ron Howard) in 1984, in which a voice is not lost, but the mermaid's name is unutterable to human ears; Disney's animated *Mermaid* in 1989; 1993's *The Piano* (Jane Campion) (though not about a singer), and the coming-of-age movies discussed above.

And these are just American films. Indian cinema, which developed initially from Hollywood musical pictures, offers some especially memorable examples. The unsuccessful Bollywood effort *Gazal* (Ved-Maden, 1964) follows talented young singer Naaz, whose suitor falls in love with her voice. When they are caught by her father, she loses her voice in fear, only regaining it when she can marry the man she loves. In the 1997 *Dance of the Wind* (Rajan Khosa), Pallavi, like her mother, has a singing career in Hindustani music; after the mother dies, Pallavi loses her voice and must search for it with the help of her mother's guru and a little girl he teaches. In 2013 Peque Gallaga and Lore Reyes, renowned directors in the Philippines, introduced *Sonata*, about an opera singer who loses her voice, retreats to her home province of Negros Occidental, and, as the filmmakers have it, "rediscovers her life" through a connection with a young boy (Ventura, 2013). The surrealist Adan Jodorowsky short *The Voice Thief* (2013) presents the story of an opera singer whose husband nearly strangles her, ruining her voice, and scours Miami for a supernatural sonic replacement. The Iraqi/Belgian short film *The Lost Voice*

(Bavi Yassin, 2013) traces the journey of Salma, a renowned Iraqi singer who loses her voice as a refugee in Belgium.

In *Trilby*, the heroine is only the instrument, the automaton of failed singer Svengali (Coll, 2010), and her new voice, the result of his magical seduction, does all he had formerly dreamed for his own incapable one. He can only control those weaker than himself, and in his Victorian context, the only figure a Jewish man can dominate is a naïve, non-Jewish European woman (Svengali, it is mentioned in the novel, had previously tried his tricks with a Jewish woman, but had ultimately failed – even a Jewish woman is portrayed as stronger). The film, released after the start of World War I in Europe and after a major influx of Jewish refugees immigrating to the U.S., supplants du Maurier's concerns about British culture with anxieties about the manipulation of white American culture, as embodied in the voice of a young woman, by foreign influences. It is noteworthy that 1915 was also the year in which *The Birth of a Nation* positioned the girl as symbolic of "both the culture being contested and the promise of a new world", and in which Mary Pickford, in *A Girl of Yesterday*, favourably contrasted older models of girlhood with the frightening trends of modernity (Driscoll, 2008: 16–17). In this context, girls' voices, in the hands of the male movers of the film industry, emerged as a paramount embodiment of conservative culture.

During the first decades of synchronously sounded film, the focus on young women's voices shifted from hearing them as symbolic of cultural victimhood to silencing them as a moral warning. Voice loss became a punishment, inflicted by the fates or God or human beings for errors of principle, for straying from certain social values. In *The Goose Woman* (1925), Louise Dresser plays opera singer Marie de Nardi, who has lost her voice following the birth of her illegitimate son. At the film's opening, twenty years have passed, and she is reviewing press and photos of her days as a star; one headline, dated 1902, reads clearly "Great Artist Will Never Sing Again: Marie De Nardi Sacrifices Voice for Motherhood". We learn that, denied her voice and the stardom she had come to crave, she had changed her name, retired to the country to raise geese, developed a drinking habit (during Prohibition), and listened obsessively to a single cylinder recording of her celebrated past. When her son accidentally breaks the cylinder, she viciously blames him for her state, and throws him out of her house. "Wasn't it enough to break my voice" she cries, "without smashing my last record of it?" After a local murder catches the public eye, she puts herself back in the spotlight claiming to be a witness, though the story she tells is fabricated. The resulting spiral of lies leads to her estranged son's arrest, though he is saved in the end.

Her voice, in this film, tells a story of a woman who sins, and moreover fights the "natural" progress of female life – the sacrifice of career for family. No good comes of her efforts. The narrative of voice loss as penance in *The Goose Woman*, which was inspired by a real-life contemporary murder case, reflects pervasive and persistent pre-Enlightenment attitudes that position disability as what Joseph Straus describes as "an outward mark of an inward moral failing" (Straus, 2011: 5). This story has not faded with time; many illnesses and other types of disability are still associated with moral failings – the phenomenon of alcoholism has been medicalized since *The Goose Woman's* era, for example, but those who suffer with it are still socially stigmatized as flawed in character, as lacking in self-control (see Straus, 2011: 6). In recent film, the disabling impact of voice loss also carries moral implications. In the 2010 film *Pure Country 2: The Gift*, voice loss is instigated by the excesses of fame, when singer Bobbie Thomas (Katrina Elam) succumbs to ego and the lure of money, to the detriment of family, faith, and the Shakespearean mandate to be true to oneself. Losing control of one's voice, one's identity, is perhaps the ultimate sign of weakness. In *Pure Country 2*, a mostly unconnected sequel to the 1992 George Strait vehicle, Bobbie is gifted, literally, by angels in charge of a squealing ball of light they identify as a beautiful voice. This voice is sent down to earth as she is born, and, as a white girl raised by a single black woman and in a black Kentucky church (perhaps inevitably), becomes a country singer. Her adoptive mother, Aunt Ella, often repeats the words we have heard the angels offer as conditions of the gift: Bobbie must not lie, she must be fair, and she must never break a promise. When she eventually fails all of these conditions – lying to procure a job, abandoning her band for a solo contract, breaking a promise to her estranged father – the gift is revoked. Furthermore, it is discovered by doctors that her larynx is congenitally deformed, and should never have been able to produce the beautiful sounds it had. A tearful conversation with a dying Aunt Ella convinces Bobbie to change her ways, work with disabled children, and learn to sing "from her heart". At a charity event, she begs the attending audience to "listen to my heart", and in the middle of her hoarse performance, the angels deem her redeemed and Bobbie begins to belt, her voice and morality restored. Like Andersen's little mermaid, she has earned a freer, truer voice through her efforts toward self-improvement.

Fifteen years after *The Goose Woman*, during the Depression and on the eve of the U.S. entry into World War II – a time when women's social roles underwent a great upheaval – *A Little Bit of Heaven* offered a new angle on voice loss and the perils of stardom. In the movie, Gloria Jean plays Midge, a tweenaged New York girl whose sudden rise to soprano fame creates trouble in her Irish working-class family. In this case, the sins are theirs, as they begin to spend their newfound wealth wildly, and to exclude old friends from their lives. Midge, incensed, pretends to lose her voice in order to persuade them to return to their old values. In Midge's scheme, voice loss becomes a strategy – and it is her family that loses her voice – and a clever, if childish, power play to right the moral scales.

Voices Lost Post-War

Following World War II, films about female voice loss appear to have declined somewhat. A remarkable exception is Nicholas Ray's 1949 noir feature *A Woman's Secret*, in which a singer's loss of voice leads her astray, even (she claims) to attempted murder. Maureen O'Hara, as Marian, is forced to give up her career when her voice deserts her suddenly in an intractable illness; instead she decides to mould and manage an aspiring ingénue named Susan (Gloria Grahame). Susan is initially impressionable and naïve, having spent all of her money on a visit to a huckster fortune teller, and hails from Azusa, California. By the time Susan is shot, she has become a kind of femme fatale in her own right, even posing a threat to Marian's unrequited interest in her friend Luke Jordan, and she is eager to leave the life Marian has shaped for her. The film can be seen, in a way, as a new perspective on du Maurier's story; Marian, in this version, takes the place of Svengali (though, I should point out, the source novel was authored by Vicki Baum, a Jewish woman), requiring and acquiring Susan as her vocal substitute. But when her proxy voice slips out of her control, she ostensibly has to silence it. In the somewhat confusing end, it is revealed that Marian has confessed falsely, and that the accidental gunshot was really Susan's responsibility. It is not explained why Marian took the blame in the first place, though perhaps it is her way of taking back control of her story, of telling it in her own voice. It may also reflect the ambiguous position of American women's voices at the time, when they had so recently sounded in the workforce and now once again called their families to dinner. Interestingly, in Baum's novel, *Mortgage on Life*,[2] Marian has lost her looks rather than her voice; the oculocentric context of film, where the star's looks sell the picture, demanded the more familiar narrative.

Though musical films faded in the U.S., the theme of women's voice loss never truly disappeared, and it is perhaps not surprising that a major resurgence occurred in the 1990s and early 2000s, as "postfeminist" cultural studies, riot grrl culture, Mary Pipher's *Reviving Ophelia* (1994) and the Spice Girls' commercial "girl power" took root in public discourse. *The Little Mermaid* of 1989 became the first in what Cassandra Stover has called a "'New Wave' of princess films" in which the world of the fairy-tale stood in for pre-feminist culture, and the teen-girl protagonist, and her voice, represented an embodiment of feminist ideals and identity (Stover, 2013: 3-4). In the late 1990s, psychologists such as Carol Gilligan (1997) discussed adolescence as a crisis of voice, when girls in particular might face many pressures and decisions regarding agency and the threat of silencing. Laurie Halse Anderson's 1999 book *Speak*, a coming-of-age story dealing with the silencing effects of rape, became standard high school reading. A flood of films about teen girl singers – including those discussed above – followed these sociological revelations, coinciding with a renewed public enthusiasm for singing. The juggernaut *Idol* phenomenon launched in the UK in 2001, succeeded by a deluge of vocal-centric programming in a trend that has not yet faded. *American Idol*, beginning in 2002, yielded three young female winners, and a collection of teen-girl finalists, in its first four seasons. As the show offered millennial Americans a sense of sociocultural voice as they voted for their next pop star (see Meizel, 2011), it also contributed to a new generation of hopeful young singers, including millions of girls. And Simon Cowell, the co-creator of the *Idols* franchise and the force behind the equally global *X Factor* format, has often been casually described as a "Svengali" in the press (for example, Hogan, 2013); marketing theorists such as Chris Hackley and Stephen Brown have taken up the habit as well (Hackley et al., 2012). For Americans, the analogy may feel especially apt, given Cowell's British foreignness and his extensive impact on popular culture.

The *Idols* singers' idols have also had something to say about women's voices. Five years before pop sensation Beyoncé declared that girls "Run the World", she debuted a newly added dramatic ballad in the film version of *Dreamgirls* (Bill Condon, 2006), in which, as the character Deena Jones (modelled on Diana Ross), she breaks free of her manager's tight hold. "Listen", she sings to him, "I followed the voice you think you gave to me/But now I gotta find my own".[3] Deena has not lost her sonic voice, but she feels that it, along with her individual identity, has been subsumed in her manager's Svengali-like manipulations. The process of finding a voice in the years surrounding the turn of the millennium was redefined, as womanhood was redefined. If we can infer anything from the history of lost voices in film, it is this consistent conclusion: a woman's voice is embedded in, sounds in, is silenced within, contemporaneous discourses of gender and agency.

Finding a Singing Voice

It should not be overlooked that what is lost by the little mermaid's cinematic daughters is the *singing* voice. Though the mermaid gives up all means of vocal communication, in all of the aforementioned films where voice loss figures, the woman does not lose the capability of speech. Marie de Nardi can still shout at her son; Marian verbally spars with her protégé; though Bobbie's speech does sound damaged, she can still talk with her Aunt Ella, and can even speak on behalf of the disabled children she begins working with; Terri still converses normally, and moratorium on singing is self-imposed; Lewellen is quiet but still speaks when spoken to. This trend raises questions about raised voices, and why it has become customary to silence women's singing onscreen instead of their speech.

Western discourse on music often positions singing as something ultimately distinct from, even beyond speech. *What you cannot say, you can sing*, the expression goes. Neurologists have found this to be literally true; since singing and speaking engage different neurophysiological processes, and since singing particularly involves the right hemisphere of the brain, it can serve as a form of therapy in aphasic patients whose left hemispheres have been damaged (Schlaug et al., 2008). Communications research in the 1970s also suggested that these processes were gendered, and that (American) women had better skills in non-verbal communication than men did, while men were more comfortable with verbal communication. Some scholars urged their colleagues to consider singing as a form of nonverbal communication, and in 1978 Peter A. Andersen, Janis F. Andersen and John P. Garrison hypothesized that in this framework, women should experience less fear of public singing than of public speaking (Andersen et al., 1978). All of this is to say that by the late twentieth century and the early twenty-first, singing (especially in the absence of other instruments) came to be understood, if problematically, as a feminine value with a biological basis.

Also by that time, singing had shifted from a male-centred public activity to a female-centred one, especially as reflected in music education. J. Terry Gates, in 1989 (the same year Disney's *The Little Mermaid* entered the conversation), traced the gendered structures of American public singing from the eighteenth century through the twentieth, proposing that with the gradual female adoption of traditionally male social roles, choral singing in schools came to be dominated by young women's voices (Gates, 1989). Girls and boys sang in equal numbers by the 1930s, but after the cultural upheaval of the following decades, singing came to be understood as a woman's pastime.[4] In *Frock Rock*, Mavis Bayton discusses the prominence of singing in women's participation in popular music – technologically external instruments such as the guitar are conventionally the domain of men, while the embodied feminine voice is the one instrument that can logically *only* be possessed by a woman. Since it *is* embodied, and women's bodies are viewed as central to their identities, women are conventionally allowed, even expected to sing (Bayton, 1998). They are also often expected to dance, simultaneously, a challenge that has led more than once to lip-synching and scandals of authenticity, furthering the gendered discourses of bodily deception and manipulated voices; here, the technological Svengali replaces the woman's voice with a more perfect simulacrum of her own. The lesson from the popular music industry is this: if women's bodies are to be controlled, then their singing voices must be as well – and if women need to regain and declare their *own* control of their bodies, of their lives, then reclaiming a voice onscreen fulfils this important purpose.

Conclusion

Examining the history of American cinema and the shifting sociopolitical landscapes in (and of) which it has projected its visions and auditions, the transformation of women's voices can be heard clearly: the singing voice has moved from symbolizing the vulnerability of identity and its susceptibility to manipulation, to embodying the *affirmation* of identity, and serving as the seat of individual agency. Deeply intertwined to twentieth-century structures of power and resistance, the lost voice, which once could only be regained in death and divine transfiguration, gives way to a found voice that cannot be claimed by any external force or person. In the years surrounding the turn of the millennium, women in film are responsible for their own voices, and can/must resist any attempts at corruption by fame and fortune, by unscrupulous music producers, by societal pressures, by the actions of men. Films dealing with the loss and rediscovery of voices remind us that, even in its most metaphorical treatments, and even on silent screens, the sonic nature of voice remains fundamental; voice is a site where *power* and *sound* are intimately connected, mutually constitutive.

The cinematic story of women's voices lost and found is, of course, nowhere near its conclusion. In the second decade of the twenty-first century, major motion picture studios have initiated a flood of dark, live-action films that, in a sense, aim to reclaim the Grimm-er literary history that Disney's hegemony has smoothed over in its animated musicals. Perhaps also capitalizing on the Broadway success of *Wicked*, the mostly Dorothy-less retelling of the film *The Wizard of Oz* (1939) in other, and Othered, women's voices – and on the success of the 1995 novel that inspired it – this trend has so far produced *Snow White and the Huntsman* (Rupert Sanders, 2012); *Hansel & Gretel: Witch Hunters* (Tommy Wirkola, 2013), and Disney's own *Maleficent* (Robert Stromberg, 2014). In March 2014, two headlines caught my attention: first, on a panel in preparation for International Women's Day, former U.S. secretary of state Hillary Clinton declared women's equality to be "the great unfinished business of the 21st century" (Frizell, 2014). A little over a week later, the next tale in line for filmic re-imagination was announced: Sofia Coppola will direct Hans Christian Andersen's "The Little Mermaid" (Gettell, 2014). While the Coppola version ultimately did not materialize due to creative differences, Disney has confirmed a 2020 release for the live-action remake, to be directed by Rob Marshall and feature 19-year-old actress and singer Halle Bailey as Ariel.[5]

About the Author
Katherine Meizel is an Associate Professor of Ethnomusicology at Bowling Green State University in Ohio. She earned her PhD in ethnomusicology at UCSB, and also holds a doctorate in vocal performance. Her research includes topics in voice and identity, popular music and media, religion, American identities, and disability studies. Her book, *Idolized: Music, Media, and Identity in American Idol* (IU Press), was published in 2011; she also wrote about *Idol* for the magazine *Slate* from 2007 to 2011. She is currently co-editing the forthcoming *Oxford Handbook of Voice Studies*, and completing a monograph for Oxford University Press titled *Multivocality: An Ethnography of Singing on the Borders of Identity*.

Notes

1. Jennifer Fleeger, in her book *Mismatched Women: The Siren's Song through the Machine*, notes that the many women who worked as inkers and painters in Disney's animation studios were virtually erased when the Computer Aided Production System was introduced during production of *The Little Mermaid*, making their jobs redundant and silencing their voices (Fleeger, 2014: 107).
2. Published serially in *Collier's* in 1946, as "The Long Denial".
3. 'Listen' was composed by Henry Krieger, Scott Cutler and Anne Preven, with contributions by Beyoncé Knowles.
4. Gates also feared that the adoption of men's values by women – such as public singing – would not stop with the feminization of choral music culture. Eventually, it seemed, because men had grown disinterested in singing, a decline in women's singing was now inevitable as well, as girls would note boys' attitudes and follow suit.
5. For further information, see https://www.oprahmag.com/entertainment/tv-movies/a28304285/little-mermaid-disney-remake-trailer-cast-premiere-date-soundtrack/ (accessed July 11, 2019).

References

Andersen, H. C. (1983 [1837]) *Hans Christian Andersen: The Complete Fairy Tales and Stories*, translated by E. C. Haugaard (1974). New York: Anchor Books.

Andersen, P., J. F. Andersen and J. P. Garrison (1978) "Singing Apprehension and Talking Apprehension: The Development of Two Constructs". *Sign Language Studies* 19: 155–86.

Anderson, L. H. (1999) *Speak*. New York: Farrar, Straus, and Giroux.

Bakhtin, M. (1981) *The Dialogic Imagination: Four Papers*, translated by C. Emerson and M. Holquist. Austin: University of Texas Press.

Bauman, H. D. L. (2008) "Introduction: Listening to Deaf Studies". In *Open Your Eyes: Deaf Studies Talking*, 1–34. Minneapolis: University of Minnesota Press.

Bayton, M. (1998) *Frock Rock*. Oxford and New York: Oxford University Press.

Bowden, D. (1995) "The Rise of a Metaphor: 'Voice' in Composition Pedagogy". *Rhetoric Review* 14/1: 173–88.

Chion, M. (1999) *The Voice in Cinema*, translated by C. Gorbman. New York: Columbia University Press.

Coll, F. (2010) "'Just a Singing-Machine': The Making of an Automaton in George du Maurier's *Trilby*". *University of Toronto Quarterly* 79/2: 742–63.

Driscoll, C. (2008) "Girls Today: Girls, Girl Culture and Girl Studies". *Girlhood Studies* 1/1: 13–32.

Eurich-Rascoe, B. L. and H. Vande Kemp (1997) *Femininity and Shame: Women, Men, and Giving Voice to the Feminine*. Lanham, MD: University Press of America, Inc.

Fleeger, J. (2014) *Mismatched Women: The Siren's Song through the Machine*. Oxford: Oxford University Press.

Frizell, S. (2014) "Hillary Clinton Kicks Off International Women's Day at United Nations. 8 March". *Time*. http://time.com/16868/clinton-kicks-off-international-womens-day-at-united-nations/ (accessed March 31, 2014).

Fryer, P. (2005) *The Opera Singer and the Silent Film*. Jefferson, NC and London: McFarland & Company, Inc.

Gates, J. T. (1989) "A Historical Comparison of Public Singing by American Men and Women". *Journal of Research in Music Education* 37/1: 32–47.

Gettell, O. (2014) "Sofia Coppola in Talks to Direct Live-Action 'Little Mermaid' Film". *L.A. Times*, March 19. http://www.latimes.com/entertainment/movies/moviesnow/la-et-mn-sofia

-coppola-to-direct-live-action-little-mermaid-film-20140319,0,6529211.story#axzz2yAX op0Rx (accessed March 31, 2014).

Gilligan, C. (1997) "Remembering Iphigenia: Voice, Resonance, and the Talking Cure". In *The Handbook of Infant, Child, and Adolescent Psychotherapy: Volume 2: New Directions in Integrative Treatment*, edited by B. S. Mark and J. A. Incorvaia, 169–94. Northvale, NJ: Jason Aronson, Inc.

Hackley, C., R. A. Hackley and S. Brown (2012) "The *X-Factor* Enigma: Simon Cowell and the Marketization of Existential Liminality". *Marketing Theory* 12/4: 451–69.

Hicks, T., with D. Wild (2007) *Heart Full of Soul: Am Inspirational Memoir about Finding Your Voice and Finding Your Way*. New York: Crown Publishers.

Hogan, M. (2013) "Simon Cowell Makes Surprise Appearance at *X Factor* Launch". *The Telegraph*, August 29. http://www.telegraph.co.uk/culture/tvandradio/x-factor/10274597/Simon-Cowell-makes-surprise-appearance-at-X-Factor-launch.html (accessed March 31, 2014).

Kim, M. and A. Y. Chung (2011) "Consuming Orientalism: Images of Asian American Women in Multicultural Advertising". In *The Kaleidoscope of Gender: Prismas, Patterns, and Possibilities*, edited by J. Z. Spade and C. G. Valentine, 263–75. Thousand Oaks, CA: Pine Forge Press.

Koplan, J. P. (2000) *Women and Smoking: A Report of the Surgeon General*. Department of Health and Human Services. Washington, DC: U.S. Government, Department of Health and Human Services.

Maurier, G. du (1899) *Trilby*. New York: International Book and Publishing Company.

Meizel, K. (2011) *Idolized: Music, Media, and Identity in* American Idol. Bloomington: Indiana University Press.

Mey, J. (1998) *When Voices Clash: A Study in Literary Pragmatics*. Berlin and New York: Mouton de Gruyter.

Pipher, M. (1994) *Reviving Ophelia*. New York: Riverhead Books.

Resnicoff, M. (1990) "Dave Davies – One of the Survivors". *Guitar Player*, March. http://www.davedavies.com/articles/gp_0390.htm (accessed March 31, 2014).

Schlaug, G., S. Marchina and A. Norton (2008) "From Singing to Speaking: Why Singing May Lead to Recovery of Expressive Language Function in Patients with Broca's Aphasia". *Music Percept* 25/4: 315–23.

Silverman, K. (1988) *The Acoustic Mirror: The Female in Psycholanalysis and Cinema*. Bloomington, IN: Indiana University Press.

Stewart, D. (1972) *The Authentic Voice: A Pre-Writing Approach to Student Writing*. Dubuque, IA: Brown.

Stover, C. (2013) "Damsels and Heroines: The Conundrum of the Post-Feminist Disney Princess". *LUX: A Journal of Transdisciplinary Writing and Research from Claremont Graduate University* 2/1: 1–10. http://scholarship.claremont.edu/lux/vol2/iss1/29 (accessed March 31, 2014).

Straus, J. N. (2011) *Extraordinary Measures: Disability in Music*. Oxford and New York: Oxford University Press.

Taylor, C. (1989) *Sources of the Self*. Cambridge, MA: Harvard University Press.

Taylor, E. and A. Landers (1989) "Interview with Ann Landers: Living By the Letter". *Time*, August 21. http://content.time.com/time/magazine/article/0,9171,958397,00.html (accessed March 31, 2014).

Ventura, D. S. (2013) "Sonata Resonates with Feeling". *The Daily Tribune*, September 11. http://www.tribune.net.ph/index.php/life-style/item/19018-sonata-resonates-with-feeling (accessed March 31, 2014).

4 Singing a Life in Bondage:
Black Vocality and Subjectivity in 12 Years a Slave

Gianpaolo Chiriacò

Since its release in October 2013, *12 Years a Slave* (Steve McQueen) has been celebrated as "easily the greatest feature film ever made about American slavery" (Debdy, 2013: 108), the one that "finally makes it impossible for American cinema to continue to sell the ugly lies it's been hawking for more than a century" (Dargis, 2013: 1). A few contrary voices have also been raised. Among them, Ruby Rich defined the film as just "Steve McQueen's newest saga of abjection" (Rich, 2013: 68), and Armond White wrote that "depicting slavery as a horror show, McQueen has made the most unpleasant American movie since William Friedkin's 1973 *The Exorcist*" (2013).[1] For the public and most of the critics alike, though, the violence in the movie is key to a poignant description of the struggle of a freeman kidnapped and brought as a slave to Louisiana in 1841.

In the so-called post-racial era, Angelita Reyes argued, "the extraordinary access to documents and information highways… enables discoveries of unknown, under-reported or once hidden narratives arising out of a monumental event – slavery" (Reyes, 2012: 165). In an interview with Henry Louis Gates Jr, McQueen stated that the movie is a product of its particular era, pinpointing the influence that the presidency of Barack Obama had on the rise of a new scenario.[2] The director is adamant, though, that his film is not about race. "I wanted to tell a story about slavery", he states; "this film is about Solomon Northup and how he survived… I hope it goes beyond race".[3] If a theme of a movie is its "common denominator" (Bandirali and Terrone, 2009: 32), then can we consider McQueen's angle as appropriate? His movie is about survival, or more precisely about strategies to survive within the context of a dehumanization based on race.

I will explore the role of the singing voice in these strategies, and in the narrative of Solomon Northup as presented by the movie. At its simplest level, the singing voice in *12 Years a Slave* signifies a distinct slave culture, with its practices and its meanings. Solomon, being a freeman from his birth, separates himself from it, but eventually embraces that culture as part of his strategy to survive. Also, McQueen, identifying the singing voice with slave culture, positions the black vocality, a distinct way of using the voice that can be considered African-

American,[4] in its original birthplace, in its original soundscape. By doing so, he instils into the American collective memory a culturally meaningful portrait of where that vocality originates, and of where it belongs.[5] This, one can argue, is a move into a dialogue about race. Many have highlighted the fact that only an international not-only-American cast, directed by a British moviemaker, could have made such an extremely merciless description of American slavery, with its perversion and its brutality.[6] I do not support this thesis. But I want to suggest that it is indeed meaningful that the cast of *12 Years a Slave* represents a sample of black Atlantic identities, as the conversation around slavery, and therefore about race, needs to be internationalized.[7]

The texts that I deal with in this chapter employ a racially offensive and abusive language, as part of a portrait of the brutal system of slavery in the plantation South. In the spirit of bearing witness that animates McQueen's cinematic production, and in compliance with scholarly accuracy, I kept such language as it is, although I am aware that my quotations may be offensive to some readers, to whom I apologize.

Commenting on Solomon's uncommon situation, the sound in the movie has been polarized in three ways. First, we find the opposition between silence and vocalization; then a dichotomy between his violin playing and singing; and finally, the sharp contrast regarding the two diegetic songs of the movie – 'Run Nigger Run' and 'Roll Jordan Roll'. These three oppositions signify on the main polarities of the plot:[8] slavery versus freedom; Solomon's performing practice in a white environment as opposed to expressions of an original slave culture; and finally the black/white racial distinctions, and the different cultural contexts that emerged from them. In addition, the singing voice provides a path into the psychology of characters. It articulates hopes and frustrations related to the main character's socio-geographical environment. Through a comparison of 'Roll Jordan Roll', interpreted by Solomon and the choir, to another scene filmed by McQueen in which the singing voice is central – Carey Mulligan's rendition of 'New York, New York' (John Kander and Fred Ebb, 1977) in *Shame* (Steve McQueen, 2011) – it is possible to underline one of McQueen's stylistic features, based on a particular use of voice. In conclusion, while relating the movie and the book, I will underline how a specific mythology of black voice and black vocal attitude is simultaneously confirmed and expanded in the movie.

The movie is inspired by the true story of Solomon Northup, written by himself and edited by David Wilson. Published the same year of his rescue, the book is part of the successful autobiographical genre of the slave narratives, made of personal accounts of individuals who had endured slavery. By telling direct experiences of slavery from the point of view of people who escaped or became free, slave narratives dispensed first-hand descriptions of the brutality of slavery as a "peculiar institution" within the debate that was animating the public discourse before the Emancipation Proclamation. They were not only factual representations of human exploitation; they were also a proof of the ability of ex-slaves to become literate, or at least eloquent. Both aspects made the slave narrative of the antebellum America a major tool of the abolitionist movement.

The plot of the movie follows the book's narrative closely, with one major difference: John Ridley's screenplay focuses more on personal struggles than on a description of the slave system (Berlin 2003). Solomon (Chiwetel Ejiofor), married and the father of three, is a free black violin player in upstate New York. He travels to Washington, DC for a job offer, where, instead of being employed, he is poisoned and put in chains. There, he is beaten and threatened by the slave-trader Burch (Christopher Berry). Rather than yielding to his initial instinct to fight, Solomon realizes that his first priority must be to survive. Transported to New Orleans under the new name Platt, he is sold to Ford (Benedict Cumberbatch), a religious man who appreciates his professional skills as well as his musical talent. The envy of Ford's oversee, Tibeats (Paul Dano), is exacerbated due to a disagreement. When Tibeats attempts to use his rawhide whip, Platt fights back, but is nearly lynched. As a result, Platt is then purchased by Epps (Michael Fassbender), a fierce slaveholder who employs violence and other tools of mental control. Epps is also engaged in a depraved relationship with Patsey (Lupita Nyong'o), a slave girl with whom he has fallen in love and whose body he subjugates through violence. Epps's jealous wife (Sarah Paulson) insists that Patsey be punished, and in one of the most appalling scenes, Platt is compelled to whip the young black woman under threats from a gun-wielding Epps. Bass (Brad Pitt), a carpenter from Canada, is the only white man in Platt's world who vilifies slavery, and it is to him that Platt finds the courage to tell his story. The letter that the Canadian sends to Saratoga brings Henry Northup, an influential white man and family friend of Solomon, to the plantation. Although Epps attempts to defend his property, Platt regains his freedom and, after a long hug with Patsey, walks to Henry's coach while the girl shouts his slave name as images of the plantation fade away. After his return to his native North, Solomon is reunited with his family. We learn that he eventually became a famous abolitionist and worked for the Underground Railroad.

Silence and Performance

The singing voices of the slaves are at the forefront from the very first scene of the movie, in which a group of slaves is singing a worksong. From then on, singing becomes a determining part in every scene of hands in the field, with a single exception that I will discuss later. Nevertheless, the narrative logic of the movie is based on silence. Solomon has to hide his origins as a free man and thus cannot speak about his original status. His silence becomes a crucial part of the movie, contrasting sharply with the musical expressions of the community of slaves. I posit that this conflict significantly contributes to making *12 Years a Slave* a portrait of slavery as we can understand it today.

Although I agree with Zachary Price on the point that the risk of making the "silence for survival" central is to reify a white hegemony (Price, 2015), I argue, with Salamishah Tillet, that depicting Solomon as a "figure of submission and survival", McQueen created "a metaphor for post-civil rights African American identities" (Tillet, 2012: 45). This is what Tillet, studying "sites of slavery" in different artistic contexts, defined as "a move… that enables post-civil rights African Americans to stage the ultimate rhetorical coup, one in which they wrestle with and eventually recuperate the primordial site of black racial inequality – slavery – as the basis for a more racially democratic future" (2012: 18).

Narratives such as that written by Frederick Douglass well describe the necessity to learn how to read and write as a way to break the bonds of captivity and to voice "the will of human heart to speak its own mind".[9] The particular condition of Solomon is such that, even though he had earlier experienced the value of the right to speak, he must now adopt a strategy of contemptuous silence. But McQueen wants to show us how this strategy is constrained by the necessity to keep a memory alive. The movie shows us how Solomon must negotiate his silence and the singing expression of a common condition, which allows him to create relationships within the slave community.

Silence, indeed, plays a big part in the book, as well. And, as we will see later, it also creates a permanent contrast with vocalizations of sorrow. However, silence in the book is a calculated response by Solomon to his situation. It is, in Solomon's view, a necessity, the consequence of logical reasoning. He knows that speaking out means sacrificing his own life, or a descent into more brutal circles of hell. The mechanical banality of evil is even more apparent in the book, as this passage clarifies:

> I was almost on the point of disclosing fully to Ford the facts of my history. I am inclined now to the opinion it would have resulted in my benefit. This course was often considered, but through fear of its miscarriage, never put into execution, until eventually my transfer and his pecuniary embarrassments rendered it evidently unsafe. Afterwards, under other masters, unlike William Ford, I knew well enough the slightest knowledge of my real character would consign me at once to the remoter depths of Slavery. I was too costly a chattel to be lost, and was well aware that I would be taken farther on, into some by-place, over the Texan border, perhaps, and sold; that I would be disposed of as the thief disposes of his stolen horse, if my right to freedom was even whispered. So I resolved to lock the secret closely in my heart – never to utter one word or syllable as to who or what I was (Northup, 2013: 57-58).

In McQueen's imagination, though, silence appears as a signifying element by itself.[10] It is the centre between an unspeakable truth and the false certainty as the status of a slave in which Solomon finds himself. The adoption of his contemptuous silence is sufficient to survive, but it does not make him part of the slave community. He has to sing to join in. In other words, he has to perform as a slave to be part of a slave culture.[11] It is the performative act of singing out that allows Solomon to construct the identity of "free slave".[12]

Being based on an image of Solomon that a contemporary public can understand, the movie is nurtured by the fragile balance between his distance from slavery and the necessity of human relationships even in bondage. Those relationships, though, take him far away from his origins and his real status as a free man. That is exactly where Solomon's struggle lies. Such struggle is perfectly portrayed, through images and singing voices, in the moment when he finally accedes to the necessity to join the choral singing of 'Roll Jordan Roll'. His singing has all the characteristics of a fight, depicting his personal difficult acceptance of his position. He initially refuses to sing and does not join the choir in their response to the call of the leader (Topsy Chapman). But slowly he accepts it, he moves his eyes around, he whispers; and then his singing becomes a grunt, a liberation, an abandonment. While he sings, he can finally express his feelings. Through this act, Solomon confirms the idea of what a slave is supposed to be: there are limited ways by which a man in bondage can express himself in the plantation South – singing is one of them. That expression of feelings is, as McQueen shows in his movie, his performance of slavery: through singing, Solomon becomes Platt. However, at the end of the song, as we will see, Platt regains the right of being Solomon again.

The dialogue with Eliza (Adepero Oduye) illuminates another emblematic aspect of the contrast between silence as a strategy and vocal expressions. Eliza is a slave woman at Ford's plantation, who has been with Solomon since they were transported together from Maryland to Louisiana. Her two children had been taken away from her in New Orleans, and she could find no consolation. Solomon is tired of Eliza's constant moans, so he asks her to hush her weeping. This results in her accusing him of having forgotten, of having erased the memory of his own children. When he strongly denies this, she accuses him: "but you make no sounds". In this fundamental statement, Eliza affirms that Solomon's attempt is a dangerous one, as his silence will eventually extinguish his memory of a better time when he and his family were free and prosperous.

The role of sounds, songs or voices, as a way to preserve a memory and therefore protecting an identity, or even preserving the existence of an identity beyond slavery, is ubiquitous in literature about African-American music.[13] As Guthrie P. Ramsey Jr has written, "cultural forms such as tales, stories, and music (especially the *performative* aspects of such) function as reservoirs in which cultural memories reside" (Ramsey, 2003: 32–33; original emphasis). Eliza is asking to Solomon/Platt to hold on to that memory, and to make some culturally meaningful noise to keep it, as a performance of black culture. When Solomon does sing, he finally makes his voice heard. The vocal performance of "reservoirs of cultural memories" in 'Roll Jordan Roll' becomes in fact his weapon in the battle for control and for agency.

Violin and Songs

Looking at McQueen's movie as a portrait of slavery and therefore of black culture in the plantation South, I would now turn my focus onto Solomon's experiences as violinist. This would shed light on another aspect related to people of African origins in 1850s America and establish other paths of analysis of the singing voice in the movie. Thanks to his practice as a professional musician, Solomon had travelled, he had visited several North American cities, and was acquainted with individuals of different classes and races. He had made himself a professional, entrepreneurial and creative man who could well interpret the socio-economic value of the dynamic and adventurous America of that time. He is a smart and ingenious individual, and these qualities, his dramatic capture and condition notwithstanding, are underlined throughout the movie. Despite McQueen's distancing the film from a discourse on race, the fact that it stresses the individual qualities of an exceptional freeman in antebellum America represents a significant difference from previous movies involving slavery. Even a film such as *Half Slave, Half Free* (Gordon Parks, 1984), based on the same book, is focused more on the collective experience of African Americans than on the subjectivity of the characters.[14]

Solomon plays violin in Louisiana, as well. He is called upon at the house of the trader Freeman (Paul Giamatti), where Solomon and other slaves are sold. He is requested to play to cover Eliza's cries when her children are taken away from her. He is also encouraged to play, in Epps's house at night, when the drunk master instructed his property to cheer up and move rhythmically. "Dance!" he shouts imperiously to his slaves, who have been wearied after an entire day in the field. Katrina Dionne Thompson argues that "the first form of American entertainment was the music, song, and dance performed by enslaved blacks for the amusement and under the coercion of whites on the Southern plantation" (Thompson, 2014: 7). Slaveholders like Epps "purposely crafted an atmosphere that induced blacks to perform… They purposely orchestrated performances on the plantation and made music and dance strategically organized aspects of plantation life" (Thompson, 2014: 80). Both Thompson and Abrahams (1993) explain how these performances were also fundamental moments in which African Americans developed strategies of resistance. It was within this context, moreover, that particularly skilled individuals – among them, musicians, singers or dancers – were able to affirm their role as cultural mediators in the plantation life.

Thompson's interpretation of race relations in the plantation South is a useful tool to understand how racial distinctions were showed in, and fundamental to, performances and performance strategies. Being able to continuously reshape the performances according to the audience was a crucial skill for black Americans. Subtle but meaningful differences in performance practices allowed blacks to gain tactical advantages while keeping vital secrets hidden from the white audience. However, here McQueen prefers to establish a sharper difference between the music played for the white audience and the music practice that is presented as quintessentially African American. If the former was enforced and included fiddle and dance, the latter was essentially sung. This substantiates the image of Solomon as an exceptional man, his subjectivity put on the forefront just like his musical skills. But at the same time, it enforces the notion that a performance of slavery gravitates around the singing voice.

The singing of the slave has often been interpreted as a more original expression, from the standpoint of white observers and from that of slave biographies as well. McQueen invites us to accept this view. The worksongs in the field, the humming of Patsey, and the song sung by the slaves for their fellow's funeral, are all part of an original slave culture that developed in the plantations, and subsequently rooted cultural productions that Americans of African origins created after slavery. Lawrence W. Levine (2007) and many other scholars after him explained how a specific culture and a specific consciousness can be traced from songs and other oral traditions. But here McQueen over-stresses the role of the singing voice as a medium. It is through vocal practices, in the humming, in the increasing excitement of the call-and-response, in the clapping, in the transformed and therefore expressive faces of singers, in resonating bodies, that the construction of "true communities of men" is relayed (Ong, 1967: 124).

The movie explained it with vivid force, suggesting that the presence of voice and of vocal performances erupts with a power that transcends the words. It is interesting to note that McQueen does not delve too specifically into the slave culture, as he is more concerned with showing the racial line of separation between the world of slaves and that of enslavers. Therefore, the singing voice, especially the act of collective singing, exemplifies the slave culture as a whole, even though it is not used to recount, for example, rituals such as the ring shout or storytelling of any sort. The essential presence of the singing voice in *12 Years a Slave* is what Michel Chion called, drawing from the psychoanalytic studies of Denis Vasse, "the vocal cord". It is a voice that "could imaginarily take up the role of an umbilical cord, as a nurturing connection, allowing no chance of autonomy to the subject trapped in its umbilical web" (Chion, 1999: 62). The image of the vocal cord is particularly effective as it reflects the extent to which that singing tradition keeps Platt alive. But it also keeps him trapped in a community to which he does not belong, but to which he depends on in order to survive. If, as said, the performative act of singing out allows Solomon to construct the identity of a "free slave", it is only by accepting the latter of the two elements – slavery – that he can get his freedom back. This is a tremendously complex relationship that McQueen so successfully describes.

Black and White Singers

The topic of a slave culture that developed through songs is explored in the movie along another axis that the singing voices signal. There are, in fact, two main non-original songs, sung during the scenes, in a diegetic pose. They might be considered classics. "'Run Nigger Run' and 'Roll Jordan Roll' are companion pieces", affirms journalist and critic Ann Powers (2013), and they both are included in the oldest, and still one of the most authoritative, collection of slave music, *Slave Songs of the United States* (Allen, Ware and McKim Garrison, 1867). The former is the first song that immediately positions us in the regime of forced labour and life. The white overseer Tibeats sings it before Solomon and other slaves, as to instil fear in their minds, to forge a scared spirit that must be maintained throughout their working hours. The choice is particularly appropriate, as the song refers to the patrollers, a militia whose task was to watch over slaves during the night, with the aim to stop any black person walking without a pass from his or her master. By singing about the patrollers, Tibeats is explaining very carefully, to the new slave Solomon and to us, what is risked by running away.

In 1925, Dorothy Scarborough described the origins of the song, reporting the words of Dr John A. Weith, a Southerner later based in New York.

> He said of *Run Nigger Run*, a famous slavery-time song, which I had heard my mother sing, that it is one of the oldest of the plantation songs. White people were always afraid of an insurrection among the Negroes, and so they had the rule that no Negro should be off his own plantation, especially at night, without a pass. They had patrols along the roads to catch truant Negroes, and the slaves called them *patter-rollers*. The darkies sang many amusing songs about the patrols and their experiences in eluding them (Scarborough, 1925: 23).

It is also appropriate that a white man is singing this song in the film. We know, in fact, that "'Run Nigger Run' became so popular that many white people sang it" (Fisher, 1953: 81). Moreover, in the context of the movie, the tune works perfectly both to explain the different roles of white males in the plantation system (the patriarchal master, the shabby overseer, the cruel patroller) and to create the fear that will reverberate throughout the movie.

Furthermore, in his iconic style, McQueen depicts – with the song – the strategy of slaveholders and overseers alike: they use a slave song to their own advantage, either for simple pleasure or to convey warnings and admonishments. Powers describes efficiently how *12 Years a Slave* depicts the interactions of blacks and whites through music:

> among the many challenges this film poses to viewers, one is to understand how music has both supported the liberation and self-expression of African-Americans and filled an imaginary space of reconciliation and even joy, where oppressors can lie to themselves about the cruelty they inflict. Music culture in America has often defeated racism and, just as often, perpetuated it (Powers, 2013).

McQueen's Tibeats sounds like a professional vocalist. His singing is almost scientific. He requires the slaves to clap their hands, a simple task that catches their attention. He establishes fear, he transmits it through his voice, he sighs, he exhales. His voice becomes vicious and then ubiquitous, when the song turns extradiegetic. As the camera moves to Ford and his reading of the Bible in front of his slaves, we experience the "powers of the acousmêtre" (Chion, 1999: 23-24). The voice of the overseer spans all over the plantation, and even beyond that. It indicates a powerful tool of mental control. Ford's and Tibeats's voices also overlap, creating an additional intersection of meanings: fear, suppression, and a tactical use of religion.

On the other end of the axis there is 'Roll Jordan Roll'. This song embodies Solomon's subjective struggle. What is important here is to understand the song's role in the narrative. "The relation of songs to narrative in plays and films varies enormously... They may set a mood or else function as scene-setting... They may act as commentary or reflection on the action" (Dyer, 2012: 9). In this case, the song both sets a scene and provides a commentary. It introduces the internal practices of the community of captives. Also, through the opposition to Tibeats's song, it enforces the frame of that relationship between whites and blacks that is so central to the narrative. The two songs complement one another, just like the two races are part of the same slave society, although in completely different roles.

In the aforementioned *Slave Songs of the United States*, 'Roll Jordan Roll' appears as the first song.[15] Whereas 'Run Nigger Run' approximately respects the musical score presented in the book, 'Roll Jordan Roll' is performed in a different way, thanks to the arrangement of composer Nicholas Britell. The performance in the movie emphasizes call-and-response. It is a more sanctified version, therefore it sets the perfect background for Solomon's voice to eventually rise up.[16]

Sissy and Solomon

The scene in which Solomon finally joins the choir in 'Roll Jordan Roll' is extremely significant within the tale, but the song also plays a fundamental part in the more intimate exploration of subjectivities. Apparently, the use of singing voices in McQueen's movies requires scenes wherein the singing voice breaks in and literally stops the sequence of events. In his study of the uses of songs in film, Richard

Dyer states that a song functions as "an interruption, a change of pace, a pause for something different" (Dyer, 2012: 9). McQueen adopts these pauses in his works, as he regularly incorporates vocal tunes to truly investigate subjectivities. The version of 'Roll Jordan Roll' that we see in *12 Years a Slave* is stylistically similar to the rendition of 'New York, New York' that occupies an equivalent position in *Shame* (Steve McQueen, 2011). The main character's sister, Sissy (Carey Mulligan), is performing the song in a club, where Brandon (Michael Fassbender) and his boss (James Badge Dale) went to enjoy the show. The long close-up on Sissy overlapped with a close-up on the face of Brandon. His expression reveals that he is particularly moved by the song, in contrast to his boss, who participates as a mere observer.

Besides technical similarities, the two scenes have more things in common. Sissy and Solomon are both musicians, they both feel under-respected, they both move in an environment that forces them to adapt their ambitions – Solomon being kidnapped into slavery, Sissy looking for a career as a singer in the big city ("If I can make it there, I'll make it anywhere"). They both sing about the socio-cultural environments in which they are impelled to live, exemplified by these specific songs. To Sissy, the song itself recalls the city, its geographical environment. In Solomon's case, 'Roll Jordan Roll', as seen, is one of the most symbolic slave songs, drawing upon the metaphors of baptism and of water as an element that brings liberation. In addition, the lyrics of the two songs suggest the image of a new birth, although one is material ("I'll make a brand new start of it") and one spiritual, as crossing the biblical Jordan leads to the promised land. Both of the scenes foster the use of metalinguistic traits: the breath, the whispering in *Shame*; the husky tones and the facial gestures of Ejiofor in *12 Years*. Yet, the close-up is very revealing – in the case of *12 Years a Slave*, it goes from Topsy Chapman who lines out the tune to the "ensemble", to Solomon's face. In *Shame*, it moves significantly from Sissy to Brandon ("top of the heap"), whose personal struggle – his sexual addiction and his perverted relationships – is embedded in his New Yorker lifestyle.

That the voice is central is also confirmed by the absence of musical accompaniment. In 'New York, New York' the piano – already quite minimal and angular – disappears in the most emphatic points. In 'Roll Jordan Roll', there is no accompaniment at all, and the close-up coincides with a lower volume of the choir. The fact that these two songs correspond to interruptions, and the fact that both Sissy and Solomon are two subjugated characters – the former being a female artist who has already tried to commit suicide; the latter being a slave, a property with no rights – signals that the singing voice here is functional to a "diegetic interiority" (Silverman, 1988: 71). It can be argued that in McQueen's aesthetic the singing voice, when it invades the visual scene through the mouths of main characters, illustrates their interior universes. In *12 Years a Slave*, by bringing the public into Solomon's subjectivity,[17] the director uses the tool of a diegetic singing voice as a sort of vocal voyeurism.

When Platt sings 'Roll Jordan Roll', at first we see Chapman's face. She starts to clap and sings the first stanza of the song. They are singing for the departure of the soul of a field hand who had died under the blasting sun. Once the leader introduces the song, the call-and-response, a fundamental element of the African-American musicality, comes to the forefront. We see the group of slaves, standing in front of the area where the dead companion has been buried, singing the song as a group. We also spot Patsey singing with a rare smile on her face – we are immediately reminded of the brief moment of calm happiness that she enjoyed while forming dolls from leaves and corn ears and humming a quiet tune. Then Platt becomes the centre of the scene.

The moments that follow are all about him. We see the inner contrast of his condition of "free slave" depicted through his surrender to the song. First, he strongly refuses, his eyes averted, his mouth closed, his hands along his hips. His determination, though, is not steady, as we see when the camera catches him. He starts moving his lips, still uncertain, still trying to tune up. As the choir increases its volume, Solomon looks around and introduces his voice timidly. He finally releases his voice completely. The focus is all on his lips and his eyes. He displays his teeth, opens his mouth more explicitly, closes his eyes, and lets his voice ring out, joining the choir of slaves. Toward the end of the scene, after several nods of his head, he is singing and he looks up, aiming at the sky, delivering his chant towards a higher level of justice. This fascination with the gestures and the slave body closely reflect the descriptions provided by colonel Thomas Wentworth Higginson. His notorious reports about his black soldiers during the Civil War, some of them ex-slaves, show a similar fascination: "the glow reflected gorgeously from their red legs & not dimingly from their shining cheeks & white teeth and rolling eyes" (Higginson, 2000: 248). The perception of the body in the voice is brightly described by Roland Barthes in his popular article on the grain of the voice (Barthes, 1977). Here, we are invited to hear the body in the voice, as we can see Platt's facial movements and how he is using them to reject the sonic invitation, and to finally project his voice. He joins the choir but at the same time tries to reach the sky. He invokes a supreme level of justice.

By signifying a particular racial, ethnic and gendered identity through his voice, Platt is portraying his struggle to resist. By performing in a distinctive and individual black voice – with his harsh tone, the call-and-response, the use of his body – Platt is looking for a final form to express his resistance, notwithstanding his apparent acceptance of the condition of bondage. Using the words of Mike Sell, here

> the Black Voice – as scream, shout, signifyin' inversion, science-dropping soapbox crusade, Negro spiritual, tragic dramatic cry, street-echoing cackle, and a myriad of other vocal modes – is understood to be the crucial lever to unhinge the spiritual and material hegemony

of whiteness... The Black voice, it was argued, would undermine to the point of collapse the most stubbornly institutionalized conceptual categories of Western thought (Sell, 2006: 278).[18]

In other words, performing vocally while in bondage does not confirm an acceptance of a slave system. It rather manifests the unbroken search for a safe space through the delivery of an uproarious vocal sound.

That Platt's signifying on that performance of black voice will finally result in his success is suggested by the fact that, once Platt has finally joined the choral performance, there is no more singing until the end of the movie. The echo of his singing voice anticipates his liberation. Even when we see again the hands in the field, at the beginning of the scene in which Platt is finally saved by Henry Northup, there are no vocal sounds, neither talking nor singing. Platt's narrative arch is eventually completed: a white man is coming to free a slave. This exceptional moment is signalled by the silence among the black crowd.

Black Utterances

I now want to focus my attention on the original story, the book published by Northup right after he returned to Saratoga. What is the role of singing in the book? Quite surprisingly, as prevalent as it is in the movie, the singing voice rarely appears in the book. There are just two occurrences of singing, and one is not presented as a personal memory of his time in slavery but rather as a more general account of tunes that were usually sung. The absence of singing is striking insofar as Northup himself is a musician, and it would be reasonable to expect a more substantial presence of songs. Even more interesting is that, at the same time that the book was published, a myth of the black singing voice was already well established.

Among the most popular descriptions of black singing was Frederick Douglass's poignant assertion that to understand slavery's violent reality one must hear the sound of slavery.[19] Young travellers and writers who were destined to be highly influential persons in late nineteenth-century America, such as Frederick Law Olmsted (1856, 1953) and Whitelaw Reid (1965), enriched their articles and books with many accounts of the powerful, exotic, sometimes "barbarous", but always enchanting, slave voices.

Shane White and Graham White have provided a stunning depiction of what slavery time may have sounded like. By consolidating the words of George Hepwort, a Union inspector in 1863 Louisiana, and Elizabeth Ross Hite, a former Louisiana slave, the two scholars provide a capturing presentation of vocal utterances: "the whole audience [after a service] swayed back and forward in their seats, and uttered in perfect harmony a sound like that caused by prolonging the letter *m* with the lips closed" (White and White, 2005: 101). Elizabeth echoed the description, clarifying the meaning: "you gotta shout and you gotta moan if you want to be saved" (102).

The movie relies on this enormous treasure of descriptions to replace the absence of singing in the book. The voices in 'Roll Jordan Roll', in worksongs, in Patsey's humming, emerge and unfold the meaning of the chant as well as its cultural and religious carriage. The often bewitched tone of the aforementioned accounts, though, obscures the racial imagination that nurtures them. Ronald Radano, studying a vast *corpus* of sources, focuses his attention on the racial distinctions and connotations on which the idea of black music developed. He also recognizes a few traits of shared space, where voices and experiences are at the forefront. In scenarios like the ones in camp meetings:

> as the songful utterances of Christians merged with the physical "cries and groans" of the struck, worshipers could be transported in a vibrant responsorial interchange of sonic-sensuous contact. It was at these sound-drenched moments of psychic precariousness that the bodily affecting force of "spiritual" encounter could produce within the frames of interracial singing a momentary glimpse of racial transcendence (Radano, 2003: 134).

While incorporating into his film crucial moments of singing, McQueen revitalizes this "sonic-sensuous contact", and uses it to portray an audiovisual image of singing a life in bondage that can be understood by his public. The effect is rather impressive because, even though this is an element of black vocality, it also "goes beyond race", as everyone can connect to the performance of the 'Roll Jordan Roll' song through either a personal experience of religious fervour or one of a passionate singing, or both.

In addition, despite the absence of singing, the voice itself plays a very important role in the book. Several vocal utterances have a remarkable position in describing the complexity of feelings of the field hands. They have been defined as slave utterances, and "include screams, falsetto, rasps, yells, calls, chants, cries, field hollers, grunts, groans, moans, keening (eerie wails), yodels, ululation and shouts – not to be confused with the ring shout or 'shout' associated with religious expression" (Payne, 2011: 884). They are ubiquitous both in the slave narratives and in the ex-slave interviews of the Federal Writers Projects, as well as in similar collections (Chiriacò 2014). They embodied the variety of possibilities of the voice as a means of expression, which has also found its way in singing practices. It would seem that these vocal expressions pertain to the world of pre-verbal expressions. This is but part of the reality, as the distinction between the word and the instrument that delivers it, the voice, is imprecise. Adriana Cavarero, in her philosophy of vocal expression, clarifies that "the semantic role of a word is saturated by a vocality that anchors it to the drives of the body" (Cavarero, 2003: 156). Within the context of slave utterances, the voice becomes also the *locus* of the relationality. Slave culture, in other words, is the space where a multivocality prevails. It is the ensemble of different voices, their interconnected differences, which constitute values and meanings, as well as the ties of meanings and values, defining the perimeter of the collective expressions in the Southern plantation.

The role of these utterances is so fundamental that *12 Years a Slave*, the book, might be read as a vocal testimony, where the voices – although not as much the singing voice, but rather the voice as a basic element of the overall depiction – are often at the forefront. A compelling example of this is the march of slaves leaving Washington for Louisiana. In Solomon's own words, it becomes a vocal and sonic contrast: "The voices of patriotic representatives boasting of freedom and equality, and the rattling of the poor slave's chains" (Northup, 2013: 21–22). McQueen transforms it visually by using the strong image of the Capitol dome as the background for the departing coffle.

A similarly powerful example of the presence of such a voice in the book is the attempt to lynch Platt by Tibeats and his companions. McQueen uses the scene to portray one of the most disturbing passages of the movie, the one in which Platt, his neck in a noose, balancing on the tips of his toes, remains semi-hung on the massive live oak for an entire day. Platt's voice is in the forefront, both in the movie and in the book: "There I still stood in the noon-tide sun, groaning with pain". The voices, the one choked in the throat of a near-lynched man and the one expressing the woman's pity, formulate a paradigm of sorrow:

> The humble creature never knew, nor could she comprehend if she had heard them, the blessings I invoked upon her, for that balmy draught. She could only say, *Oh, Platt, how I do pity you*, and then hastened back to her labors in the kitchen (Northup, 2013: 77–78).

This paradigm of sorrow, and yet the wealth of the possibility to express it in all the implications and nuances, is what the black vocality here described represents at its most expressive point, later to be employed in a variety of musical and performative styles.

What McQueen's interpretation of the book unravels is a representation of how these vocal sounds, which are frequently described on print within the slave narratives and other accounts, found their way into vocal practices. The movie, therefore, confirms and simultaneously expands the idea of a black vocality as it has been structured by scholars and performers alike. Such a practice, in its original slave environment, is not separated from the social conditions. It is not separated from the soundscape of slavery. Quite the opposite, it resonates in, and it comes from, the physical space in which the slave society operated. As Carlo Serra indicates, in his investigation of the relationship between traditional vocal practices and space, there are streams of identification that cannot be disconnected. "We can silently assume that the chant is an intermediary element. It is hyper-hyphenated. It can connect the human being with the voice of nature and therefore suggest a stream of identifications" (Serra, 2011: 105).

The connections between voices and soundscape in the plantation culture of the South remains an uninvestigated one. Such a study would contribute to a more profound understanding of the role that singing voices played in structuring the American slave culture. Northup gave us what might be considered a clue to where this exploration might lead, in his poignant, sonic description of Epps's land: "It is the literal, unvarnished truth, that the crack of the lash, and the shrieking of the slaves, can be heard from dark till bed time, on Epps' plantation, any day almost during the entire period of the cotton-picking season" (Northup, 2013: 117). While this exploration still has to be pursued, it is my argument that – by positioning it in the iconic sequences of the movie, and by transferring it from the book to the vocal performances – McQueen inserts such a vocality in a wider frame. He redefines it as a means of expression that finds its way in singing, as a socially meaningful practice, and as a culturally specific symbol. Simultaneously, McQueen positions black vocality in its original soundscape, making a strong contribution to the contemporary conceptualization of a traditional African-American singing voice. This is a fundamental stone for the reconstruction of a collective memory that is an indispensable tool to move "beyond race".

About the Author
Gianpaolo Chiriacò is a Lise Meitner researcher at the Archive of Popular Music-Universität Innsbruck. He is mainly interested in the history and anthropology of black singing voices, and in musical expressions of Afro-Italian identities and communities. He has been a fellow researcher at the University of Chicago and worked for three years at the Center for Black Music Research (Columbia College Chicago) thanks to a Marie Skłodowska-Curie Fellowship. He authored the book *Voci Nere. Storia e antropologia del canto afroamericano* (2018) and curated the symposia "Black Vocality: Cultural Memories, Identities, and Practices of African-American Singing Styles" (www.afrovocality.com). Chiriacò taught ethnomusicology and popular music at the University of Salento, where he also earned his PhD, and at the Freie Universität Bolzano-Bozen.

Notes
1. According to many journalists and some of the people present at the awards ceremony hosted by the New York Film Critics Circle, Armond White shouted insults towards Steve McQueen during the event, as he was stepping on stage to receive the award as best director. McQueen did not pay attention to the hostile words during that night, but afterwards, when Arsenio Hall reported them to him, he commented on the insults (https://www.indiewire.com/2014/01/watch-12-years-a-slave-director-steve-mcqueen-stays-classy-when-asked-about-armond-whites-comments-248517/, accessed June 1, 2020).
2. His exact words are: "one cannot underestimate the influence that President Barack Obama has had on all these recent films on African-American life" (Gates, 2013).

3. Director Steve McQueen made this claim during the press conference after the film's premiere at the Toronto International Film Festival. The question was: "can we talk about race in America?" In the video of the conference, McQueen's embarrassment is visible, as he argues that such a broad question overshadowed his movie (https://www.youtube.com/watch?v=qbHVhXlbYWA). A few months later, during the Academy Awards ceremony, he affirmed: "everyone deserves not just to survive, but to live".
4. During the symposium "Black Vocality: Cultural Memory, Identities, and Practices of African-American Singing Styles", held at Columbia College Chicago, September 24-25, 2013, as part of the international project project ROTVOSCIAME (The Role of Traditional Vocal Styles in Reshaping Cultural Identities Related to African Diasporas in America and Europe, http://www.afrovocality.com), the following working-definition of black vocality, drawing upon Meizel's study (2011a: 269), was used: "the set of vocal sounds, practices, techniques, values, qualities, meanings – as well as the entirety of the different combinations of them – that factor in the making of a black culture and in the negotiation of a black identity". Here, I use the same definition to investigate the role of black vocality in *12 Years a Slave*. For further discussions of singing and vocality within African-American contexts, see Chiriacò (2018), Eidsheim (2019), Griffin (2004), Jones (2019), Mentjes (2019), Newland (2014), Sebron (2018).
5. For a discussion about voice as a marker of race and identity, see Meizel (2011a, 2011b), Meizel and Scherer (2019), Eidsheim (2008, 2012, 2019), and Dunn and Jones (1994).
6. "Steve was the first to ask the big question, 'Why has there not been more films on the American history of slavery?' producer and actor Brad Pitt said last night at the film's world premiere at the Toronto Film Festival. 'And it was the big question it took a Brit to ask'" (Van Syckle, 2013).
7. The director is also concerned with bringing modern slavery to the public discourse. In the aforementioned acceptance speech of the Academy Award for Best Picture, McQueen said: "I dedicate this award to all the people who have endured slavery, and the 21 million people who still suffer slavery today".
8. When I use the expression "signify on", I rely on the concept of signifyin(g) in black culture, as theorized by Gates (1988), and developed within the musical context by Samuel A. Floyd, Jr (1995). The general definition that I am using here considers the signifyin(g) in the form of a reference to a culture or a subculture, whose meaning is expanded through the use of rhetorical figures.
9. These words come from the acceptance speech of Nikky Finney for the 2011 National Book Award. Her description of the effects of the slave codes, especially of the prohibition on becoming literate, is exceptionally touching (https://www.youtube.com/watch?v=Y2q15iiL79g).
10. Following Bresson's famous maxim, "the soundtrack invented silence" (Bresson, 1986: 38), scholar and composer Riccardo Giagni affirmed: "It is therefore in the sound film that the game of silence and hidden sound emerges as a newness and as an absolute truth". The original words are: "è dunque nel cinema sonoro che il gioco del silenzio e del suono nascosto emergono con una novità e una verità assolute" (Giagni, 2015: 22). It is interesting to note that silence is a singularly effective tool in *Hunger* (Steve McQueen, 2008), his first feature-length film. For a better understanding of Steve McQueen's aesthetics and artistic practices, see McQueen (2003, 2009, 2010, 2013).
11. My interpretation of silence as denial of the right to speak, and of the performance of slavery as a strategy to survive, is based on the works of two scholars: Judith Butler and

Shoshana Felman (Butler, 1997; Felman, 2003). Here I also use the concept of slave culture as it emerges from seminal works such as Levine (2007) and Stuckey (1987).

12. The condition of "free slave" is accurately described, in an article that appeared the day after the Academy Awards ceremony, by Henry Louis Gates Jr, who also worked as historical consultant for the production (Gates, 2014).
13. See, for example, Floyd (1995), and Fabre and O'Meally (1994).
14. *Half Slave, Half Free*, originally titled *Solomon Northup's Odyssey*, was produced for public television in 1984. A perfect example of the different focus is Solomon's last speech. Before leaving the plantation forever, he addresses his companions, and expresses his hope to save everybody, "to make a magic that would take us all". This monologue is not in the book, and it would be simply unimaginable in McQueen's movie. See also Ebiri (2013).
15. It also appears in other important collections, such as Work (1940: 199).
16. The rendition provided by John Legend, in *12 Years a Slave* (2013), the album that he produced, with "music from and inspired by the movie", is closer to the version reported by the old collection. In the same album, one can hear the original orchestral soundtrack composed by Hans Zimmer, and criticized by Ramsey (2013), who writes: "ironically – and there's no elegant way to put this – the string music that often accompanies scenes in which we are encouraged by the director to relate to Northup's emotional interior are the same chords in this summer's worldwide pop hit 'Get Lucky'. Yes – as in 'We're up all night to get lucky'". Although Ramsey admits that the "flat-lined" music represents "a decision that may have highlighted to some viewers how numbness may have become a strategy of survival", he is uncompromising in his criticisms. He states: "those of us who believe we know better about the emotional worlds of the enslaved from our studies may have found this move a missed opportunity". Even though Zimmer's score does sound uninvolved, and definitely not innovatory, one can argue that the emotional remove of the orchestral parts creates a fertile contrast with the presence and relevance of singing.
17. Although McQueen's focus on Solomon as a subject and on his struggle to survive is a prolific "move", to use Tillet's definition, towards a reshaping of memories of slavery, the concept of subjectivity is a problematic one when it emerges from a slave narrative. On the one hand, the role of David Wilson in the writing of *12 Years a Slave* might have been more substantial than he affirms in the 'Editor's Preface' (see Olney, 1984), therefore raising questions related to what we really know about the subjectivity of Solomon Northup. On the other hand, as Sabine Broeck effectively demonstrates in her analysis of John Locke's *Treatises*, the concept of subject, inherited as it is from the Enlightenment, requires a deeper understanding of how the slave trade might have affected the reasoning of European intellectuals who are considered founding fathers of modern thought. The "hermeneutics of epistemological suspicion from the point of view of the desubjectification of African human beings", for which she argues (Broeck, 2004: 245), poses interesting questions for anyone who aims at analysing representations and perceptions of black vocality.
18. That Ejiofor's voice here is redolent of black vocal performance practices is confirmed by various theorizations of African-American vocal styles. Stewart (1998: 6) defines the specific effect, that Ejiofor is moderately using, as a grunt, and he explains: "they [the grunts] are usually used during musical moments where their presence adds emotional emphasis or heightens the emotional drama of the music". Scholar and composer Andrew Legg confirms Stewart's view but uses a different term, gravel. "Gravel in the voice, [a device] used by many singers, is a commonly applied general characteristic

that also functions as a means of creating an impassioned emphasis and added intensity to a word or phrase" (Legg, 2010: 108). Definitions from African-American vocalists sometimes refer to the strong, powerful groan emphasized in their technique as "heavy voice" (Beauchamp 2010: 8). By using these vocal devices within the specific context, Ejiofor confirms both the intensity of feelings and the cultural identity expressed, and constructed, in his performance.

19. "If any one wishes to be impressed with the soul-killing effects of slavery, let him go to Colonel Lloyd's plantation, and, on allowance-day, place himself in the deep pine woods, and there let him, in silence, analyze the sounds that shall pass through the chambers of his soul, – and if he is not thus impressed, it will only be because there is no flesh in his obdurate heart" (Douglass, 1845: 14).

References

Abrahams, R. D. (1993) *Singing the Master: The Emergence of African-American Culture in the Plantation South*. New York: Penguin.

Allen, W. F., C. P. Ware and L. McKim Garrison (1867) *Slave Songs of the United States*. New York: Simpson & Co.

Bandirali, L. and E. Terrone (2009) *Il Sistema Sceneggiatura: Scrivere e Descrivere i Film*. Turin: Lindau.

Barthes, R. (1977) "The Grain of the Voice". In *Image, Music, Text: Essays Selected and Translated by Stephen Heath*, edited by R. Barthes, 179–89. New York: Hill and Wang.

Beauchamp, L. T., Jr. (2010) *Blues Speaks: The Best of the Original Chicago Blues Annual*. Urbana and Chicago: University of Illinois Press.

Berlin, I. (2003) *Generations of Captivity: A History of African-American Slaves*. Cambridge and London: Harvard University Press.

Bresson, R. (1986) *Notes on the Cinematographer*. London, Melbourne and New York: Quartet. Original edition: R. Bresson (1975) *Notes sur le Cinématographe*. Paris: Gallimard.

Broeck, S. (2004) "Never Shall We Be Slaves: Locke's Treatises, Slavery, and Early European Modernity". In *Blackening Europe: The African American Presence*, edited by H. Raphael-Hernandez, 235–47. New York and London: Routledge.

Butler, J. (1997) *Excitable Speech. A Politics of the Performative*. New York and London: Routledge.

Cavarero, A. (2003) *A Più Voci: Filosofia dell'espressione vocale*. Milan: Feltrinelli.

Chion, M. (1999) *The Voice in Cinema*. New York: Columbia University Press. Original edition: M. Chion (1982) *La voix au cinéma*. Paris: Editions de l'Etoile.

Chiriacò, G. (2014) Voice Map: Emotional Geography of African-American Vocality. Online: https://www.afrovocality.com/voice-map/ (accessed June 1, 2020).

Chiriacò, G. (2018) "To Become Human: A Comparative Investigation into Lena McLin's Vocal Pedagogy and the Italian School of Vocologia Artistica". In *Singing: The Timeless Muse. Essays on the Human Voice, Singing, and Spirituality*, edited by D. C. Wiley, 47–59. Gahanna: Inside View Press.

Dargis, M. (2013) "The Blood and Tears, not the Magnolias". *New York Times*, October 18, Section C, p. 1.

Debdy, D. (2013) "Fighting to Survive: *12 Years a Slave* and *All Is Lost*". *The New Yorker*, October 21, pp. 108–109.

Douglass, F. (1845) *Narrative of Life of Frederick Douglass, an American Slave. Written by Himself*. Boston: Anti-Slavery Office.

Dunn, L. C. and N. A. Jones (1994) *Embodied Voices: Representing Female Vocality in Western Culture*. Cambridge, New York and Melbourne: Cambridge University Press.

Dyer, R. (2012) *In the Space of a Song: The Uses of Song in Film*. Abingdon, Oxon and New York: Routledge.

Ebiri, B. (2013) "A Tale Twice Told: Comparing *12 Years a Slave* to 1984's TV Movie *Solomon Northup's Odyssey*". *Vulture*. http://www.vulture.com/2013/11/12-years-a-slave-vs-gordon-parks-1984-solomon-northups-odyssey.html (accessed January 30, 2016).

Eidsheim, N. S. (2008) "Voice as Technology of Selfhood: Towards an Analysis of Racialized Timbre and Vocal Performance". PhD dissertation. San Diego: University of California.

Eidsheim, N. S. (2012) "Marian Anderson and Sonic Blackness in American Opera". In *Sound Clash: Listening to American Studies*, edited by K. Keeling and J. Kun, 197–227. Baltimore: Johns Hopkins University Press.

Eidsheim, N. S. (2019) *The Race of Sound: Listening, Timbre, and Vocality in African American Music*. Durham, NC and London: Duke University Press.

Fabre, G. and R. O'Meally (1994) *History and Memory in African-American Culture*. Oxford and New York: Oxford University Press.

Felman, S. (2003) *The Scandal of the Speaking Body: Don Juan with J. L. Austin, Or Seduction in Two Languages*. Stanford, CA: Stanford University Press (1st edition 1983). Original edition: S. Felman (1980) *Le Scandale du Corps Parlant: Don Juan avec Austin, ou, la Séduction en deux Langues*. Paris: Editions du Seuil.

Fisher, M. M. (1953) *Negro Slaves Songs in the United States*. Ithaca, NY: Cornell University Press.

Floyd, S. A., Jr (1995) *The Power of Black Music: Interpreting Its History from Africa to the United States*. Oxford and New York: Oxford University Press.

Gates, H. L., Jr (1988) *The Signifying Monkey: A Theory of African-American Literary Criticism*. Oxford and New York: Oxford University Press.

Gates, H. L., Jr (2013) "Steve McQueen and Henry Louis Gates Jr. Talk *12 Years a Slave*". *The Root*, December 24. https://www.theroot.com/steve-mcqueen-and-henry-louis-gates-jr-talk-12-years-a-1790899438 (accessed June 1, 2020).

Gates, H. L., Jr (2014) "*12 Years a Slave*: Trek from Slave to Screen". *The Root*, March 3. https://www.theroot.com/12-years-a-slave-trek-from-slave-to-screen-1790874787 (accessed June 1, 2020).

Giagni, R. (2015) *L'ascolto delle Immagini: Silenzio e Suono nell'"Audiovisione*. Rome: Arcana.

Griffin, F. J. (2004) "When Malindy Sings: A Meditation on Black Women's Vocality". In *Uptown Conversation: The New Jazz Studies*, edited by R. O'Meally and F. J. Griffin, 102–125. New York: Columbia University Press.

Higginson, T. W. (2000) *The Complete Civil War Journal and Selected Letters*. Chicago: University of Chicago Press.

Jones, A. L. (2019) "Singing High: Black Countertenors and Gendered Sound in Gospel Performances". In *The Oxford Handbook of Voice Studies*, edited by N. S. Eidsheim and K. Meizel, 35–51. Oxford and New York: Oxford University Press.

Legg, A. (2010) "A Taxonomy of Musical Gestures in African-American Gospel Music". *Popular Music* 29/1: 103–129.

Levine, L. L. (2007) *Black Culture and Black Consciousness. African-American Folk Thought from Slavery to Freedom*. Oxford and New York: Oxford University Press (1st edn 1977).

McQueen, S. (2003) *Speaking in Tongues: 7 Février–23 Mars 2003*. Paris: Musée d'Art Moderne de la Ville de Paris.

McQueen, S. (2009) *Giardini. Notebook. British Pavilion Venice Biennale 2009*. London: British Council.

McQueen, S. (2010) *Queen and Country*. London: British Council.
McQueen, S. (2013) "A Book of Courage". Foreword to Northup (1853).
Meizel, K. (2011a) "Powerful Voices: Investigating Vocality and Identity". *Voice and Speech Review* 7/1: 267–74.
Meizel, K. (2011b) *Idolized: Music, Media, and Identity in* American Idol. Bloomington and Indianapolis: Indiana University Press.
Meizel, K. and R. C. Scherer (2019) "Fluid Voices: Processes and Practices in Singing Impersonation". In *The Oxford Handbook of Voice Studies*, edited by N. S. Eidsheim and K. Meizel, 77–95. Oxford and New York: Oxford University Press.
Mentjes, L. (2019) "Ululation". In *Remapping Sound Studies*, edited by G. Steingo and J. Sykes, 61–76. Durham, NC and London: Duke University Press.
Newland, M. K. (2014) "'Sounding Black'. An Ethnography of Racialized Vocality at Fisk University". PhD dissertation. New York: Columbia University.
Northup, S. (1853) *Twelve Years a Slave: Narrative of Solomon Northup, a Citizen of New York, Kidnapped in Washington City in 1841, and Rescued in 1853*. Auburn: Derby and Miller, republished in S. Northup (2013) *12 Years a Slave*. New York: Penguin.
Olmsted, F. L. (1856) *A Journey in the Seaboard Slave States, with Remarks on their Economy*. London: Sampson Low.
Olmsted, F. L. (1953) *The Cotton Kingdom: A Traveller's Observations on Cotton and Slavery in the American South*. New York: Knopf.
Olney, J. (1984) "*I Was Born*: Slave Narratives, their Status as Autobiographies and as Literature". *Callaloo* 20: 46–73.
Ong, W. J. (1967) *The Presence of the Word: Some Prolegomena for Cultural and Religious History*. Minneapolis: University of Minnesota Press.
Payne, A. (2011) "Slave Utterances". In *Encyclopedia of African American Music*, vol. 3, edited by E. G. Price, III, T. L. Kernodle and H. J. Maxile, 884–85. Santa Barbara, Denver, Oxford: Greenwood.
Powers, A. (2013) "*12 Years a Slave* is This Year's Best Film about Music". *NPR Music*, November 13. http://www.npr.org/blogs/therecord/2013/11/12/244851884/12-years-a-slave-is-this-years-best-film-about-music (accessed January 29, 2016).
Price, Z. (2015) "Economies of Enjoyment and Terror in *Django Unchained* and *12 Years a Slave*". *The Postcolonialist* 2/2. http://postcolonialist.com/culture/economies-enjoyment-terror-django-unchained-12-years-slave/ (accessed January 30, 2016).
Radano, R. (2003) *Lying up a Nation: Race and Black Music*. Chicago and London: University of Chicago Press.
Ramsey, G. P., Jr (2003) *Race Music: Black Cultures from Bebop to Hip-Hop*. Berkeley and Los Angeles: University of California Press.
Ramsey, G. P., Jr (2013) "There Was Music in *12 Years a Slave*? Yes. It Sounds Like *Get Lucky*". *Gawker*, November 8. http://gawker.com/we-re-up-all-night-to-get-lucky-or-there-was-music-in-1-1460666699 (accessed January 29, 2016).
Reid, W. (1965) *After the War: A Tour of the Southern States, 1865–1866*. New York: Harper & Row.
Reyes, A. (2012) "The Slave's Cabin: From the Back of the Big House to the National Register of Historic Places". In *Afterimages of Slavery: Essays on Appearances in Recent American Films, Literature, Television, and Other Media*, edited by M. D. Allen and S. D. Williams, 164–82. Jefferson and London: McFarland.
Rich, B. R. (2013) "Outrages and Obsessions: A Report on Festival Season". *Film Quarterly* 67/1: 67–72.
Scarborough, D. (1925) *On the Trail of Negro Folk-Songs*. Cambridge: Harvard University Press.

Sebron, C. (2018) "Singing and the Multicultural Platform". In *Singing: The Timeless Muse. Essays on the Human Voice, Singing, and Spirituality*, edited by D.C. Wiley, 79–88. Gahanna: Inside View Press.

Sell, M. (2006) "The Voice of Blackness: The Black Art Movement and Logocentrism". In *Staging Philosophy: Intersections of Theater, Performance, and Philosophy*, edited by D. Kranser and D. Z. Saltz, 278–300. Ann Arbor: University of Michigan Press.

Serra, C. (2011) *La Voce e lo Spazio. Per un"estetica della voce*. Milan: Saggiatore.

Silverman, K. (1988) *The Acoustic Mirror: The Female Voice in Psychoanalysis and Cinema*. Bloomington and Indiana: Indiana University Press.

Stewart, E. L. (1998) *African-American Music: An Introduction*. New York: Schirmer Books.

Stuckey, S. (1987) *Slave Culture: Nationalist Theory and the Foundations of Black America*. New York and Oxford: Oxford University Press.

Thompson, K. D. (2014) *Ring Shout, Wheel About: The Racial Politics of Music and Dance in North American Slavery*. Indiana, Chicago and Springfield: University of Illinois Press.

Tillet, S. (2012) *Sites of Slavery: Citizenship and Racial Democracy in the Post-Civil Rights Imagination*. Durham, NC and London: Duke University Press.

Van Syckle, K. (2013) "Brad Pitt: 'It Took a Brit' to Ask the Right Question on Slavery". *Rolling Stone*, September 7. http://www.rollingstone.com/movies/news/brad-pitt-it-took-a-brit-to-ask-the-right-question-on-slavery-20130907 (accessed January 30, 2016).

White, A. (2013) "Can't Trust It". *CityArts. New York's Review of Culture*, October 16. http://cityarts.info/2013/10/16/cant-trust-it/ (accessed January 30, 2016).

White, S. and G. White (2005) *The Sounds of Slavery: Discovering African American History through Songs, Sermons, and Speech*. Boston: Beacon Press.

Work, J. W. (1940) *American Negro Songs: A Comprehensive Collection of 130 Folk Songs, Religious and Secular*. New York: Howell, Soskin & Co.

5 Ghost Singers:
The Singing Voice in Korean Pop Cinema

Sarah Keith and Alex Mesker

Introduction

In the last decade, Korean popular music (K-pop) has become increasingly visible outside of Korea; firstly in East Asia, and more recently beyond Asia and in the West. Its impeccably produced music videos and songs, featuring young and attractive "idol" singers sporting extravagant fashions, represent a burgeoning popular culture industry and a modern, cosmopolitan sensibility. Set in this context, the films examined here explore tensions and ambiguities related to the singing voice in K-pop. Horror film 화이트; 저주의 멜로디 (*White: The Melody of the Curse*) (Gok Kim and Sun Kim, 2011) and romantic comedy 미녀는 괴로워 (*200 Pounds Beauty*) (Yong-hwa Kim, 2006) detail the trials of young female singers.

> Sun-ye: What's with the sad face? Is something wrong?
>
> Eun-ju: [browsing a lengthy book of karaoke songs] There are so many... All these people were singers. Where are they all now?
>
> Sun-ye: Singers are just a seasonal act. Especially idols.
>
> (*White: The Melody of the Curse*)
>
> Hanna: I have to stay hidden. It's my voice that makes people happy... Don't be mistaken. My real job is a singer.
>
> (*200 Pounds Beauty*)

In the first quote, Eun-ju muses on the number of forgotten singers who have tried to succeed in the industry and failed; her vocal coach Sun-ye reminds her of the transitory nature of fame in an industry which thrives on passing fashions. In the second, Hanna, an overweight part-time phone sex operator and "ghost singer" for a well-known K-pop idol, reflects on how her appearance requires that she "stay hidden" despite the attractiveness of her voice. This chapter will explore the tensions surrounding the singing voice in these films, focusing on how portrayals of pop singers within the K-pop industrial model illustrate underlying anxieties surrounding modernity and individual identity.

South Korea and *Hallyu*

Before discussing the singing voice in the two films under analysis, some background is required to contextualize the development of popular music, film and culture in South Korea (henceforth Korea). Since the 1990s, Korean popular culture exports – particularly pop music, television series, and films – have grown in popularity across Asia, and, more recently, beyond Asia. This phenomenon, often referred to as *Hallyu* (meaning "Korean Wave"), has its basis in a host of complex political and economic factors.

The history of Korea in the twentieth century is characterized by rapid and far-reaching cultural, social, political and economic change. Having been occupied by Japan for the first part of the century, Korean music and film have been subject to Japanese influences; the post-war boom in Korean filmmaking has been attributed in part to Japanese-educated Korean directors (Russell, 2008: x), while early popular musics such as *yuhaengga* were heavily influenced by Japanese *enka* ballads (Howard, 2002: 81). After the end of World War II, the Korean War and subsequent division of the peninsula into a communist North and U.S.-allied South brought with it cultural influences from the USA. Military bases imported Western music, and the American army touring circuit introduced Korean musicians to jazz, country and rock (Russell, 2008: 141), which thrived on what D. Kim (2012: 23) calls an "unconditional preference" for U.S. culture at the time.

In the second half of the twentieth century, the film, television and music industries were subject to varying amounts of government intervention and censorship. Following the end of Japanese occupation in 1945, Japanese record companies were replaced by Korean companies, and a ban on Japanese popular music endured until the late 1990s (Howard, 2008: 81, 93). A politically aware "underground" music scene existed, most notably in the 1970s and 80s, albeit primarily through live performance with no presence in mainstream broadcast media (D. Kim, 2012: 45). The film industry was likewise subject to state intervention; under Korea's military government in the 1970s and 80s, film companies were "censored and harrassed" (Russell, 2008: 4), driving most to bankruptcy. Following this decline, a quota was enforced in 1993 stipulating that at least 40% of screenings consist of local content (Russell, 2008: 5) in an attempt to revive the industry. Similar quotas were imposed on television stations, limiting the number of American imports and cultivating the production and increased quality of Korean programmes (Kim, 2011: 169).

The democratization process of the late 1980s and accompanying loosening of censorship (D. Kim, 2012: 65) is recognized as a key stage in the evolution of Korean popular media. Although censorship and foreign media distribution restrictions were still in place, relaxed travel restrictions for Koreans and the proliferation of recorded, rather than broadcast, music (Howard, 2002: 86, 88) resulted in increasing musical diversity. Howard recounts this change in Korean popular music throughout the 1980s and 90s, shifting away from heavily-censored televised ballads towards more foreign-influenced forms, including rap, reggae and hip-hop.

From the 1990s onwards, Korea's increasingly democratic government, alongside diminishing restrictions on foreign media imports and the country's relatively rapid recovery from the Asian financial crisis (Koo and Kiser, 2001: 33), ushered in a new period of cultural and economic openness, as well as globalization (Choi, 2010: 15). The beginnings of *Hallyu* can be identified in this timeframe. Governmental protectionism and financial support of local cultural industries (Kim, 2011: 172), combined with the country's growing GDP, had created a strong infrastructure for producing film, television and music. A longtime export economy, firstly in heavy industry, then lighter industries such as electronics manufacturing, Korea thus began to shift towards exporting cultural industries as well. Neighbouring Japan was the first significant export market, with television drama *Winter Sonata* and Japanese-speaking K-pop artists, such as solo female singer BoA and male group Tohoshinki, experiencing remarkable popularity. Korean pop music in particular had, and still has, a strong focus on export to Japan; its music market is significantly larger than Korea's, where piracy has been identified as "severely hampering the development of the legitimate music market" (IFPI, 2006) and driving the recording industry into decline (D. Kim, 2012: 10). As industries focused on export, *Hallyu* pop music, television and film offer representations of a globalizing Korea, portraying images of cosmopolitanism (Cho, 2011: 386) and sophistication.

Korean pop music, the singing voice in K-pop and its portrayal in film are bound up with Korea's unique recent history. Understanding pop music, singing and film in this context goes beyond an analysis of individual creative expression; it builds on diverse historical factors, a growing national awareness and contemporary anxieties, and creative industries which are *industries* in the literal sense of the word.

The Voice in K-pop

K-pop today encompasses a variety of genres, including acoustic ballads, hip-hop, rap, electronic and dance music, and rock-influenced styles. It can be most accurately defined by its non-musical features, particularly the industrial nature of its construction. The typical K-pop idol singer is manufactured; he or she is recruited at an early age (even pre-teen) by a management agency based on a promising voice, dance ability, or simply looks; trained intensively (similar to the Motown artist development model [Warwick, 2007: 51]) in singing, dance, MCing, language instruction and media presence; and (usually) placed within a group managed by the agency. A group's style is developed by their management, including clothing and overall "look", as well as album-specific concepts. Aspiring singers, called "trainees", remain in this preparatory stage for around five years before their public debut, and will often live together as a group in dormitories both before and after their public debut.

Compared to Western pop, where programmes such as *Countdown* (Australian Broadcasting Corporation) and *Top of the Pops* (British Broadcasting Corporation) have long since disappeared, K-pop is still heavily performance- and television-oriented. This is in part due to the longstanding broadcast of music variety programmes on Korean network TV, which endures today via various weekly music countdown shows as well as year-end spectaculars produced by broadcasters including KBS, SBS and MBC. These usually involve live performances (albeit occasionally lip-synced or doubled) in front of an audience, and live voting. Performers are expected to be able to perform convincingly and accurately, and train rigorously to do so.

This intense training-to-debut formula (often referred to as the "trainee system"), its emphasis on performance and media-readiness, and its near-ubiquitous use across K-pop management companies, is arguably K-pop's most distinguishing feature compared to other pop musics. As D. Kim (2012: 83) notes, this established model "differs significantly from how musicians entered the field and performed within the conventional system for popular music". The end result is not simply one of music and creative expression; it also illustrates how K-pop "is only made possible through the capital power of a monopolistic cultural industry" (D. Kim, 2012: 84).

The powerful industrialization underlying K-pop is somewhat at odds with popular understandings of the voice as a personally expressive medium. Popular music scholars such as Frith (1998: 199) have discussed the use of the voice as a way "to assess that person's sincerity", while Barthes' well-known concept of *grain* describes the singer's bodily presence in the voice. In popular music particularly, the voice is often understood to convey authenticity, emotional state and personal identity (Welch, 2005: 255). In K-pop, however, D. Kim (2012: 124) notes that audiences "commonly [recognize] that idol singers' music [is] created in an industrial fashion through the strategies of talent agencies, regardless of any sense of identity or the artist's spirit as a musician". This disembodiment of the voice is particularly noticeable in the prevalent "dance-pop" genre, as Fuhr (2013) notes in his study of ethnicity in Korean popular vocal music, asserting, "these synthesized voices... bear notions of absence and alienation. They appear as evocations of the dehumanized, de-ethnicized, or simply desired body" (280). The voice in

K-pop is explicitly shaped via the trainee system to sing in a way that meets the commercial demands of popular music, which itself is influenced by Western popular music trends. Whereas discussions of vocal enculturation (see Hughes, 2013) typically focus on individual experience, including traditions, emotions, and a representation of self (ibid.), enculturation in the K-pop voice is conversely imposed on the singer's voice by the demands of the market. This split between the individual and the voice, identity and vocality, and the conflict between self-expression and industrialization in contemporary K-pop provide a rich source of material for exploration in the films under consideration here.

A number of films have addressed contemporary Korean music in recent years. Documentaries such as *Our Nation: A Korean Punk Rock Community* (Timothy R. Tangherlini and Stephen J. Epstein, 2002) and 소규모 아카시아 밴드 (*Sogyumo Acacia Band's Story*) (Min Hwan-kee, 2009) have addressed the punk rock and indie genres, respectively. More recently, 나인뮤지스 오브 스타 엠파이어 (*9 Muses of Star Empire*) (Lee Hark-Joon, 2012) focused specifically on the K-pop idol system, documenting the early career of girl group 9 Muses. Feature-length K-pop "concert movies" have also been produced, such as 아이엠 (*I.AM*) (Choi Jin-seong, 2012), documenting SM's[1] Madison Square Garden concert as well as behind-the-scenes footage, interviews and rehearsals.

The films considered here, meanwhile, are fictionalized portrayals of singers within the K-pop industry. Both *White: The Melody of the Curse* and *200 Pounds Beauty* articulate and dramatize concerns about the singing voice in a highly commercialized context. These films have been selected as they are both concerned specifically with K-pop idol production, rather than other forms of Korean popular music, and are both comparatively recent (post-*Hallyu*) productions that experienced some commercial success.[2] In these films, the singer and the singing voice are used as a means for expressing anxieties about contemporary popular culture, and a way to explore wider concerns about modernization, identity and image.

Korean Horror and *White: The Melody of the Curse*

As mentioned earlier, the Korean cinema industry was subject to heavy government intervention from the 1950s until the 1980s, and was encouraged to produce "wholesome movies" (Park, 2012) aligned with public interest and upholding moral values. Following democratization throughout the 1980s, the late 1990s saw a surge in the number of Korean horror films, to the point where horror arguably became the genre most often associated with Korean contemporary cinema (Conrich, 2010: 107). Alongside successful thriller/horror productions such as 올드보이 (*Oldboy*) (Park Chan-wook, 2003) and 추격자 (*The Chaser*) (Na Hong-jin, 2008), vengeful ghost stories have been a staple of Korean horror since the 1960s (Odell and Le Blanc, 2008: 18). More recently, this subgenre has been stylistically influenced by Japanese horror (Conrich, 2010: 108), sharing tropes such as the long-haired female vengeful ghost character. This figure appears in Korean productions including 여고괴담 (*Whispering Corridors*) (Park Ki-hyeong, 1998)³ and 폰 (*Phone*) (Ahn Byeong-ki, 2002). *White: The Melody of the Curse* (henceforth *White*) continues this well-established vengeful ghost theme, situating it in the world of K-pop. The protagonists are a group of young idol singers, whose developing career is interrupted by a series of supernatural events. The film depicts well-known aspects of idol life, including overwork and exhaustion, in-group (and inter-group) conflict and competition, issues of image and authenticity, mental health, and punishing physical and vocal routines. At the core of the film is the members' rivalries, as each vies for the role of leader (the "main").

White focuses on the fictional K-pop idol group Pink Dolls.⁴ Its four members are Eun-ju (the eldest of the group), Shin-ji (the principal dancer), A-rang (the "visual", meaning the prettiest member), and Jenny (the best vocalist). The film opens with Pink Dolls performing to an unimpressed audience. Afterwards, their manager informs them that an unnamed sponsor has provided them with a new dormitory and rehearsal space. Soon after moving in, Eun-ju finds an old VHS tape hidden behind a wall. Playing it to the group's producer and manager, they find that it contains an old music video for a song called 'White' (Lee Ho-yang [Shinsadong Tiger], 2011). Their manager decides that the mysterious song will become Pink Dolls' next single, stating, "There's thousands of these old songs out there… it's just another song without an owner".

Pink Dolls perform 'White' on a television show, and the audience's response indicates that the song has hit potential. The group subsequently becomes embroiled in an internal conflict between the members over who should be the group's "main". During rehearsals and recording for the song, Pink Dolls start to experience a series of events culminating in injury, psychotic episodes and group members' hospitalization. Jenny, recording vocals during a late-night recording session, is found choked by a microphone cable; A-rang is impaled on a camera harness during a music video shoot; and Shin-ji is crushed by a camera rig during filming for a television show. Images of a female ghost (*gwishin*) foreshadow these events, leading sole remaining member Eun-ju and her friend, the group's vocal coach Sun-ye, to discover that the vengeful ghost is Jang Ye-bin, the leader of the original group depicted on the VHS tape, who died in a fire within their dormitory. Being the only remaining member of the group, Eun-ju prepares to debut as a solo artist (called "White") on a television show. After seeing the ghost once more during her performance, she is trampled to death by panicked fans following a blackout.

As a horror film, *White* is unusual in that it foregrounds the voice, and the "haunted" song, as the focus of the entire film; the vengeful ghost targets those who sing her song, seeking revenge on those who would take credit for her work (the titular song 'White'). Music is used sparingly otherwise, with the only other original compositions heard during the film's introduction and final scene. The film is also notable because it draws on members of the industry which it also explicitly critiques. *White* stars an established K-Pop idol (actress, model and singer Ham Eun-jung of girl group T-ara in the role of Eun-ju) and features cameos from other real-world groups and personalities (including girl group After School and 2PM member Lee Junho). The film illustrates not only the "horror" of *gwishin*, but also the horrors of K-pop idol life. *White* thus explores two primary anxieties surrounding the voice in K-pop; firstly, the song 'White', originally written and sung by the ill-fated ghost, shows how the (particularly female) singing voice is treated as an "ownerless" commodity within the industry, positioning personal ownership against commercialization. It additionally illustrates the hardships that trainees endure in order to achieve a "voice", and become the "main" of a group. These two topics will be explored in the following sections.

Ghost Voices, Postcolonialism, and Han

As Kim and Berry (2000: 53) discuss, Korean cinema has been greatly influenced by postcolonialism and concerns surrounding modernity. Using the example of *Whispering Corridors* (1998), Kim and Berry point out how the film "invokes a deep historical disquiet about Korea's modernity" (2000: 54), particularly how traditional, pre-modern and Confucian values can be reconciled with modern values, including female sexuality and social mobility. Cagle (2009) describes this tension as a result of globalization, which demands that Koreans "surrender their cultural identity and become 'global' citizens" (130), resulting in an erasure of tradition which "recalls Korea's traumatic past as [an] occupied and oppressed nation" (ibid.). This, in turn, creates *han*, a national trait unique to Korea which represents an internalized anger, consciousness of ongoing trauma, and lack of resolution (ibid.).

Anger, resentment and revenge are common features of South Korean horror film, particularly in the vengeful ghost subgenre, which echoes themes found in traditional Korean allegorical folklore. At its core, *White* is a modern form of a *cheonyeo gwishin* (처녀귀신, virgin ghost) horror story, a centuries-old form of revenge story prevalent in Korean culture which describes the ghost of a deceased human who is unable to go to the underworld without completing something that they must do on earth (Chung, 2011). *Cheonyeo gwishin* are deemed unfulfilled because they have died unmarried, and *White*'s association of K-pop with this variety of ghost underscores the young, virginal nature of K-pop idols, whose agency contracts typically do not allow them to date.

The primary reason for the *gwishin*'s revenge in *White*, however, is the appropriation of her song by the members of Pink Dolls. The lack of fulfilment leading to her vengefulness is therefore not only that she died young and unmarried, but also that her identity as a singer is being denied. This highlights the contradiction between the industrialized process of K-pop production which often ignores the individual artists' personhood (D. Kim, 2012: 124), with the function of the song and the voice as an embodied and personally expressive instrument (Welch, 2005: 255), as shown in the following scenarios.

When listening to the song 'White', lead vocalist Jenny asks "Who sang this? That's quite high". Despite the melody being above her comfortable vocal range, she enters the recording studio and forces her voice to achieve the required pitch; the manager asks, "Can you raise it to a nasal tone? I can still hear a head voice – let's try it again". Heavily reliant on a herbal medicine drink to treat her stressed voice, Jenny takes a sip before trying again. As she sings the highest note, the *gwishin*'s fingers are shown encircling her neck, and her voice transforms to a scream. Later that night, Eun-ju is drawn to the studio by Jenny's high-pitched screaming/singing, where she discovers that Jenny is being asphyxiated by a hanging cable. In this series of events, no consideration is given to Jenny's vocal range or health; furthermore, her reliance on herbal medicine is used to excuse the incident, having supposedly caused hallucinations leading to her asphyxiation. Jenny's domination by Pink Dolls' manager and her self-medication shows the disjunction between her own needs and vocal characteristics, and the requirements of the K-pop production process.

Later, trying to discover the identity of the original singer, vocal coach Sun-ye visits the recording studio alone. Closely inspecting the music video footage, she discovers that the audio and image do not sync, stating, "The lips and song don't match – especially there. You can't open your mouth that wide at that pitch". Her investigation leads her to conclude that the *gwishin*, and the song's owner, is not the "main" Jang Ye-bin but another unknown member of the group who provided vocals for the song.[5] The vengeful ghost's actions, stemming from the denial of her authorship, can be interpreted as an expression of *han*. Here, *han* has arisen through the tension between the erasure of identity (in this case, personal and vocal rather than cultural identity) and the hallmarks of modern and globalized K-pop production.

The voice, as an expressive and embodied instrument, is inextricably linked with personal identity. Set in the neoliberal context of the K-pop idol system, however, *White* shows the voice treated as a bodiless product. The increasing use of the term *vocality* in recent music scholarship (Meizel, 2011: 267) contradicts this conception of the voice as an entity separable from the singer and its bodily production; as Meizel (2011: 269) writes, vocality encompasses "the act of vocalization and the entirety of that which is being vocalized – it is a set of vocal sounds, practices, techniques, and meanings that factor in the making of culture and the negotiation of identity". Barthes' description of the "grain" of the voice (1977) likewise asserts the relationship between the voice and individual identity. The separation of the voice from its owner, and the denial of vocality and personal identity, is the driving narrative force in 'White'; the titular song's lyrics express this through the lyric "stop trying to erase me" (날 지우려 하지마).

Hardship Narratives in K-pop

Unresolved *han* can also be discerned in the hardships faced by Pink Dolls throughout *White*. In order to succeed as a K-pop group, they need to endure personal trials including rigorous vocal and physical training, as well as relinquishing their personal autonomy. The film depicts all decisions being made by management, including designation of group roles, repertoire, styling, and other creative choices, which leads to ongoing conflict between members, anxiety and exhaustion. It offers a systematic critique of the industry, framed within horror tropes. More unusually, the film's events draw substantially on actual well-known industry practices.

Numerous disreputable industry practices are alluded to in *White*. Firstly, the industrialized audition and "trainee system", where thousands of hopefuls compete for limited opportunities, is reflected in the "forgotten" group whose VHS tape is discovered by Eun-ju, and the producer's statement that "there are so many of these old tapes floating around". Restrictive contracts, which limit the agency of individual artists, are also depicted as Pink Dolls' activities are shown to be controlled exclusively by their management. The nature of this training and subsequent indenture to an agency has become public knowledge through a number of high-profile recent legal cases, leading to the term "slave contract" which describes particularly restrictive agreements.[6]

White also alludes to the industry's focus on youth, and the practice of "retiring" members once they are too old. K-pop groups, relying on current musical trends and physically demanding dance routines, are necessarily youth-focused and older members are often replaced or removed once they reach a certain age. Being the eldest of the group, Eun-ju is teased by other Pink Dolls members. The interchangeability of individual members and roles further explains why Pink Dolls members are vying for the "main" position, as this is less easily replaced. The conflict between Pink Dolls' members, including verbal abuse and accusations of sabotage, also has parallels to real-life occurrences.[7]

Further aspects of *White*'s "horror" are grounded in industry practice. Crowded living conditions are common, and fires have occurred in groups' living quarters.[8] Eun-ju is also exhorted by her manager to meet with the group's anonymous sponsor, obliquely referring to the exchange of sexual favours in return for improving Eun-ju's future career prospects. The importance of favouring influential industry figures is well-known, and cases have arisen where managers have exploited idols in this manner.[9] Another key feature of idol life portrayed in *White* is injury, as experienced by three Pink Dolls members leading to their withdrawal from the group. Idols in K-pop are frequently injured, ranging from sprained ankles and injured necks, to concussions; idols may go on temporary hiatus if the injury is serious, but more often will participate in activities in a reduced capacity.

These "horrors" of K-pop, as shown in both *White* and in actual practice, are however not necessarily at odds with the industry's interests. In actuality, most K-pop fans are aware of the "darker" features of the industry and it can be argued that there is an interest in promoting these characteristics. The hardships endured by trainees and idols are made public in order to develop identification, empathy, sympathy, and even pity from fans towards artists, instilling them with a desire to support artists both emotionally and financially. In an industry where an idol singer's look, sound and overall persona are developed by their management, the publicized hardships they endure build an authenticity which would otherwise be lacking.

These hardships also relate to core Korean cultural values. Competitiveness is highly ingrained in Korean society;[10] simultaneously, Confucian values emphasize continual striving for self-improvement and developing virtue. This manifests through hard work and devotion to perfection (in this case, climbing the "trainee system" ladder through endless rehearsals). Furthermore, while Western pop may involve elements of rebellion, disrespect for authority, and conspicuous consumption, K-pop idols are required to embody humility, a strong work ethic and traditional values. This once again embodies and negotiates the tension of *han*; while K-pop represents a globalized and cosmopolitan industry and music, it simultaneously reinforces traditional values and an intense work ethic.

The portrayal of the singing voice in *White* elucidates underlying themes within K-pop idol production. The hardships that Pink Dolls undergo, based in real-world industry practices, are tolerated in the hope that their voices will be heard and will endure in an environment which thrives on competition and continual novelty. The voice is also shown as a marker of identity and individuality, guaranteeing security to the "main" position of the group and offering the primary clue as to the identity of the *gwishin*; it is also subjected to the vagaries of the industry, being stolen, abused and erased. This contrast illustrates the tension between the voice as a personally expressive instrument, and one that is shaped and owned by commercial and industrial concerns.

Romantic Comedy and *200 Pounds Beauty*

200 Pounds Beauty (henceforth *Beauty*) is a 2006 melodramatic romantic comedy which, like *White*, focuses on the voice, its function as a marker of identity and its treatment in the K-pop industry. It is loosely based on the Japanese manga カンナさん大成功です! (*Kanna's Big Success!*) by Yumiko Suzuki.[11] Like Korean horror, romantic comedy/romance more generally is recognized as a genre with broad appeal both within Korea and wider Asia (Choi, 2010: 85), though the genre has not been as widely discussed in scholarly circles. *Beauty* fits alongside other romantic comedies such as 엽기적인 그녀 (*My Sassy Girl*) (Kwak Jae-Yong, 2001) and 동갑내기 과외하기 (*My Tutor Friend*) (Kim Kyeong-hyeong, 2003), where two seemingly mismatched lead characters eventually, following a series of humorous events and misunderstandings, develop romantic feelings for each other. Like *White*, *Beauty* is set in the K-pop milieu, but instead of focusing on trainees, its protagonist is a ghost singer for an established idol. The film's plot focuses on the connection, and disconnect, between the singing voice, individual identity, and the corporeal (and particularly female) body.

The film's protagonist, Hanna, is romantically obsessed with her boss, Sang-jun. Sang-jun is the producer and manager for K-pop idol Ammy, and employs Hanna to serve as Ammy's ghost singer, both in concert and in recordings. Vocally, Hanna is a competent singer in the pop idiom. Her repertoire ranges from breathy delivery to belting and is comparable to Western pop singers such as Janet Jackson and Debbie Harry, both of whose songs – 'Miss You Much' (Janet Jackson, James Harris III and Terry Lewis, 1989) and 'Maria' (Jimmy Destri, 1999) – are covered in *Beauty*. Hanna also has an after-hours job as a phone sex operator. Significantly overweight, she has attempted various weight-loss strategies but has concluded that her efforts are futile. Her best friend Jung-min, a back-up singer, tells Hanna that she is a "reject" who has no hope with Sang-jun due to her appearance; nonetheless, Hanna believes that Sang-jun's kindness to her may be an indication of a latent romantic interest. Jealous of their closeness, Ammy humiliates Hanna by gifting her an unflattering outfit (ostensibly from Sang-jun) which Hanna then proudly wears to a social gathering with Sang-jun. On finding this out, an irritated Sang-jun reminds Ammy of their reliance on Hanna, asking, "Do you miss the days of being a back-up dancer?" Ammy retorts, "The bitch gets on my nerves", to which Sang-jun replies, "If so, *you* sing". He goes on to say, "She's talented, but ugly and fat. You're untalented, but gorgeous and sexy... She exists for you".

Following her humiliation, Hanna tries to commit suicide, but is interrupted by a telephone call from one of her phone sex clients, a high-profile cosmetic surgeon. Visiting him, she asks, "Don't you recognize my voice?" and blackmails him into performing expensive "full-body makeover" surgery by showing him an audio tape of their conversations and by threatening to commit suicide if he refuses. A year later, Hanna emerges from surgery as a "natural"-looking beauty. Meanwhile, her long disappearance has caused Ammy's second album to be postponed.

The now-unrecognizable Hanna makes contact with best friend Jung-min, who informs Hanna about Ammy's stalled career, stating, "They're looking hard for your replacement". Hanna responds, "I can be the replacement. They'll like me, since I have the same voice". Auditioning using the name "Jenny", and inventing a back-story of having recently returned from the United States, Hanna impresses Sang-jun. He decides to launch Jenny as a singer in her own right, describing her as "an image of innocence... a natural beauty". Meanwhile, Ammy is still looking for Hanna but is losing hope. Sang-jun tells her to focus on acting, but Ammy responds, "I'm a singer... I want to be a singer!" Sang-jun mockingly replies, "You realize that now?"

Just before Jenny's debut concert, Sang-jun receives a letter (implicitly from the jealous Ammy) threatening to expose Jenny as the former overweight ghost singer Hanna. Despite this, Sang-jun decides to go ahead with the concert. He tells Jenny, "This isn't for me, nor Ammy. It's your show – do it for yourself". Jenny interrupts the show's opening to confess to the audience her actual identity as Hanna:

> I was an ugly, fat girl. So... I sang for someone else, hiding in the back. Then I got plastic surgery. From head to toe – everything. Now that I'm pretty... I can sing. I've been in love. I was so happy being Jenny. But I'm sorry. I ruined it... I don't know who I am anymore... Jenny isn't here. But if you wanna hear that fat, ugly girl sing... Please, listen to me sing once and for all.

The film closes by showing how Jenny's confession, rather than ending her career, gained her a substantial new audience.

Cosmetic Surgery in K-pop

Despite purportedly being a romantic comedy, there are "horrific" elements to *Beauty*'s plot. Hanna attempts suicide, is labelled a "reject", ugly and fat, and undergoes extreme cosmetic surgery; partway through the film, her best friend Jungmin also attempts suicide following a break-up with her boyfriend, and in a short scene following the film's closing credits, requests a full makeover from Hanna's surgeon. While *White* draws on the trainee system as an authenticity-forming hardship narrative, *Beauty* depicts extreme surgery as a form of self-sacrifice in order to achieve the same ends.

Cosmetic surgery in Korea has received significant media attention in recent years. An increasing number of women (as well as men) are open to the practice, with an estimated 20% of women in Seoul having undergone a cosmetic procedure (Choe, 2011). C. N. Kim (2012) associates this rise in cosmetic surgery with a broader trend towards neoliberalism, which is simultaneously associated with the commercial production of K-pop. "Before-and-after" images comparing idols' appearances pre-training and post-debut abound on the internet, and it is well-known that many idols elect, or are urged by their management, to undergo cosmetic surgery alongside physical training and dietary control as part of sculpting their appearance (Oh and Park, 2012). In *Beauty*, even the supposedly natural Ammy is revealed to have had breast implants.

The underlying reasons for the popularity of cosmetic surgery in Korea are many. One commonly cited factor is wanting to achieve a more "Western" appearance, a motive that is critiqued by Holliday and Elfving-Hwang (2012).

Park (2007) suggests that the practice has a basis in the gendered Confucian notion of self-sacrifice, where femininity is linked with self-denial and subservience to patriarchal ideals; discussing *200 Pounds Beauty*, he asserts that Hanna's surgery serves as a "ritual death" enabling her to be reborn as a beauty (62). Elsewhere, Woo (2004) associates beautiful appearance with competitive power, and proposes the notion that "all means are legitimate in the aspiration towards beauty" (62). Both *Beauty* and *White* demonstrate the same legitimation of controversial practices, whether cosmetic surgery, the trainee system, or ghost singing, as valid means to an end of creating the perfect K-pop idol product. The relation of cosmetic surgery, embodiment, and the voice (the literal singing voice, and the individual "voice") in *Beauty* is therefore both gendered and highly relevant to K-pop idol reality.

Ghost Singing, Ownership, and Vocal Identity

As in *White*, *Beauty* also addresses tensions between vocal ownership and identity. The voice is firstly shown as an "ownerless" commodity via Hanna's ghost singing work for Ammy. Although the initially successful Ammy is attractive (possessing a lucrative contract from a cosmetics company) and a competent dancer and performer, she lacks singing ability. Fulfilling the role of ghost singer, Hanna becomes an integral part of Ammy's overall "package". Her existence is framed in terms of Ammy's career and persona; this is demonstrated by Sang-jun's comment, "She exists for you". Hanna's phone sex work also shows the disconnect between the corporeal and the voice; in response to a client's request to tell him her "body size", Hanna responds, "You'll be amazed... my bust is 34 inches, waist is 24, and hip is 36". Ultimately, Hanna becomes her own "ghost singer", constructing Jenny both as a new persona and a physical body to hide behind.

At the same time, the voice is positioned as a marker of identity. Notably, despite Hanna's complete reinvention of her persona and physical self as Jenny, her vocal identity remains her single constant characteristic; this is shown through her successful audition for the role of Ammy's ghost singer. Similarly, her voice identifies her as her plastic surgeon's phone sex provider, as she asks him, "Don't you recognize my voice?" The invention of Jenny, however, poses problems for the authenticity of Hanna's voice. Although she possesses both the physical appearance and vocal ability necessary for an idol singer, she lacks confidence in her new persona, which adversely affects her singing. The trials of her existence as Hanna, and then as Jenny, are thus portrayed as contributing to the enculturation of her voice. In a recording session with Jenny, Sang-jun shows her an old video of Hanna, and asks, "What do you feel from her song?" Jenny replies, "Her song carries her heart, for someone that she loves". Sang-jun responds, "Can't you sing like her? You care too much about how you look", implying that Jenny's newly confident character is unable to vocally express the emotions that she felt as Hanna. This disconnect between the physical body, identity, and the voice is finally reconciled at the end of the film. Before surgery, Hanna is deemed grotesque; post-surgery, Jenny is accepted only while she maintains the pretence of being "natural", but has lost the vocal expressivity she had as Hanna. Once her use of cosmetic surgery is discovered, Jenny's "deceptive" body is viewed as monstrous by Sang-jun, and her narrative redemption only occurs during her final public admission stating that she no longer wants to exist as Jenny, confessing to her true identity as an "ugly, fat girl".

Conclusion

The treatment of the singing voice in fictionalized K-pop cinema reveals anxieties around the voice and identity, as well as broader concerns around Korea's modernity and contemporary culture. Significantly, these concerns surrounding the singing voice are framed in a female context. Although masculinity in K-pop has been covered, especially its visual aspects (Jung, 2011), these examples reveal how critiques of femininity in K-pop are closely associated with issues surrounding the voice, and in particular, questions of identity and ownership. The singing voice in K-pop cinema can further be interpreted in terms of the theorized national trait, *han*. Much as Korea's cultural identity has been complicated by its colonial history, these films show the conflict between conventional understanding of the voice as an embodied and unique instrument, and the pressures of modern-day capitalism, consumerism and globalization. In *Beauty*, Hanna realizes that she is viewed as a "product" rather than an individual, and reflects how her value as a singer changes before and after extreme surgical intervention; in *White*, the nameless *gwishin*'s suicide note reveals how her "dance and song were taken", leading her to commit suicide "as a last resort". The tension between the contemporary K-pop industry's negation of individual identity – whether through cosmetic surgery or through eradication of the creative self – and the persisting importance of vocal ownership, is therefore highlighted as an emerging and ongoing site of contention.

About the Authors

Dr Sarah Keith is a Senior Lecturer in Music and Media at Macquarie University. Her research areas include Korean and Japanese popular music and culture, the Australian music industries, and music and cultural policy. Sarah's current research focuses on Korean popular culture within Australia.

Dr Alex Mesker is an Associate Lecturer in the Department of Media, Music, Communication, and Cultural Studies at Macquarie University. He completed a Masters in 2007 on compositional strategies for electronic music, and a PhD in 2017 on the use of sound and music in 1960s television cartoons. His research interests span computational arts, animation, and screen soundtrack studies.

Notes

1. SM Entertainment is one of the largest K-pop entertainment agencies, and possesses a roster of high-profile artists.
2. *White: The Melody of the Curse* grossed over US$5 million domestically, debuting at position #5 and staying in the top 10 for 5 weeks, while *200 Pounds Beauty* grossed over US$37 million domestically, staying in the #1 position for 2 weeks and the top 10 for 8 weeks.
3. The fourth sequel of *Whispering Corridors*, 여고괴담 4: 목소리 (*Whispering Corridors 4: Voice*) (Choi Ik-hwan, 2005) is notable as it also uses the voice as a focus for horror; the plot centres on a murder mystery which, if not solved, will result in the loss of the protagonist's voice.
4. This name typifies conventional girl group naming in K-pop, and may be a portmanteau of actual K-pop groups "A Pink" and "5dolls".
5. This practice of "ghost singing" is a well-known procedure in K-pop; in *White*, vocal coach Sun-ye also acts as a ghost singer in Pink Dolls' live performances, covering for weaker singers.
6. The most well-known cases involve the groups TVXQ (also known as DBSK/Tohoshinki) and Super Junior, where group members have successfully sued their management agency for overwork, underpayment, lack of creative control, and overly long contracts.
7. As an example, girl group T-ara (which includes lead *White* actor Ham Eun-jung) was embroiled in a bullying scandal in 2013, which saw the departure of member Hwayoung after a number of incidents including abusive tweets and on-camera persecution.
8. Small fires have reportedly broken out in the living quarters of groups FT Island and Sistar; more seriously, a fire in 2012 in group M.I.B.'s dorm resulted in the deaths of two stylists.
9. Actress Jang Ja-yeon, following a string of these incidents enforced by her manager, eventually committed suicide in 2009, describing the occurrences and naming perpetrators in a final letter.
10. For example, this focus on competitiveness is apparent in the phenomenon of *hagwon* (cram schools), where school-aged children are commonly sent to improve their academic performance.
11. This manga was also adapted into a Japanese film in 2009, but set in the fashion industry.

References

Barthes, R. (1977) *Image, Music, Text*, trans. Stephen Heath. New York: Hill and Wang.
Cagle, R. L. (2009) "The Good, the Bad, and the South Korean: Violence, Morality, and the South Korean Extreme Film". In *Horror to the Extreme: Changing Boundaries in Asian Cinema*, edited by J. Choi and M. Wada-Marciano, 123–44. Hong Kong: Hong Kong University Press.
Cho, Y. (2011) "Desperately Seeking East Asia amidst the Popularity of South Korean Pop Culture in Asia". *Cultural Studies* 25/3: 383–404.
Choe, S. (2011) "In South Korea, Plastic Surgery Comes Out of the Closet". *The New York Times*, November 3. http://www.nytimes.com/2011/11/04/world/asia/in-south-korea-plastic-surgery-comes-out-of-the-closet.html (accessed February 18, 2014).
Choi, J. (2010) *The South Korean Film Renaissance: Local Hitmakers, Global Provocateurs*. Middletown, CT: Wesleyan University Press.

Chung, S. (2011) "Chilled to the Bone: Korean Ghosts and Urban Legends". *The Korea Blog*, August 22. http://koreanetblog.blogspot.com/2011/08/chilled-to-bone-korean-ghosts-and-urban.html (accessed May 25, 2020).

Conrich, I. (2010) "Gothic Bodies and the Return of the Repressed: The Korean Horror Films of Ahn Byeong-ki". *Gothic Studies* 12/1: 106–115.

Frith, S. (1998) *Performing Rites: On the Value of Popular Music*. Cambridge, MA: Harvard University Press.

Fuhr, M. (2013) "Voicing Body, Voicing Seoul: Vocalization, Body, and Ethnicity in Korean Popular Music". In *Vocal Music and Contemporary Identities: Unlimited Voices in East Asia and the West*, edited by C. Utz and F. Lau, 267–84. New York: Routledge.

Holliday, R. and J. Elfving-Hwang (2012) "Gender, Globalization and Aesthetic Surgery in South Korea". *Body and Society* 18/2: 58–81.

Howard, K. (2002) "Exploding Ballads: The Transformation of Korean Pop Music". In *Korean Pop Music: Riding the Wave*, edited by K. Howard, 80–98. Honolulu: University of Hawai'i Press.

Hughes, D. (2013) "An Encultured Identity: Individuality, Expressivity and the Singing-self". *Australian Voice* 15: 13–19.

IFPI (International Federation of the Phonographic Industry) (2006) *The Recording Industry 2006 Piracy Report: Protecting Creativity in Music*. http://www.ifpi.org/content/library/piracy-report2006.pdf (accessed February 20, 2014).

Jung, S. (2011) *Korean Masculinities and Transcultural Consumption: Yonsama, Rain, Oldboy, K-Pop Idols*. Hong Kong: Hong Kong University Press.

Kim, C. N. (2012) *K-Pop: Roots and Blossoming of Korean Popular Music*. Seoul, Korea: Arts Council Korea.

Kim, D. (2012) "Reappropriating Desires in Neoliberal Societies through KPop". Masters Thesis in Asian American Studies, University of California, Los Angeles.

Kim, S. and C. Berry (2000) "'*Suri suri masuri*': The Magic of the Korean Horror Film. A Conversation". *Postcolonial Studies* 3/1: 53–60.

Kim, M. (2011) "The Role of the Government in Cultural Industry: Some Observations from Korea's Experience". *Keio Communication Review* 33: 163–82.

Koo, J. and S. L. Kiser (2001) "Recovery from a Financial Crisis: The Case of South Korea". *Federal Reserve Bank of Dallas Economic and Financial Review*, Fourth Quarter 2001: 24–36.

Meizel, K. (2011) "A Powerful Voice: Investigating Vocality and Identity". *Voice and Speech Review* 7/1: 267–74.

Odell, C. and M. Le Blanc (2008) *Horror Films*. Harpenden, UK: Kamera Books.

Oh, I. and G. Park (2012) "From B2C to B2B: Selling Korean Pop Music in the Age of New Social Media". *Korea Observer* 43/3: 365–97.

Park, S. U. (2007) "Beauty Will Save You: The Myth and Ritual of Dieting in Korean Society". *Korea Journal* 47/2: 41–70.

Park, S. H. (2012) "Establishing a National Identity from Above: Film Production and Wholesome Movies in South Korea, 1966–1979". *Journal of Japanese & Korean Cinema* 4/1: 53–67.

Russell, M. J. (2008) *Pop Goes Korea: Behind the Revolution in Movies, Music, and Internet Culture*. Berkeley, CA: Stone Bridge Press.

Warwick, J. (2007) *Girl Groups, Girl Culture: Popular Music and Identity in the 1960s*. Abingdon, UK: Taylor and Francis.

Welch, G. F. (2005) "Singing as Communication". In *Musical Communication*, edited by D. Miell, R. MacDonald and D. J. Hargreaves, 239–60. Oxford: Oxford University Press.

Woo, K. J. (2004) "The Beauty Complex and the Cosmetic Surgery Industry". *Korea Journal* 44/2: 52–82.

6 Voices of Sheila:
Resignification in Filmic and Non-filmic Contexts

Nina Menezes

Bollywood, India's Hindi-language film industry, is recognized worldwide for its vibrant, sometimes over-the-top song-and-dance sequences.[1] On first exposure to a Bollywood film, most foreign audiences might find the musical interpolations extraneous or unrealistic. However, Ranjani Majumdar argues that it is important to analyse these sequences because they are central to the film narrative (Majumdar, 2005: 98). A typical Hindi film today contains five to seven songs, each remarkably heterogeneous, drawing on diverse popular music sources, both Indian and foreign. Among the many genres of Hindi film song today, there is one, in particular, that has tantalized audiences for decades: the item number.

In the late 1990s, the proliferation of film song programmes on MTV and other cable television channels found filmmakers enticing audiences in an exceptional way. They began spending excessively on the visualization of songs to ensure the film's "repeat value" (Ganti, 2013: 98). In Bollywood, the term "item number" typically refers to big-budget, overtly sexual music videos, which depict objectified images of the female body. Although the term item number emerged only in the late 1990s, the genre had existed and evolved since the early years of Indian cinema. During the beginning of the 1930s, filmmakers began to capitalize on the marketing power of sexuality in films like *Zarina* (Ezra Mir, 1932). Song-and-dance sequences became a standard in Hindi cinema from the late 1950s, and many view these as the precursor to today's item numbers.

This chapter analyses a single song-and-dance sequence, 'Sheila Ki Jawani' (Sheila's Youth/Oomph), from the Bollywood film *Tees Maar Khan* (Farah Khan, 2010). The film received poor reviews and was criticized as "a disappointment", with its "farcical comedy" and "over-the-top characters".[2] However, 'Sheila Ki Jawani' topped the popular music charts for seven months and was rated "the hottest item song of the year".[3] While most Indian audiences refer to 'Sheila Ki Jawani' (Vishal Dadlani and Shekhar Ravjiani, 2010) as an item number, a closer analysis reveals that it is not typical of its genre. The singing voice and elements of parody work together to problematize the generic category of item numbers.

'Sheila Ki Jawani' draws on a variety of Indian and non-Indian musical traditions. This chapter goes on to examine some of the musical elements drawn from these traditions. Gendered associations from these prior contexts are transferred, creating a highly-gendered, musical, textual, visual pastiche. Hindi film songs often move beyond their filmic contexts; they are re-mediated and re-enacted at social and cultural gatherings and enjoy a life of their own. Finally, this chapter examines some of the popular re-enactments and resignifications of 'Sheila Ki Jawani' by the original actress (Katrina Kaif), playback singer (Sunidhi Chauhan) and Hindi cinema fans. In doing so, it discusses how the singing voice functions in Hindi cinema and how female voices, in particular, aurally reinforced the conventional visual gender dichotomies of the "virtuous" lady and the vamp.

Singing Voices and Dancing Bodies in Hindi Cinema

> The voice is the site of perhaps the most radical of all subjective divisions – the division between meaning and materiality... The sounds the voice makes always exceed signification to some degree, both before the entry into language and after. The voice is never completely standardized, forever retaining an individual flavour or texture – what Barthes calls its "grain" (Silverman, 1988: 44).

In the quotation above, Silverman offers a psychoanalytic perspective of vocality. She draws on Roland Barthes's much-quoted essay, "The Grain of the Voice" (1977), which explores the dialectic between the meaning and materiality of vocal production. Barthes locates the "grain" more specifically in the voice. For him, "The 'grain' is the body in the voice as it sings, the hand... the limb as it performs" (Barthes, 1977: 188). Barthes's notion of the grain is particularly relevant to the disembodied voice and serves as a point of departure for understanding the voice in Hindi cinema.

Indian cinema in the early twentieth century drew heavily on the stage conventions of Indian theatrical traditions. An acting career during the early years of Indian cinema demanded acting, singing and dancing skills. However, in the late 1940s, owing to technological innovations, audio-visual tracks began to be recorded separately, thus allowing performers to specialize. Actors were no longer required to sing and obtained roles chiefly on the merits of their appearance and acting skills. The specialized singers who served as voice surrogates for these actors came to be called "playback singers". During the process of filming, the singer's pre-recorded tracks were played back over a loudspeaker, allowing actors to lip-synch their parts.

In *The Voice in Cinema* (1999), Michel Chion's concept of "playback" provides an understanding of how the disembodied voice functions. Chion describes the relationship between the singer's voice and the actor's body. In playback, the actors:

> make their bodies sing, speak, move... precisely to the voice... In playback there is someone before us whose entire effort is to attach his face and body to the voice we hear. Playback is a source of direct, even physical emotion... Playback marshals the image in the effort to embody. In playback, the body confesses to being the puppet brought to life by the voice (Chion, 1999: 156).

In Hindi cinema, the singing voice is artificially reconstructed through an actor's body as the actor lip-synchs to the playback singer's voice. Perhaps this cinematic technique in Hindi cinema is not any different than that employed in Hollywood musicals in the 1950s and 1960s (Bharathan, 1995: 69). It is necessary to highlight, however, that Indian audiences of Hindi cinema are remarkably perceptive to the voice emerging from the body of an actor, and can often recognize to which singer it belongs. It is the audience's awareness of the source of the singing voice which serves as a reminder that it is disembodied and mediated by technology. In Hindi cinema, the split between the actor's body and the singer's voice does not "rob the singer of the opportunity to reclaim his or her voice" (Siefert, 1995: 57). In the late 1940s, as women entered the public realm of the film industry to become professional playback singers, they negotiated notions of space, identity and stardom. Far from being invisible, female singers, in particular, developed a "voice recognizability" (Majumdar, 2009: 189, bestowing on them a degree of aural stardom. However, female playback singers' voices also conveyed "certain moral and emotional traits" (ibid.).

The Female Body in Hindi Cinema – the Heroine, the Vamp, and the Item Girl

Early Indian cinema focused on the depiction of tales of gods and goddesses from Hindu mythology (Dwyer, 2006: 15). Although Hindi cinema has developed into several genres over the last few decades, contemporary plots and characters still bear mythological resonances. According to Amita Nijhawan, stereotypical images of women in Bollywood and regional Indian cinema draw on the dichotomies of Sita and Menaka represented in Indian mythology. Sita, the heroine figure, is the ideal modest wife who obeys and upholds her husband's word as supreme. Menaka, her "alter ego", is someone who beguiles men with her charm and overpowering sexuality (Nijhawan, 2009: 101).

While the mythological dichotomies of Sita and Menaka shed light on the construction of the ideal Indian woman and her alter ego in Hindi cinema, historical and cultural formations have also influenced these archetypes. Early Indian cinema actively engaged in shaping images of the ideal Indian woman and her "other". In the years that followed India's independence in 1947, the status of women in society became an important marker in the construction of India's image as a modern nation. Through social and political ideologies and through social reform, notions of an "ideal womanhood" were clearly imagined. Sangeeta Datta argues that the "nationalist project constitutes the female body as a privileged signifier and various struggles are waged over the meaning and ownership of that body" (2000: 73). During this period, Hindi cinema actively took part in constructing the rigid binaries of the ideal woman and the vamp through images, styles and settings. The heroine, who was the epitome of all virtue and purity, conformed to patriarchal norms of Indian-ness, and was presented as the ideal Indian woman. The song sequences she inhabited were in the confines of a domestic sphere, in the midst of nature, or in some fantastic pristine setting. The role of the vamp became a standard in Hindi cinema during the 1960s, 70s and early 80s (Pinto, 2006). The vamp stood diametrically opposite to the heroine. She was marked by an exotic foreignness, depicted as the symbol of uncontrolled sexuality and associated with everything deviant, modern and Western. The vamp's body suggested excess, desire and vice. Her song sequences inhabited "hypersexualized yet illicit space", such as the privacy of the bedroom, a nightclub or a bar (Majumdar, 2005: 80). Female actors who played the role of the virtuous heroine never played the role of the vamp and vice-versa (Majumdar, 2005; Pinto, 2006). This began to change in the 1980s and 90s, when the astronomical wages for starring in an item number saw many heroines happy to take on these previously maligned roles.

An item number is most often strategically inserted into the film for seemingly commercial purposes: it may or may not be relevant to the plot. As the main attraction, the "item girl" often makes a cameo appearance in the film. She is depicted in skimpy clothing, with a heaving bosom and revealing cleavage as she lip-synchs to suggestive lyrics and dances to vibrant rhythms with swaying hips and pelvic thrusts. She typically performs for a mostly-male audience. The hero in this scene is usually just a spectator; though he may engage in a few dance steps with the item girl.

Female Playback Singing in Hindi Cinema – the Lady, the Vamp, and the Item Girl

The development of playback singing as a profession in Hindi cinema brought women into the public sphere. Female playback singers were doing something remarkable by entering the studio, previously a male public domain. These women were not only transgressing cultural norms of respectability, but were also performing a genre not considered high-cultural music (Weidman, 2007: 139). In the late 1940s, a voice monopoly emerged in the Hindi film music industry where a handful of singers dominated for almost four decades (Majumdar, 2009: 176). Pavitra Sundar attributes two main reasons for the development of this voice monopoly. Firstly, a number of wealthy individuals who sought to either protect or multiply their illegal wartime profits began investing in individual singers and actors. Secondly, a mass emigration of performers from the industry took place during the India–Pakistan partition in 1947, leaving the film industry with just a handful of individuals to reorganize it. This voice monopoly appeared to be more pronounced in female playback singing (Sundar, 2008: 147–67).

Two female playback singers who held such a monopoly in the Hindi film music industry for almost four decades were Lata Mangeshkar and her younger sister Asha Bhosle. Lata Mangeshkar's voice was markedly different from her predecessors' throaty vocal quality. With its unique, high-pitched, lighter, resonant and lyrical timbre, Mangeshkar's voice was lauded as the ideal female voice. Freed from any associations with immorality or sexuality, it represented the disembodied femininity, respectability and innocence of the heroine in the film (Majumdar, 2001; Sundar, 2008; Weidman, 2012). Mangeshkar's popularity and rise to stardom also coincided with the years that followed Indian independence, earning her the reputation as the "voice of the nation" (Majumdar, 2001; Sundar, 2008). Asha Bhosle's more versatile voice provided a perfect counterpoint to that of her sister. In the 1950s, when leading playback singers refused to lend their voices to characters of the fallen women, Bhosle's was frequently employed (Beaster-Jones, 2015: 106). Bhosle's playful, seductive voice was thus reserved chiefly for the character of the vamp and the more exotic, modern women who were depicted singing and dancing in night clubs in Hindi cinema. Early in the sisters' careers, music director Anil Biswas is believed to have remarked, "Asha's voice has body, Lata's soul" (Beaster-Jones, 2015: 106). It was with Mangeshkar's and Bhosle's contrasting voices that "voice casting" emerged – the process where singers' voices were consistently matched with particular roles in Hindi cinema. Filmmakers and audiences strongly associated Bhosle's voice with the vamp figure in the 1960s, 70s and 80s. Voice casting thus further reinforced the visual dichotomies of the heroine and the vamp.

In the 1990s, the item numbers in Hindi cinema saw the voice of the item girl taking on a lower, projected, declamatory, throaty, sexualized timbre. More recently, a husky, breathy tone, perhaps modified by digital pitch correction, has also become common. Independent of the visual depiction, the voice of the playback singer constructs a "bodily presence", acquiring associations to "womanly sexuality and womanly authority" (Weidman, 2012: 310). With this as a background, the chapter now provides a detailed analysis of the song 'Sheila Ki Jawani', highlighting unique characteristics that make it atypical of its genre.

Is 'Sheila Ki Jawani' an Item Number?

Bollywood film *Tees Maar Khan* (2010), directed by Farah Khan is a re-make of Vittorio De Sica's 1966 film *Cassia Alla Volpe* (*After the Fox*) (Mishra, 2013: 186). *Tees Maar Khan* narrates a love story between a conman, Tabrez (Akshay Kumar), and his ambitious girlfriend, Anya (Katrina Kaif). Anya's sole desire is to become a glamorous heroine in the film industry. Strategically placed within the first half hour of the film, 'Sheila Ki Jawani' offers a temporary break from the monotonous farcical comedy. While most film-going audiences would consider 'Sheila Ki Jawani' as an item number, a close analysis reveals that the song is not typical of its genre. The song, framed as an item number within the film itself, can be read as a parody of item numbers. In this *mise-en-abîme*, 'Sheila Ki Jawani' parodies the male-centric film industry and its perspectives on female sexuality.[4]

The scene that precedes 'Sheila Ki Jawani' depicts internationally-renowned conman Tabrez arriving on an airplane in Mumbai after having successfully hoodwinked two Central Bureau of Investigation officers and his fellow passengers. He is received by his minions only to discover that Anya, his girlfriend, is being filmed as the item girl Sheila, at Mehboob studio. Concerned that the lecherous director will take advantage of Anya, Tabrez and his friends rush to the studio to save her. They barge into the studio and join in the singing and dancing, re-introducing the elements of farcical comedy. Their repeated attempts to rescue Anya prove unsuccessful. The film crew and security banish Tabrez and his friends from the scene while Anya continues filming the final shot for the item number. Throughout the filming of the song, the ditsy Anya, now playing the role of the sexually assertive "Sheila", demonstrates by her actions that she can single-handedly deflect any unwanted male attention. However, once the filming of the song ends, Tabrez enters once again, beats up the director, and carries the hysterical Anya off the set. Anya is denied any agency and is rescued from being "Sheila". Table 1 lays out a structural analysis of the visual, textual and musical elements depicted in the song.

Figure 1: Men swooning around Sheila on the rotating bed on the stage

6 Voices of Sheila   95

Table 1: 'Sheila Ki Jawani' *(Tees Maar Khan)* – musical, textual and visual analysis

Time	Music	Lyrics Plain text – original English lyrics Text in *italics* – translated from Hindi	Visual Description
00:00 – 0:08	Instrumental Introduction • *Qawwālī* style harmonium melody and tabla • Ganpath festive percussion ensemble Shakers and synthesizers		*Mise-en-abîme* Sheila wrapped in satin sheets on a red rotating bed. Fit young men dressed in ripped, black, revealing outfits swoon around her. They move ecstatically to the pulsating rhythms, while the director of the film looks on, lecherously.
00:09 – 0:18	Voice: Refrain Sheila Instruments: harmonium and Ganpath percussion ensemble	Refrain Section: a (Sheila) I know you want it, But you're never gonna get it *I won't fall into your hands* *Believe it or not,* *The whole world is crazy for my love.*	Sheila sings and sways while the men swoon towards her on the rotating bed on stage.
00:19 – 0:26	Instrumental Interlude: Prominently features festive Ganpath percussion		Sheila and men move energetically on the rotating bed.

Table 1: 'Sheila Ki Jawani' (*Tees Maar Khan*) – musical, textual and visual analysis (cont.)

00:27 – 0:34	Voice: Refrain Sheila	Hey you, Refrain Section: a (repeated)	Sheila in a belly dancing costume sings and dances, while the men dance around her. The elaborate stage setting is adorned with transparent curtains, lights and chandeliers.
00:35 – 0:46		Refrain Section: b *I feel like I should treat myself gently and tenderly I don't need anyone else, I love myself.*	
00:47 – 0:50	Voice: Sheila (spoken, Auto-tune)	What's my name? (3)	
00:51 – 1:09		Refrain Section: c My name is Sheila *Sheila's youth / oomph* I'm too sexy for you *I won't fall into your hands* No, no, no, Sheila *Sheila's youth* I'm too sexy for you *I won't fall into your hands*	

Table 1: 'Sheila Ki Jawani' (Tees Maar Khan) – musical, textual and visual analysis (cont.)

1:10 – 1:43	Instrumental Interlude: Harmonium and percussion interlude		Tabrez breaks open the door to the studio. Entering he sees the director of the film blowing kisses at Sheila. Tabrez yells out: "He is molesting her with his eyes. Get her off the stage." and attempts to rescue Sheila. But Sheila and the men continue dancing the item number, now in Western cabaret / burlesque style with outfits to match. Tabrez and his friends mug the dancers who are preparing to join the rest on stage. Stealing their uniforms, they immediately assume character, singing and dancing with the rest of the ensemble.
1:44 – 2:02	Voices: Sheila & Male Chorus	Section A Silly, silly, silly, silly boys Oh oh oh (Male Chorus) You're so silly (Sheila speaking) *They follow me* Oh oh oh (Male Chorus) *When I look at them,* *Their words seem so hollow* *Every trick is ineffective on me*	Tabrez dances with Sheila in the centre while she sings and dances.

Table 1: 'Sheila Ki Jawani' (*Tees Maar Khan*) – musical, textual and visual analysis (cont.)

Time	Voice	Lyrics	Visual
2:03 – 2:12	Voice: Tabrez & Male Chorus Qwwaalli style with clapping	Male Qawwālī Chorus 1 *I craved for this, It feels like ages Your gaze feels like raindrops Oh this thirsty heart*	Tabrez and his friends form a ring around Sheila, singing, dancing and clapping their hands in *qawwālī* style.
2:13 – 2:35	Voices: Sheila and Chorus	Modified Refrain – Section a I know you want it But you're never gonna get it I won't fall into your hands Modified Refrain – Section c Sheila... (Chorus) Sheila's youth / oomph I'm too sexy for you I won't fall into your hands No, no, no, Sheila Sheila's youth / oomph I'm too sexy for you I won't fall into your hands	Tabrez and his friends are dragged away by security and Sheila in Marathi style costume dances with the male dance ensemble.
2:36 – 2:50	Instrumental Interlude		Fusion styles of dance, costume and music, Sheila is lowered on stage *Deus ex machina* style. The director looks on lecherously and blows kisses at her.

Table 1: 'Sheila Ki Jawani' (*Tees Maar Khan*) – musical, textual and visual analysis (cont.)

2:51 – 2:59	Voice: Sheila	Section B *Money, car, luxurious mansion,* *I need a man who can gimme all that* *Empty pockets and broke* *No, no I don't, I don't like it like that*	In a style of musical theatre, Sheila sings with the dancers, dancing at the fringes of the stage and on elevated platforms above the stage.
3:00 – 3:08	Voice: Tabrez & friends (in Auto-tune and *Qawwālī* style)	Male Qawwālī Solo (Tabrez) *Let's get out of here,* *I'll give you everything* *I'll bring the whole world at your feet* *I'll fulfill all your dreams* *None will be unfulfilled* *You know I'm going to love you like that*	Tabrez enters again, this time swinging like Tarzan on a rope, grabbing Sheila in arms.
3:09	Voice: Sheila (spoken)	Whatever...	
3:10 – 3:18	Voice: Tabrez	Male Qawwālī Chorus 1	Tarbez's friends dance, sing and clap their hand in *qawwālī* style.

Table 1: 'Sheila Ki Jawani' (*Tees Maar Khan*) – musical, textual and visual analysis (cont.)

3:19 – 3:43	Voice: Sheila	*Refrain Section: a*	Tabrez is dragged off the stage. Sheila's change of outfit is another Marathi-style costume.
		Refrain Section: b	
3:44 – 3:46		What's my name? (3) (Speaking)	
3:47 – 4:15		*Refrain Section c x (2)*	The dancers and Sheila are splashed with water. They carry her moving away from the stage towards the crowd and the filming crew. The director joins in with everyone else cheering and toasting Sheila with their large non-descript mugs containing beer, cola or coffee. She rejects the director with her "I'm WAY too sexy for you". Tabrez is seen on the fringes bribing a security officer. He puts up a fight, manages to enter the set and carries the hysterical Anya off on his shoulders.

The first visual shot in 'Sheila Ki Jawani' is a staged bedroom (private space), in a film studio (public space) (Figure 1). The staged bedroom and the film studio filled with men are suggestive of the male voyeuristic aesthetic of item numbers. The lecherous male director ogles at Anya, who plays the role of Sheila, the item girl. Anya/Sheila dances, surrounded by an entirely male cast and crew, emphasizing the male-dominated film industry. While the depiction of the director in this scene (*mise-en-abîme*) is a lecherous man, the actual director, producer and choreographer of the film *Tees Maar Khan*, Farah Khan, is female. In a promotional video on the making of the song, composer Vishal Dadlani and lyricist Shekhar Ravjiani explicitly attribute the concept for the title and song to Farah Khan.[5] Within this farcical comedy, what we encounter is an attempt to parody a male-centric film culture. Though Sheila is objectified in a male-dominated space, we cannot dismiss the authorial voice of Farah Khan resonating in the song. Instead of any previous paradigmatic norms of the non-respectable item girl depicting sexual availability through her dancing body, Sheila is unquestionably sexually assertive. She flaunts her body, simultaneously rejecting the men around her: "My name is Sheila... I'm too sexy for you... I know you want it, but you're never gonna get it... you're never gonna get my body".

Similarly, the vocal qualities of the playback singer Sunidhi Chauhan challenge the conventions of item numbers. Chauhan's powerful, projected quality, linked to folk idioms, along with the loud, technologically-mediated disco-based music are familiar sonorities of contemporary item numbers. But we also encounter Chauhan's high-pitched voice, a quality commonly associated with the virtuous heroine. As presented, therefore, in the song Anya/Sheila is both heroine and item girl. But Anya is, by no stretch of the imagination, the ideal heroine; neither is she the typical item girl. As Anya (the heroine) she is allowed to explore the power conventionally associated with the item girl's voice. As Sheila (the item girl) she enjoys the soft and lyrical vocal qualities traditionally linked to the heroine. Previously rigid vocal categories typically associated with the figures of the heroine and the vamp are now more fluid in 'Sheila Ki Jawani'. The singing voice and the body subversively reject conventions; in this rejection a space is created to explore a more integrated female identity.

Item numbers typically employ a single genre or style, depicting male perspectives on female sexuality. 'Sheila Ki Jawani', however, draws on multiple traditions: Marathi *lavani*, Bhojpuri folk, belly dancing, and Western forms, such as cabaret and burlesque. Each is highly-gendered in meaning, either appropriated or subverted to depict Sheila's assertive identity. The following section first describes the concept of resignification in music, and then highlights some of the gendered associations transferred from prior musical contexts in 'Sheila Ki Jawani'.

Resignification and Music

In the semiotic process, meaning is derived from signs. Resignification is a particular form of semiosis wherein new signs are taken from their original contexts and inserted into other semiotics progressions. In the process, resignification changes the meaning of what has been appropriated. The borrowed element is no longer foreign, but becomes integral to the identity that is being configured (Manuel, 1994: 250). Peter Manuel explains that:

> On a strictly musical level, appropriation can involve the active alteration, however subtle, of acquired styles, as competent imitation gives way to creative syncretism and further evolution. More importantly, however, appropriation is a socio-musical process, involving the resignification of the borrowed idiom to serve as a symbol of a new social identity (Manuel, 1994: 274).

Resignification does not imply a false representation or inauthenticity, but rather it provides opportunities for unlimited semiosis. In *The Role of the Reader*, Umberto Eco (1995) emphasizes the openness of texts. Eco's preoccupation is not about individual interpretations, but rather he points to the multiple meanings a text can produce: "the repeated action responding to a given sign becomes in its turn a new sign, the representamen of a law interpreting the former sign and giving rise to new processes of interpretation" (Eco, 1995: 195). It sets off a new chain of unlimited semiosis based on new texts, signs, and new interpretations. "Semiosis explains itself by itself: this continual circularity is the normal condition of signification and even allows communicational processes to use signs in order to mention things and states of the world" (Eco, 1995: 198).

Resignification in 'Sheila Ki Jawani'

'Sheila Ki Jawani' draws heavily on the erotic elements from the *lavani* tradition and Bhojpuri folk songs. These folk songs draw attention to female sexuality and the female form. Anya/Sheila draws attention to her body through the lyrical content of the song. The powerful declamatory style, the projected quality of Sunidhi Chauhan's voice, the energetic rhythms, and some of the costumes and dance styles are reminiscent of these folk song traditions.

In the "making of" video of the film, director Farah Khan explains that the rhythmic drumming of a local band playing on the streets of Mumbai for the Hindu religious Ganpath festival caught her attention and she decided to incorporate these elements in 'Sheila Ki Jawani'.[6] The Ganpath festival celebrates the (re)birth of the elephant-headed god, Ganesh, associated with success, knowledge and the destruction of evil. Interestingly, Ganesh is the son of Parvathi, the goddess who embodies *shakti*, "power" or "empowerment". The *dholki* is a traditional drum used in the Ganpath festival. This drum is highly-gendered and considered female, while the performers in the festival are exclusively male. Doubleday (2008) argues that gendered meanings are often constructed within relationships between human and musical instruments. She examines ways in which gendered meanings are invested in instruments, and considers how male exclusivity and domination shape gendered spaces (Doubleday, 2008). Whether intentionally resignified or not, the aesthetic of power associated with the *dholki* ensemble is appropriated and made to empower Anya/Sheila.

The harmonium plays a prominent role in the song as part of another male-dominated tradition – the *qawalli*. When Tabrez and his friends attempt to rescue Anya/Sheila, they sing and dance around her, employing the call-and-response technique from this musical tradition: their intention is to protect Anya from the lecherous gaze of the film director and crew. We first encounter the exotic sounds of the harmonium in the introduction to the song, as a two-measured phrase which is repeated and replete with chromaticism (see Figure 2).

Figure 2: Author transcription of harmonium introduction from 'Sheila Ki Jawani'

For the film audience this is their very first visual encounter with Anya. Anya/Sheila gyrates through the course of the song, linking this chromatic melody to her female sexuality. The chromaticism marks her as the sexual "other" to the hero Tabrez's diatonic male self. This chromatic harmonium melody linked to the male-dominated *qawalli* tradition is appropriated and linked to Anya's more assertive sexual identity. This act serves to subvert the existing gender hierarchies, and momentarily empowers the item girl through her performance of the item number. Notably, the chromatic melody repeatedly heralds Anya's appearance throughout the film, becoming her leitmotif; its associations to sexuality serve as a continual reminder to the audience. Because of the use of parodic elements in the film, Anya is allowed to express her sexuality as heroine; she is after all an atypical heroine in Hindi cinema.

In their indexical relationship, all these borrowed traditions aurally and visually illustrate and create a highly-gendered musical, textual and visual pastiche; they evoke a power, sexuality and otherness which become common codes associated with Sheila. There is no doubt that a fine line exists between the power in asserting sexuality and objectification. However, there could not be a clearer articulation of female empowerment for an item girl or a heroine in Hindi cinema.

In addition to Manuel's definition of resignification, Turino's concept of semantic snowballing also provides a good model for understanding how a single musical unit might symbolize and compete for new meaning over time:

> when former indexically related objects are not present... new elements in the situation may become linked to the same sign... indices continually take on new layers of meaning while potentially also carrying along former associations – a kind of semantic snowballing (Turino, 1999: 235).

Just as 'Sheila Ki Jawani' draws on multiple influences and gives them new meaning through their new associations, so 'Sheila Ki Jawani' is given new meaning through its many re-enactments in popular culture.

Non-filmic Re-enactments of 'Sheila Ki Jawani'

As a form of popular music in India, Hindi film songs move beyond their filmic contexts. Film audiences remediate and re-enact film songs at social and cultural gatherings. As these songs circulate in new contexts, they create new meanings and take on a life of their own. Weidman points out that "there has been relatively little attention paid to the way in which film songs are performed – sung and danced" outside their filmic contexts (Weidman, 2012: 307). To address this lacuna, this chapter now examines some of the popular non-filmic performances of 'Sheila Ki Jawani' in popular culture. Apart from the renditions by the original playback singer (Sunidhi Chauhan) and female actor (Katrina Kaif), the song has also enjoyed considerable attention from fans and aspiring singers and dancers.

Figure 3: Actress Katrina Kaif performing a live Marathi style version of 'Sheila Ki Jawani'

A growing trend at Bollywood film events has seen actors perform live renditions of their hit songs. At these events, actors typically dance to the original movie soundtrack. Female actor/dancer Katrina Kaif's Marathi version of 'Sheila Ki Jawani' at the Max Stardust Film Award ceremony (2011) offers a flamboyant spectacle.[7] Kaif's body, her entourage of dancers, the extravagant stage sets and costumes overshadow the playback singer's voice.

Even though Bollywood is located in the Western state of Maharashtra, it frequently draws on a variety of pan-Indian and foreign musical elements in order to appeal to a wider audience. The choice of a Marathi style for the film awards ceremony showcased local folk music and dance traditions and was perhaps a deliberate attempt by organizers to claim Sheila as their own. The soundtrack for this event is a pastiche of the original vocal and percussion tracks interspersed with tracks from other popular Bollywood item numbers. To emphasize the local Marathi flavour, instruments like the *dholki* (percussion) and *tutari* (bugle) feature prominently. The Marathi lavani dance style and other local folk dance styles, costumes and settings enhance the audio-visual experience (see Figure 3).

Similarly, playback singer Sunidhi Chauhan's live performances depict noteworthy alterations from her filmic soundtrack. Unlike the original track where her voice is disembodied, her stage renditions draw attention to the body.[8] Before Chauhan begins singing, she tantalizes her audience, inviting them to interact with her:

> **Chauhan** (speak-singing into the microphone): Ain't nobody got a body like...
>
> **Audience** (screaming): Sheila!
>
> **Chauhan**: Everybody want my body, I'm...
>
> **Audience** (screaming): Sheila!
>
> **Chauhan**: Drive you crazy, cos my name is...
>
> **Audience** (screaming): Sheila!

Although, in her original track, Chauhan's voice was disembodied, in her live renditions her voice is evidently embodied by her physical presence – visible and centre stage (see Figure 4). "Sheila" is evoked in and through Chauhan's voice and body. Unmediated by hi-tech studio equipment, Chauhan emphasizes and at times re-directs the focus to her voice. Her voice resonates in a public space, oozing with female sexuality: Chauhan emits howls, grunts, sighs, and husky, breathy interjections, making her voice sound even more sensual than in the original film. Her voice is charged with sexual energy as she arouses her audience. There is a marked difference between Chauhan's filmic and non-filmic renditions. While the former inspired a break from the item number tradition, the latter appears to regress to the norm by reinforcing vocal qualities conventionally associated with item numbers. In this instance, it can be seen that non-filmic covers have the potential to modify the context and meaning of the original film song.

Figure 4: Playback singer Sunidhi Chauhan performing 'Sheila Ki Jawani' live

Resignification of 'Sheila Ki Jawani' by Independent Popular Music Artists

Rave iBand is a four-member band based in the cosmopolitan city of Bangalore. The band has created a unique "iDentity" by being the first band in Asia to use smartphones and tablets to create music that is quintessentially of the "iAge".[9] Devices of communication commonly utilized for social networking become powerful, creative tools providing numerous possibilities to make and share musical meaning. Riccha Paul, the female lead singer, sings into an iPhone. Her all-male accompanists employ iPad apps (piano, guitar, flute, percussion, DJ and sampler apps) as alternatives to traditional instruments, in their version of 'Sheila Ki Jawani' (see Figure 5).

Rave iBand's performance is a slow, smooth jazz blues version in duple meter, in contrast to Chauhan's vivacious filmic and non-filmic versions in the meter of 4/4. Like Chauhan's live performances, however, this cover also re-directs the attention to the singer's voice. Riccha Paul's rich, low, velvety, projected voice draws on some of the earthy aspects associated with jazz and blues.

During the 1920s and 30s, American female jazz and blues singers such as Ida Cox, Bessie Smith and Billie Holiday sang of pain, suffering and heartbreak. Some audiences have inadvertently linked their performing bodies and voices to hyper-sexualized images from vaudeville and variety shows (McGee, 2009: 32). In India, jazz had similar associations. Jazz was first introduced to select Indian audiences during the 1930s. Bradley Shope (2013) argues that the demand for this live entertainment influenced the character and content of cabaret and nightclub song-and-dance sequences in Hindi films during the 1940s and 50s. In Hindi cinema, jazz not only provided an exotic element, but also led to the construction of audio-visual dichotomies for female characters, more specifically linking jazz and cabaret to the figure of the vamp.

Figure 5: Rave iBand performing their live jazz version of 'Sheila Ki Jawani'

While most covers of 'Sheila Ki Jawani' feature re-enactments by female singers and dancers, the Dubai-based Indian male rock band, Rooh, offers a quirky re-mix music video in reaction to the original song.[10] The group composed their own lyrics except for the refrain a) and c) (see Table 1, above) which are modified from the original to present their male perspective. The lead singer's rock-inflected voice, with its glottal constriction, builds up to the refrain "her name is Sheila", evoking desire and raw sexuality. Their remix, like other renditions, triggers off a chain of associations – rock, Sheila, sexuality, etc.

Rooh's music video begins with the band members narrating how in their drunken revelry at a night club the night before, they pursued a girl named Sheila, who rejected them. The setting shifts between the discotheque from the previous night to a dilapidated building the next morning where they sing of their rejection, "All I wanted is a number, all I got was a name... her name is Sheila" (see Figure 6). The audience never sees Sheila, the object, even though she is objectified. In the final shot of the music video the boys, groggy from the night before, reveal the humour of the entire incident. Drunk and blinded by their obsession for

Sheila, they realize that they had been pursuing a man with long hair. The man turns around and punches one of the boys in the face awakening them to reality.

Traditionally, in an item number, the woman and her body are objects of the male gaze. However, in Rooh's video, Sheila is never visible. The audience only hears about her through their rock-inflected male voices. From a male perspective, the band employs the conventional rock trope to evoke male sexual desire. They do not merely sing of desire and the object of desire, but their voices, in turn, represent a sexualized vision to be desired: "Ooooo... you know you want it, I know I'm gonna get it, *mere haath tu tu aani* (you'll have to fall into my hands/give in)". The use of auto-tune and the sheepish smile on the lead singer's face are open to interpretation, but one cannot discount the use of parody.

Since 2010, the original 'Sheila Ki Jawani' has been very popular and has inspired several re-mediations. Audiences have ogled Sheila, participated in singing her praises by joining in and singing the chorus, and have obsessively created and re-created her in many ways. Rooh's music video presents the perspective of an audience reacting to Sheila. As an audience they, too, have been obsessed with Sheila. In their parodic rendition, the band mocks audiences' obsession with Sheila and her song. While in the original filmic context, the parody of the song was directed toward item numbers and its male voyeurs, by shifting the gender perspective in their re-mix, Rooh parodies Sheila's ardent fans.

Figure 6: Rooh's parodic music video to 'Sheila Ki Jawani'

Conclusion

Audiences often refer to the Bollywood song 'Sheila Ki Jawani' as an item number, yet it is not typical of its genre. Parody is employed to replace stereotypical norms of the sexually-available item girl with a sexually-assertive Sheila who rejects her patrons. Although Sheila is objectified, her song draws on highly-gendered musical, textual and visual traditions, and in the process, subverts them. This recalls Judith Butler's point wherein resignification has the potential to defuse power not by banning it, but by reworking its meaning (Butler, 1997: 15). Through the act of subversion, Sheila sees herself as the empowered item girl.

'Sheila Ki Jawani' appears to be a particularly vibrant link in the chain of unlimited semiosis. In using resignification, the original composer, Dadlani, allays the risk of being overly explicit; he merely presents sexually-charged indices. Audiences familiar with these borrowed musical traditions have already formed associations with these elements and can read between the lines to construct meaning. The multiple traditions drawn upon in 'Sheila Ki Jawani', in turn, make the song ripe for further resignification:

> The appropriation and resignification of musics by urban subcultures themselves embody their own complex and often internally contradictory senses of symbol and simulacrum. These expressive works at once celebrate meaning and meaninglessness, play and nostalgia, pathos and jouissance, in a synthesis that goes much deeper than the paradigmatic dualities of "tradition and innovation", or "commercialism and authenticity" (Manuel, 1995: 228–29).

Most re-enactments of 'Sheila Ki Jawani' are performed by female singers and dancers. While these renditions offer instances of the unlimited potential for resignification through their choice of genre and style, they are, however, "complex and often internally contradictory" (ibid.). Performances of the song by women tend to regress to the norms of item numbers; they subtly perpetuate stereotypical notions of female sexual availability rather than allowing it to empower them as women. Their verbal utterances appear incongruent with their gestures and vocal timbre. Perhaps the contradiction lies in having to perform for multiple audiences, but mostly those who uphold patriarchal values. In most of the videos found on YouTube, the class and age of these women performers appear to play a significant role in determining whether these covers or re-mixes subscribe to or subvert tradition.

The power of resignification as a tool forces musicians to make decisions. Both film music director Dadlani's original version, and Rooh's re-mix, through their use of parody and resignification, have complicated meanings. The audience is provoked to contemplate, rather than passively consume. Both versions "at once celebrate meaning and meaninglessness, play and nostalgia, pathos and jouissance" (Manuel, 1995: 229). The theory of resignification recognizes that meaning can never be permanently fixed and that meanings change for reasons outside the control of any single author or composer (Butler, 1997: 15). Resignification can occur for a variety of reasons, some intentional and some not. In and through the process of resignification, 'Sheila Ki Jawani' participates, actively, in the chain of unlimited semiosis.

About the Author

Nina Menezes graduated with a PhD in Music (Ethnomusicology) and a doctoral minor in voice performance from the University of Florida in 2018. A leading soprano soloist from Chennai, South India, her live and studio career resulted in creative collaborations with some of India's internationally renowned film music directors such as A.R. Rahman and Ilaiyaraaja. Her voice features on several award-winning film soundtracks for Bollywood and Kollywood cinema. Over the years, such opportunities have provided a unique perspective in her research on Indian film music production and its cover culture. Nina currently teaches World Music at the University of Tampa and applied voice lessons at the Conservatory, Berkeley Preparatory School in Tampa.

Notes

1. This chapter emerged from a paper I presented at the Society for Ethnomusicology Southeast and Caribbean Chapter conference in spring 2014. I express my gratitude to my mentor Dr Larry Crook, Professor Emeritus, at the University of Florida, for his encouragement. Thank you, Diane Hughes, Mark Evans, Sarah Norman, and the anonymous reviewers for your thoughtful comments.
2. See http://www.koimoi.com/reviews/tees-maar-khan-review-by-komal-nahta/ (accessed November 20, 2013).
3. See https://timesofindia.indiatimes.com/entertainment/hindi/bollywood/news/Hottest-Item-numbers-of-Bollywood/articleshow/9149575.cms (accessed August 2, 2020).
4. See https://www.youtube. com/watch? v=ZTmF2v59CtI (accessed November 21, 2013).
5. See https://www.youtube.com/watch? v= WNki7 rwSA4I (accessed November 21, 2013).
6. See https://www.you tube.com/watch? v= WNKi7rwSA4I (accessed November 21, 2013).
7. See https://www.youtube.com/watch?v=7L7 d-3mzerc (accessed December 5, 2013).
8. See https://www.youtube.com/watch?v=stNw1cVw Sc (accessed November 23, 2013).
9. See http://ukasiaonline.blogspot.com/ 2012/02/ rave-iband-music-for-iage.html (accessed December 5, 2013).
10. See https://www.youtube.com/watch?v=RAXLR-MSrzw (accessed December 5, 2013).

References

Barthes, R. (1977) "The Grain of the Voice". In *Image, Music and Text*, edited by S. Heath, 179–89. London: Fontana Press.

Beaster-Jones, J. (2015) *Bollywood Sounds: The Cosmopolitan Mediation of Hindi Film Song*. New York: Oxford University Press.

Bharathan, R. (1995) *Lata Mangeshkar: A Biography*. New Delhi: USB Publishers Distribution Ltd.

Butler, J. (1997) *Excitable Speech: A Politics of the Performative*. New York: Routledge.

Chion, M. (1999) *The Voice in Cinema*, translated by C. Gorbman. New York: Columbia University Press.

Datta, S. (2000) "Globalization and Representation of Women in Indian Cinema". *South Asian Popular Culture* 28/3: 71–82.

Doubleday, V. (2008) "Sounds of Power: An Overview of Musical Instruments and Gender". *Ethnomusicology Forum* 17: 3–39.

Dwyer, R. (2006) *Filming the Gods: Religion and Indian Cinema*. New York: Routledge.

Eco, U. (1995) *The Role of the Reader: Explorations in the Semiotics of Texts*. Bloomington: Indiana University Press.

Ganti, T. (2013) *Bollywood: A Guidebook to Popular Hindi Cinema*. New York: Routledge.

Majumdar, N. (2001) "The Embodied Voice: Song Sequences and Stardom in Popular Hindi Cinema". In *Soundtrack Available: Essays on Film and Popular Music*, edited by P. Robertson Wojcik and A. Knight, 161–81. Durham, NC: Duke University Press.

Majumdar, N. (2009) *Wanted Cultured Ladies Only!: Female Stardom and Cinema in India, 1930s-1950s*. Illinois: University of Illinois Press.

Majumdar, R. (2005) *Bombay Cinema: An Archive of the City*. Minneapolis: University of Minnesota Press.

Manuel, P. (1994) "Puerto Rican Music and Cultural Identity: Creative Appropriation of Cuban Sources from Danza to Salsa". *Ethnomusicology* 38/2: 249–80.

Manuel, P. (1995) "Music as Symbol, Music as Simulacrum: Postmodern, Pre-modern, and Modern Aesthetics in Subcultural Popular Musics". *Popular Music* 14/2: 227–39.

McGee, K. A. (2009) *Some Liked It Hot: Jazz Women in Film and Television, 1928-1959*. Connecticut: Wesleyan University Press.

Mishra, S. (2013) "Negotiating Female Sexuality: Bollywood Belly Dance, 'Item Girls' and Dance Classes". In *Belly Dance around the World*, edited by C. E. McDonald and B. Sellers-Young, 181–96. North Carolina: McFarland & Company Inc.

Nijhawan, A. (2009) "Excusing the Female Dancer". *South Asian Popular Culture* 7/2: 100–10.

Pinto, J. (2006) *Helen: The Life and Times of an H-bomb*. New Delhi: Penguin.

Shope, B. (2013) "Latin American Music in Moving Pictures and Jazzy Cabarets in Mumbai, 1930s to 1950s". In *More than Bollywood: Studies in Popular Music*, edited by G. D. Booth and B. Shope, 201–215. New York: Oxford University Press.

Siefert, M. (1995) "Image/Music/Voice: Song Dubbing in Hollywood Musicals". *Journal of Communication* 45/2: 44–64.

Silverman, K. (1988) *The Acoustic Mirror: The Female Voice in Psychoanalysis and Cinema*. Bloomington: Indiana Press.

Sundar, P. (2008) "Meri Awaaz Suno: Women, Vocality, and Nation in Hindi Cinema". *Meridians* 8/1: 144–79.

Turino, T. (1999) "Signs of Imagination, Identity, and Experience: A Peircian Semiotic Theory for Music". *Ethnomusicology* 43/2: 221–55.

Weidman, A. (2007) "Stage Goddesses and Studio Divas in South India: On Agency and the Politics of the Voice". In *Words, World, and Material Girls: Language, Gender, Globalization*, edited by B. S. McElhinny, 131–55. New York: Mouton de Gruyter.

Weidman, A. (2012) "Voices of Meenakumari: Sound, Meaning and Self-Fashioning in Performances of an Item Number". *South Asian Popular Culture* 10: 307–318.

7 Before #MeToo:
Hearing Vulnerability

Diane Hughes and Mark Evans

Introduction

The #MeToo[1] hashtag went viral in 2017. This signified a growing awareness of workplace misconduct and exposed detrimental power relationships within various sectors of the entertainment industry. Gendered power play, misogyny and sexual transgression quickly became "key topics"[2] in the #MeToo tweeting and sharing of personal stories. The oppressed were heard as their perpetrators were progressively ousted.[3] The movement now serves as a significant and recognized marker of workplace health and safety and related issues. It also raises questions as to who enabled such abuses of power, for how long and why? In this chapter, we explore abuses of power and sector hypocrisy in cinematic representations of singers in various music industry contexts. The contemporary music industry has long been fraught with a "low degree of regulation [in which industry] 'standards' have not always paralleled other business entities as to ethical business protocols" (Golden, 2001: 9). The post-digitization fragmentation of the label-centric music industry (Hughes et al., 2016: 1), along with the potential for multiple levels of artistic control, frames the complexity of the contemporary music environment. These issues, combined with "questionable business practices, music lyrics and subject matter, and [general] validation of riskier social norms" (Golden, 2001: 2), create further layers of risk and emphasize the potential vulnerability for those involved.

Filmic narratives, whether fictional or documentary presentations, provide a powerful medium through which to explore topics related to exploitation in the music industries. From the feature-length documentary to the inclusion of singers as fictional representations of those industries, the cinematic depiction of singing in contemporary music practices forms the focus of this chapter. Several films have been selected for analysis and comparison as each provides a unique perspective and context. The films – *Nashville* (Robert Altman, 1975), *Music and Lyrics* (Marc Lawrence, 2007), *Begin Again* (John Carney, 2013), *Beyond the Lights* (Gina Prince-Bythewood, 2014) and *20 Feet from Stardom* (Morgan Neville, 2013) – collectively represent over four decades of workplace representations of singers.

The inclusion of fictional cinematic representations that depict ingrained sector issues aligns with many of the sector realities identified and featured in the documentary, *20 Feet from Stardom*. Each film also serves to acknowledge the pervasiveness of singing in popular culture, and highlights an underlying audience predilection for celebrity and fame.

The chapter begins by examining recent discussions in popular music studies and cultural movements that have called out inappropriate but entrenched behaviours associated with contemporary music, singing and/or singers. The analysis of each filmic narrative informs a particular music industry context – such as vocal artistry, artistic control, song creation – in which hypocrisy, institutional norms and gender issues are exposed and/or questioned. Within these contexts, and extending well beyond its acoustic properties or embodied expression, "singing" is often situated as the protagonist in ways that seek to contextualize or consider its potential commodification and manipulation. Such mistreatment extends to the related multiplicity of detrimental industry practices and, for some singers, the ensuing complications. Our discussion concludes by outlining the collective and recurrent themes that identify and reveal – and hear – vulnerability.

Vulnerability in the Music Industries

Vulnerability, whether that be an outcome of endemic misogyny, prejudice or harassment, is particularly relevant for female sector workers.[4] The music industries have long been fraught with sexual misconduct under the guise of industry personnel and associated "rock star" behaviours. A panel at South by Southwest (SXSW) in 2018 examined "the pervasiveness of sexual misconduct and how this aggression affects the psyche of women working in music in regards to performance, promotions, equal pay and influence".[5] Although acknowledging that #MeToo had not received the same exposure as it had in other sectors, the panel addressed the ways in which #MeToo extended to the music industries. Challenging industry pre-conceptions and the sector's somewhat siloed structure, the panel discussed the male-dominated power play that largely controls these industries and noted the lack of human resources or similar industry reporting lines due to the transient workplace. Other industry representatives[6] pointed to this and discussed touring and the potential vulnerability that ensues through the often insecure and transient environment. This second SXSW panel also signalled behaviours that stemmed largely from the gendered powerplay within the workplace and discussed a particular song, an "empowerment anthem"[7] called 'Time's Up'[8] (Kalie Shorr and Lacy Green, 2018). The song was performed and recorded by members of a Nashville collective of female singer-songwriters, Song Suffragettes. The opening of the song's video presents a visual signpost of "no trespassing". Here, the song provides a "distanced" and powerful intermediary – as it signifies a "conversation that is at times hard and painful to discuss"[9] – through which to explore sector issues, particularly those that pertain to female vulnerability and related concerns. Such concerns were corroborated by the Preatures' vocalist, Isabella Manfredi, who discussed how the industry's gendered power play precludes or makes difficult the reporting of issues such as sexual misconduct.[10]

Gender biases, discrimination and sexist behaviours have been longstanding industry concerns. The potential vulnerability of being female in a male-dominated industry poses considerations for many industry contexts. In 2017, Gordon discussed the way that sexist behaviours can undermine "the value and important role women play in the music industry".[11] Domanick, in a 2018 music industry discussion, further suggested that "sexual misconduct is built into the foundation of the music industry" and highlighted the male dominance *over* and *within* the industry:

> Little consolidated data is available about the gender breakdown of the American music industry, but Census Bureau data points to an imbalance: within the sound recording industry, for example, which includes record labels and publishing groups, women make up 28 percent of the workforce [DATA USA, 2016]. The workforce tends to skew even more male at the highest levels. Recent reports from the UK [UK Music, 2017] and Australia [Cooper, Coles and Hanna-Osbourne, 2017] found that women remain underrepresented there; according to a 2016 survey by the UK Music Diversity Taskforce, women occupy 30 percent of senior executive positions and 40 percent of senior management positions, despite comprising more than half of entry-level roles.[12]

While gender-biases and resultant levels of discrimination are evident (Cooper, Coles and Hanna-Osbourne, 2017), research into the music industries (for example, Hughes et al., 2016; van den Eynde, Fisher and Sonn, 2016) identifies that workers within the music and related industries, including singers, are susceptible to myriad adverse sector conditions. One such condition is the culture of substance abuse that exists within the industries. Artist, Lily Allen, commented that "the whole culture of music is, whether we like it or not, geared around alcohol and drugs".[13] Research in Australia (van den Eynde, Fisher and Sonn, 2016)[14] and in the UK (Gross and Musgrave, 2016)[15] further suggests that mental health issues manifest in the face of structureless, precarious and adverse sector conditions (Gross and Musgrave, 2016: 13):

> musicians could be up to three times more likely to suffer from depression compared to the general public… working in, or having ambitions to work in, the music industry, might indeed be making musicians sick, or at least contribute towards their levels of mental ill-health (Gross and Musgrave, 2016: 5).

Vulnerability is also evident in a personal reluctance to make perpetrators accountable. Certainly, the perception of isolation and a hesitancy to report incidents or adverse conditions is deduced by Allen to be due, in part, to:

> long-term contracts… Like, 15 years. There isn't an HR place to go to because everyone's self-employed. You can't go to the record company, nobody there's looking after you. Management's not looking after you, you're all on your own.[16]

Similarly, the personal and legal costs of taking action are highlighted by Kesha who in 2014 made harassment and abuse allegations against her mentor/producer, Dr Luke. While Kesha reportedly received public support from other artists, a 2016 court ruling failed to grant an injunction that would have ended her contractual obligation to Dr Luke.[17]

In an industry where workplace conditions can be unregulated and when incidents may be unreported, filmic representations become even more significant. The portrayals and narratives discussed in this chapter and the emergent themes identified through our analyses – both respectively and collectively – expose various manifestations of vulnerability in the music industries.

Filmic Representations and Contexts

The films discussed below – *Nashville* (1975), *Music and Lyrics* (2007), *Begin Again* (2013), *Beyond the Lights* (2014) and *20 Feet from Stardom* (2013) – present a multiplicity of contexts and time periods through which to explore the music industries and consequential vulnerability. The fragility of singing and singers is revealed largely through aspects of performance, recording, songwriting, touring, and other industry realities. Popularity and control are often explored in representations of gendered, misogynistic environments in which manipulation and exploitation are unmistakably evident. Within this milieu, vulnerability in singing may be heard as a hesitancy to sing, as breathy vocal tone, or as being musically insecure. The vulnerability of singers is also evident through exploitation and misrepresentation. Such vulnerability occurs alongside themes of digital disruption, substance abuse, gender biases, sexist behaviours, musical commodification and career uncertainty.

Nashville (Robert Altman, 1975)

Nashville paradoxically portrays both singing and the singing voice in ways that reflect more broadly the film's diegetic action. Rush (1990) extrapolates:

> *Nashville* uses simple, unidirectional parody to create alien discourse within the diegetic world. But that discourse does not challenge the

> narrating frame. It turns a single mirror on the world outside the film, creating a parodied reflection but ignoring the question of what gives the mirror authority in the first place (Rush, 1990: 11).

Such "parodied reflection" is evident from the moment the film begins with an "advertisement" for the film, including the cast and aspects of the soundtrack. At once, we are cognizant of and tacitly accept the commodification of singers and songs. On the one hand, singing is revered in the film and acclaimed through its celebritized status. In stark contrast, an inability to sing well translates to personal humiliation and exploitation. It is, however, through the defenceless characters of Barbara Jean (Ronee Blakley) and Sueleen Gay (Gwen Welles) that the singing voice is most exposed. Struggling with mental health issues and from being controlled by her husband-manager, Barnett (Allen Garfield), Barbara Jean is ultimately unable to sustain professional performances and appearances; objectified by her lack of singing ability, Sueleen is coerced into stripping.

Throughout the film, singing successes are juxtaposed with the vulnerability of aspiring singers, artistic singing with politicized voice, cultivated image with naturalness, and sincerity with the "aesthetically bankrupt" (Cardullo, 1976: 315). Altman's pervasive use of irony exposes underlying insecurities. This is most evident through the vulnerable Barbara Jean and the Vietnam veteran (Scott Glenn) who, even though he carefully watches out for Barbara Jean, is ultimately unable to save her. There is also the dedicated ageing husband who misses his wife's passing, and the BBC reporter, Opal (Geraldine Chaplin), who misses the actual assassination and asks those around her "what happened?". Irony and contrasts are also extensively evident in the film's diegetic singing. For example, the singing voice of Henry Gibson, who plays Haven Hamilton, is professional and provides a striking contrast to the amateur, out-of-tune and vulnerable singing of Sueleen. Similarly, the irony of the seeming sincerity expressed by philanderer Tom Frank (Keith Carradine) is striking when he sings 'I'm Easy' (Keith Carradine, 1975). In this context, it is his "victims" that are vulnerable.

Nashville is situated in the label-centric recording industry of the 1970s. While most of its characters are involved in country music in some way, other characters serve to provide social, political and/or industry commentary. The film tracks the trajectories of twenty-four characters within a five-day time frame in the music-centred city of Nashville. Here, the industry context of analogue recording technology is also symbolic as Rick Altman[18] (1991) asserts:

> Modeling his narrative on the 24-track recording technology commonly used within the music industry, Altman builds his story around 24 independent characters... Created as an ode to country music for the American bicentennial, *Nashville* is also a tribute to the twenty-four track sound technology that dominates the music industry (Altman, 1991: 104).

Nashville's script was based on research undertaken by Altman's collaborator and scriptwriter, Joan Tewkesbury (Altman, 1991: 123). The noticeable and deliberate political theme throughout the film was undoubtedly in response to a government in crisis.[19] It was also at a time when the then troubled Nixon (1974) politicized country music in a speech at Nashville's Grand Ole Opry:

> What country music is, is that first it comes from the heart of America, because [Nashville] is the heart of America, out here in Middle America. Second, it relates to those experiences that mean so much to America. It talks about family, it talks about religion, the faith in God that is so important to our country and particularly to our family life. And as we all know, country music radiates a love of this Nation, patriotism. Country music, therefore, has those combinations which are so essential to America's character at a time that America needs character... And country music does that (Nixon, 1974: 280-81).

Altman's representation of country music is far more complex than the nationalistic sentiments espoused by Nixon. Altman introduces country singing by panning a recording studio during a contrived rendition of '200 Years' (Richard Baskin and Henry Gibson, 1975) by singer, Haven Hamilton. The song is rendered as a symbolic testimony of "its own hollow patriotism" (Cardullo, 1976: 317); the singing is authoritative even in the lower vocal range and dynamically builds as the melodic lines become higher to culminate in the lyrical affirmation of '200 years'. The star status afforded the sequined Haven extends to his high-handed treatment of those observing the session. Haven directs the recording session and admonishes the vulnerable piano player who struggles to play within such a stringent, musically notated and constrained recording environment. This scene is juxtaposed with the freely improvised gospel singing being recorded in the adjacent studio. Even in relation to the gospel singing, there is a distinct difference between the "gospel" and higher register singing of Linnea Reese (Lily Tomlin) and the black gospel choristers who sing with clear tone and rhythmic energy. Such contrasts attest to a cinematic "reality [that] is multiple" (Altman, 1991: 121). At times, the satire is overt such as when the aspiring and previously ignored singer, Winifred (Barbara Harris) takes the stage following Barbara Jean's assassination and sings 'It Don't Worry Me' (Keith Carradine, 1975). Winifred's singing begins tentatively as if reflecting her own vulnerability and provides a direct contrast to the rich vocal timbre of Barbara Jean's singing just prior to her being shot. Haven's response to the shooting is to engage the crowd in singing and after Winifred's initial hesitancy of having a microphone thrust in her hand by Haven, the crowd positively responds to her voice which gains authority as others join in clapping and singing. In doing so, they collectively ignore the inappropriateness of the lyrical content. Altman reasoned:

> I saw that as both sides of a coin. When they say, "It Don't Worry Me" after that assassination, I think it indicates how quickly you can get over something and become apathetic about it. But I think it also talks about, in equal intensity, the fact that people carry on (Altman as quoted in Kloman and Michaels, 1983: 22).

Ironically, these events occur at a rally for the politician, Hal Phillip Walker, who never physically appears in the film but who remains pivotal to the film and the interrelatedness of its characters. Again, Altman's use of panning relegates the viewer to observing rather than being immersed in the action which perhaps makes the onscreen vulnerability at times more palatable. This voyeuristic viewpoint likewise aids the effectiveness of Altman's vignettes such as Sueleen's coerced striptease and Linnea's singing with her deaf children. The voyeuristic stance is reinforced by the political van that keeps roving the streets amplifying recorded rhetoric in a way that makes other diegetic voices silent: "the narrating voice disguised as alien discourse, simply imposed over a compliant diegetic world, that lacks any voice to speak back" (Rush, 1990: 8).

Music and Lyrics (Marc Lawrence, 2007)

Music and Lyrics explores career sustainability within the evolutionary ethos of pop music and related industry practices. The romantic comedy opens with a dated and clichéd music video featuring the then popular male duo, PoP! Some fifteen years later, the film segues into the fading career of the duo's lead singer, Alex Fletcher (Hugh Grant). Unlike his former band mate's successful solo career and its associated merchandising, Alex is invited to be a contestant on a fictitious television show, "Battle of the '80s Has-Beens". It becomes apparent that the opportunity to sing on this show is only afforded to the winner of an on-air boxing match. The comical boxing analogy is multi-layered as it serves to stress the competitiveness of industry expectations and posits consideration of mass-mediated humiliation versus entertainment. The film then focuses on the rejuvenation of Alex's career through various opportunities, collaborations and performances. Much of the comedic narrative in *Music and Lyrics* is satirically based and touches on themes of superficiality, exploitation and career longevity.

Singing and songwriting as industry practices feature in *Music and Lyrics*. The narrative is centred on an invitation to write a song for contemporary pop star Cora Corman (Haley Bennett). There are stringent parameters for the song's creation including its title, 'Way Back Into Love' (as an acknowledgement of Cora's recent break up), the song's creative turnaround time of a week and its ability to be performed as a duo with Cora at Madison Square Garden. The inherent irony in these parameters is compounded by the competitiveness of Cora's invitation as it extends to other "retro" artists as well. Alex's manager, Chris Riley (Brad Garrett), endorses Cora's invitation as, if successful, it would provide currency to counteract Alex's fading career and image. Several aspects of commercial songwriting are highlighted in Cora's invitation including the commissioning of a song, the structuring of a song to suit an artist, and the potential constraints of imposed project timelines. The context of the invitation also positions the competitiveness and commodification of pop music more broadly.

The struggle for Alex to write the melodic component becomes quickly apparent. He is also concerned about potential songwriting collaborations. This not only typifies the two key songwriting components of melody and lyrics, but also highlights the often tenuous collaborative songwriting process. To complicate matters, Alex has not written anything in a long time. After one failed attempt to collaborate on the song, Alex turns his attention to Sophie Fisher (Drew Barrymore) who arrives at his apartment to care for his plants. Sophie improvises and sings while watering the plants. Here, her singing voice is natural and spontaneous, unaffected by vocal technique or purposeful production. Alex quickly recognizes Sophie's potential for writing lyrics and asks her to collaborate. Over the course of writing, Alex confides in Sophie about his past and about the industry. This includes his former band mate's success by recording solo three original PoP! songs, Alex's own failed solo album, his spiralling career and financial ramifications, the need to perform "nostalgia" gigs and his resultant substance abuse. Sophie's response is that she understands what it is like to live with "a shadow overhead". This forms the germ of their song for Cora and typifies how a song may be incidentally created. When Sophie has difficulty in meeting Cora's final request to write another verse, Alex says that "in the end it's all just business… that's why they call it the music business". It is here that Sophie's vulnerability in being coerced into extending the song is markedly evident.

Additional aspects of the music sector recurrently feature through portrayals of singing and performance. Most notably is the contrast between Sophie's "natural" but initially hesitant and soft diegetic singing during the song's demo recording and Cora's "pop" affected voice. Cora's character presents a female pop vocal that is both produced and predictable. When performing a sexualized interpretation of Alex and Sophie's song, however, Cora's vocal aesthetic is naïve, almost atonal. Her singing later morphs into the produced and perfected vocal aesthetic expected of a contemporary pop singer. Similarly, Alex's diegetic singing for the demo is contrasted by his almost soulless theme park performance where his singing competes with park rides and other distractions. It is at the theme park when Alex is required contractually to sing an encore that his impassive singing is most evident. This is marked by a lack of dynamic variance and enthusiasm. Other industry aspects and themes include image and hype,[20] career diversification, the ramifications of fading or failing careers, the impact of negative public critiques, the difficulties of sustaining successful collaborations, dealing with writer's block, and maintaining integrity.

Integrity is also explored through the link between and cinematic emphasis on the song's creative integrity and intent. After their song is submitted, Alex and Sophie receive an invitation to meet at Cora's studio to discuss the song where Cora performs a new introduction to 'Way Back Into Love' (Adam Schlesinger, 2007). Here, Cora dances provocatively but this time it is to Indian rhythms. Despite Cora's justification that her interpretation meets audience expectations, Sophie objects to Alex's acceptance of their song's sexualized performance. Their ensuing discussion centres on artistic control, vision and integrity. In many ways, Cora and Alex are victims of music industry expectations and music commodification. However, when they finally perform at Madison Square Garden, 'Way Back Into Love' is sung as it was originally written. This stripped-back performance aligns with Sophie's creative vision and allows the respective singing by Alex and Cora to prominently feature.

Begin Again (John Carney, 2013)

Begin Again portrays the fading career of music entrepreneur, Dan Mulligan (Mark Ruffalo). The narrative signifies a disrupted profession caused by the digitization of music. Throughout the film, there are continual references to industry changes. Dan's "nuture and foster" approach to artist development is criticized by his business partner for being outdated and no longer viable. Dan, however, believes that the contemporary industry needs "vision not gimmicks". Here, Dan is referring to the disruption caused by digitization which is at odds with his own notion of artist development that solely relied on creative and musical ability. Dan's artistic foresight is hindered by financial problems and substance abuse that, together with his failed marriage and troubled daughter, are depicted as industry fallout. Dan's fading career in artist development and label management is contrasted by the emerging careers of Dave Khol (Adam Levine) and Gretta James (Keira Knightley). Much of the film's industry context is centred on Dan's artistic vision, his guidance of Gretta's development and their subsequent recording project.

Digital recording, and contemporary industry practices, underscore the narrative in *Begin Again*. This is evident at the film's outset where temporal interchanges enable the opening scene to be revisited from Dan's perspective and an alternative musical arrangement of Gretta's original song is heard. While Dan listens to Gretta sing, he imagines other instruments accompanying her, musically layering Gretta's singing with piano, drums, cello and violin. He changes position so that he can stand in front of Gretta and "conduct" his imagined orchestrated performance. This mirrors the musical process of audiation or predictive musical hearing (Gordon, 1999).

It is through Dan's artistic vision that much of the industry practices and their impact are further portrayed. Dan constantly critiques current practices that focus on promotional tactics rather than the actual music. He also discusses the personal demands and cost of being involved in music. Such involvement is portrayed as being incompatible with long-term relationships and family life. Dan's own failed marriage highlights this incompatibility which is also reflected in Gretta's failed relationship with Dave. Of particular industry interest is the debate around the importance of visual image versus Gretta's stance on music being about "ears not eyes" and about "authenticity". Dan's cynical approach is typified by his belief that it is the visual elements that attract an audience to listen and that then allows the music to "do its real work".

The theme of artistic control is further elaborated through the interplay between Gretta and her former boyfriend, Dave. From the outset, Dave is manipulated by both industry expectations and his assigned industry personnel. His record label sets out to minimize Gretta's involvement in his career. The opposing musical trajectories of Gretta and Dave highlight *commercial* versus *independent* intent, *security* versus *vulnerability*. After Dave records a studio album while touring, Gretta comments on how its production has compromised their initial personal and musical connection and views Dave's recording as being overproduced "stadium pop". In contrast, Gretta records her live album through a series of single tracks recorded in different New York settings including in Central Park, on the subway and on a Manhattan roof top.

Singing and songs feature throughout the film. The naturalness and simple treatment of Gretta's recorded voice and songs provide a stark contrast to Dave's studio-produced recordings and sound. This is underscored by Gretta's connection to song lyrics and the intent of "original" songs that are often presented through her singer-songwriter perspective. The independent aspects of Gretta's album, however, not only relate to artistic choices and recording processes but also reflect contemporary independent industry practices through the album's eventual distribution. Having being told by Dan's former label that she would receive only a dollar for every album sold if she were to sign a distribution deal, Gretta chooses instead to independently release the album. She intends to sell the album for a dollar and to equitably divide the sales revenue amongst the contributing musicians as a "legitimate back-end deal". According to Dan, this decision is like "going to war" with industry practices. Here, the once vulnerable Gretta takes a stand against imposed industry control – not only of her vocal sound and recorded product – but also of her image and artistry.

Beyond the Lights (Gina Prince-Bythewood, 2014)
Within a popular music context, *Beyond the Lights* is a provocative portrayal of singing, the singer and career sustainability. The narrative focuses on industry expectations and the related experiences of singer, Noni Jean (Gugu Mbatha-Raw). Noni's characterization centres on a number of contrasting intents and ideals. Perhaps the most significant of these is Noni's apparent success which is set against

her personal desperation. Associated contrasts include industry aims versus individual goals, control versus powerlessness, glamour versus simplicity, and commodification versus artistic pursuit. For example, police officer, Kaz Nicol (Nate Parker), thwarts Noni's suicide attempt while Noni's mother and manager, Macy Jean (Minnie Driver), continues her manipulative and incessant control of Noni and her career. Macy's managerial tactics align directly with the directives and commercial interests of Noni's male-dominated record label. The personal and professional control of Noni by the ambitious Macy is somewhat mirrored by Kaz's father Captain David Nicol (Danny Glover) as he constantly engineers political aspirations and strategies on behalf of his son, Kaz. In both examples, manipulation and control are often seen to take precedence over seemingly altruistic intention.

The commodified and generic intentions of other people are portrayed in relation to Noni's narrative and hypersexualized image[21] which is particularly evident in her appearance, song lyrics and dance moves. Noni struggles with this public and created persona. She is confronted by the expectations of photo shoots where she is encouraged to provocatively pose. Macy, in her role as manager, endorses such "opportunities". However, Noni is clearly uncomfortable with objectification. This extends to her seductive posing and image as she performs with her boyfriend, Kid Culprit (Machine Gun Kelly), a rapper. Following a Billboard awards ceremony, it is the stylist who covers Noni as soon as she is out of the view of paparazzi. The objectified portrayal of Noni, however, continues even after her suicide attempt. For example, a record executive threatens to cancel Noni's scheduled album launch as Noni is "the girl that every guy wants and every girl wants to be [the label is] selling fantasy here and suicide ain't sexy".

Noni's struggle with her mental health and wellbeing is underscored by a crafted selection and inclusion of specific songs. This began with the film's inception as reportedly Prince-Bythewood played 'Beneath Your Beautiful' (Labrinth, Mike Posner and Emeli Sandé, 2012) and 'Save Me' (Andrew Wansel, Nicki Minaj and Warren Felder, 2010) as she developed *Beyond the Lights*.[22] Indeed, Prince-Bythewood acknowledges that every script she has written has had "its own playlist".[23] The significance that Prince-Bythewood places on songs is highly relevant as it not only reflects the contemporary industry practice and focus of *the song* versus *the album*, but also serves to highlight the ways in which songs may be consumed, that is, through individualized playlists. The choice of specific commercially released songs by contemporary female artists that feature in the film's soundtrack is significant. These include 'Fly Before You Fall' (Cynthia Erivo and Michael Lister, 2014), 'Shelter' (Romy Anna Madley Croft, Oliver David Sim and James Thomas Smith, 2011; performed by Birdy), 'Don't Let Me Down' (Amel Larrieux and Laru Larrieux, 2009) and 'I am Light' (India Arie, 2013). Prince-Bythewood also acknowledges that her discovery of Nina Simone's 'Blackbird' (Herbert Sacker and Nina

Simone, 1966) changed "the trajectory of the film" as originally Noni was going to sing an original song in Mexico:

> Once I found 'Blackbird', I realized that I thought it was better that in that moment [in the Mexican karaoke bar] she's going back to trying to be the singer she had hoped to be when she was a little girl and then at the end she sings her original song.[24]

The imagery provided by the inclusion of Nina Simone's 'Blackbird' (1966) is highly expressive as it is through Noni's singing of 'Blackbird' that the audience is introduced to extreme vulnerability and the plight of oppressed black women in Western society. The opening scene is set in the south London area of Brixton, an area known for civil unrest during the 1980s and 1990s (Gray, 2009: 151). Here, Macy takes Noni to a hairdresser to prepare her for a talent quest the following day – a "Youth Talent Quest" – where a young Noni (India Jean-Jacques) first sings an *a cappella* version of 'Blackbird'. She is portrayed as a girl who loves to sing; her singing voice is clear and unaffected. During the subsequent awards scene, Noni's haunting singing voice is underscored by low-level audio and vision of the award announcements. Noni is awarded first runner up. Macy encourages Noni to throw away her trophy and demands to know whether Noni wants to be a runner up or a winner. This sets the tone for Noni's ensuing struggles and manipulation.[25] Throughout *Beyond the Lights*, the manufactured pop voice is set against Noni's natural singing ability and as the film progresses, Noni's adult pop singing voice is technologically affected. Here, her singing bears little resemblance to the integrity of Noni's younger singing voice. The integrity only later returns when a broken and vulnerable Noni again sings 'Blackbird' in the Mexican karaoke bar where she almost whispers at the beginning with a distinct breathy tone. Being an *a cappella* version, her full singing voice becomes exposed; there is an intensive "b" plosive in the lyric "body" which reflects emotionality and vocal integrity. While fragility is evident in the softer dynamics, a higher intensity and dynamic is utilized as the song's emotional intensity builds. Certainly, as Noni becomes stronger and begins to control her artistic vision, she "finds" her own voice through both singing and songwriting. Much of Noni's narrative, however, is explored through her heavily treated and affected singing as opposed to her singing voice that is musically and personally expressive. In many ways, *Beyond the Lights* focuses on the literal and metaphoric symbolism of Noni finding herself through finding her "authentic" singing voice. This intent is highlighted in the film's trailer[26] and in the directorial aim to emphasize female empowerment.[27]

Other industry practices were also instrumental in development and preparation for filming *Beyond the Lights*. Prince-Bythewood explained that the intention was to surround Mbatha-Raw with "the real people in the industry".[28] Choreographer, Laurieann Gibson, was involved in Mbatha-Raw's preparation and for her role as a pop singer, Mbatha-Raw also worked with music producer, singer and songwriter, The-Dream. Mbatha-Raw had never been in a recording studio before her role as Noni and found the process challenging:

> the music hours are very different... a lot of late nights, a lot of early, early hours of the morning... in the music studio. But it was great because you know that's really... what those artists do... It's the first time [I'd] sung in this style... It was a challenge... but part of the character's world.[29]

20 Feet from Stardom (Morgan Neville, 2013)

Our inclusion of the documentary, *20 Feet from Stardom*, validates many of the issues and themes explored above through the discussion and exposure of real-world experiences. The film simultaneously celebrates singing achievements while exposing the negative realities of singing within contemporary music industries – namely, manipulation, exploitation, hypersexualization and commodification. These "realities" echo those identified in the previous fictional narratives. *20 Feet from Stardom* portrays the stories of professional and predominantly female backing or backup singers – including Merry Clayton, Lisa Fischer, Judith Hill, Darlene Love, Janice Pendavaris and Táta Vega. The featured singers provide insight through their respective roles and commentaries on a sector that largely determined their relevance and prominence. This is reflected in the metaphoric film title which symbolizes both their on-stage placement and their often subjugated professional status. Diffrient (2017) deduces that:

> those titular twenty feet also hint at the larger history of race relations and sexual politics in twentieth-century America, where the divisionist discourses and segregationist policies that civil rights activists fought against found their musicological equivalent in concert venues and recording sessions (Diffrient, 2017: 26).

Much of the film's commentary is delivered through interviews with artists such as Bette Midler, Stevie Wonder, Sheryl Crow, Bruce Springsteen and Mick Jagger. Each artist emphasizes the significance of backing singers and the role they have played in the development of popular music. This includes the desire for many rock artists to emulate the "freedom" of their sound (see Claudia Lennear and Darlene Love quotations in Neville, 2013). The commentary also questions why many singers remained in the background. Lisa Fischer, after receiving a Grammy award, says that it was poor timing in that it took too long to release a second album. Others, including Springsteen, talk about the need to have an ego in order to take the "conceptual leap" (Springsteen as quoted in Neville, 2013) to become a solo singer. In the contemporary scene, however, the call for backing vocalists, at least in recording contexts, is not as extensive as it was in analogue production.

Digital production enables lead singers to layer their own harmonies or for background vocals to be technologically created. Digital production also enables the sung pitch to be altered (Hughes, 2015; Bill Maxwell as quoted in Neville, 2013).

Prior to improvised soul and gospel infused backing vocals, backing singers for recordings performed vocal parts that were usually notated and, when sung, resulted in a structured, musically accurate and somewhat predictable harmonic sound. The introduction of black American backing singers in the 1960s brought a level of vocal freedom not previously heard (see Stevie Wonder as quoted in Neville, 2013). Certainly, their singing was not confined to the written score. They typically complemented the often male lead vocals by providing vocal intensity, harmonic layering, responding phrases[30] and additional, often brighter, vocal timbre. Unsettling their effectiveness were the manipulative strategies that resulted in subversive singer attributions. This is clearly apparent in the reflections on 1960s record producer, Phil Spector, and in his particular treatment of Darlene Love (formerly Wright). Love had recorded vocals that were ultimately attributed to other artists. She recalled one particular "ghosted" track, 'He's a Rebel' (Gene Pitney, 1962), where her lead vocals were attributed to The Crystals. On the back of the song's success, Love signed with Spector and, at his instigation, changed her surname from Wright to Love. Arguably, this name change emphasized seductive potential and allure. Love's first release was supposed to be 'He's Sure the Boy I Love' (Barry Mann and Cynthia Weil, 1962). However, when the record was released it was again attributed to The Crystals. Describing such attribution as "debilitating to the spirit [when] no one knows that you did it" (Susaye Greene, as quoted in Neville, 2013), the process of ghosted recordings was reflective of an unstructured and unregulated industry. In Love's particular case, Warren Zanes, a music historian included in the film, also confirmed the gendered power play: "You couldn't fit two stars in the room at the same time. So Phil Spector really kept [Love] in a box. The best material she was putting out wasn't even coming out under her name" (Zanes, as quoted in Neville, 2013).

As evident in the assigning of Love's stage name, genderization also encompassed stereotypical expectations. For many female singers, genderization extended to group names such as Ray Charles' "Raelettes" and Ike and Tina Turner's "Ikettes". However, industry expectations surrounding image and performances made some female singers uncomfortable. Singer, Stevvi Alexander, commented that "I just get chills when I think about how I was just so demoralized at the outfits... we were basically naked". Similarly, Lynn Mabry noted that the dress code was often to "make guys" excited: "There are still artists right now that view a back-up singer as eye candy. Personally, that's not back-up singing, that's just playing a role" (Mabry, as quoted in Neville, 2013).

The singing featured throughout the documentary testifies to the value and communicative ability of singing more broadly. Bill Maxwell, a vocalist contractor, espoused in the film:

> The human voice is the most pure expression coming from your own being. There's nothing between your soul and your ability and your body and them. It's not being camouflaged by a trumpet or a saxophone or a guitar. It's pure and that's why [singers are] so sensitive about it, because they're putting it out there (Bill Maxwell as quoted in Neville, 2013).

It is this physical embodiment that adds to a potential level of personal vulnerability as singers and their voices are often so prominent in performance. A resolute passion for singing was evident in all the featured singers in *20 Feet from Stardom*. Theirs is a type of singing that is a collective experience. Singer, Lynn Mabry, also explained that it is backing singers that add "life" so that singing provides "a person to person connection" (Mabry, as quoted in Neville, 2013). Judith Hill, a contemporary singer-songwriter featured in the documentary, epitomizes a soul-infused vocal. Hill's voice, like so many of the other featured singers, is strong, musical and highly communicative in the expressive techniques she embodies. Evident in her performance of her original song, 'Desperation' (released as a single in 2013), Hill personifies emotive angst through which a level of vulnerability is heard in her soulful pleas.

Recurrent Themes

Our analyses explored cinematic representations of many sector issues and themes relating to singing, singers and songs. We purposefully included films which identified the potential vulnerability for both females and males. The latter, however, largely pertained to susceptibility due to substance abuse and failing careers. For females, on the other hand, themes of powerlessness and manipulation, hypersexualization, artistic control and surviving in a gendered industry were consistently evident. Similarly, the prevalence of female backing vocalists featured in *20 Feet from Stardom* and their support of predominantly male lead vocalists is indicative of stereotypical industry generated norms/expectations. Such expectations have been entrenched for decades which is supported by the respective time periods of our cinematic representations. Indeed, each of the cinematic portrayals revealed issues subsequently identified and responded to by cultural movements such as #MeToo and Times Up. It is curious, and discouraging, that popular film has been pointing out the vulnerability and exploitation of contemporary singers for so long. Long before #MeToo, the evidence was plainly before our eyes and ears. In seeking to depict the life and experience of singers, concerning behaviours and associated industry contexts were routinely showcased.

Identified in our analyses were industry issues including "misogyny, sexism and gender-based abuse, along with isolation, fear of the unknown and varying levels of security (personal and financial)" (Hughes et al., 2016: 93). Similarly, additional industry research has identified that "poor working conditions... contribute towards high levels of anxiety and depression given the precarious nature of the work, an inability to plan one's time/future, the nature of self-employment, anti-social hours, exhaustion, and, crucially, low or often zero pay" (Gross and Musgrave, 2016: 13). This precariousness was evident in each of the cinematic portrayals that respectively questioned career sustainability.

The intent and relevance of hearing vulnerability in contemporary cinema revealed a multiplicity of contrasting contexts. The singing voice could at once be political and sexualized, emotive and exploited, inspired and exhausted, fictional and real; the songs could be literal and metaphoric, or inconsequential and measured. These contrasts were set alongside notions of vocal authenticity against constructed sound, natural against manufactured ability, honesty against gimmickry. While each film encompassed adverse working conditions and industry expectations, the theme of losing, regaining or maintaining a metaphorical voice/sense of self-worth through singing was prominent. The impact of the technologies on singing was also evident particularly in the cinematic depictions of differing recording practices including digital versus analogue, home recording versus commercial studio, in situ versus portable and accessible recording technology. Cumulatively, our research identifies that cinematic representations of singing, singers and songs are diverse, complex and often contradictory. Yet the synergies between such representations reveal that despite the potential for industry manipulation and commodification, the quest for vocal and artistic integrity is highly sought and valued. It is when this quest is compromised, paused or shattered that vulnerability is most evident.

About the Authors
Diane Hughes is an Associate Professor in Vocal Studies and Music at Macquarie University. Vocal health and wellbeing are a focus of her work; her research interests include singing contexts such as industries and recording, vocal artistry, emotion in song, the singer-songwriter and vocal pedagogy. She co-authored *The New Music Industries: Disruption and Discovery* (2016) with Evans, Morrow and Keith, published by Palgrave Macmillan. She is an advocate for music education and for multidisciplinary voice studies more broadly.

Professor Mark Evans is Head of the School of Communication at the University of Technology Sydney. He is Series Editor for the Genre, Music and Sound book series published by Equinox Publishing. Recent books include *Sounding Funny: Comedy, Cinema and Music* (with Phillip Hayward), *Moves, Movies and Music: The Sound of Dance Films* (with Mary Fogarty), and *The New Music Industries: Disruption and Discovery* (co-authored with Hughes, Morrow and Keith), published by Palgrave Macmillan.

Notes

1. Prior to its # inclusion, MeToo began in 2006 as the "me too" movement. Its founder, Tarana Burke, discussed that the motivation behind the movement was to support survivors of sexual abuse. See https://metoomvmt.org/about/#history (accessed September 3, 2019). The subsequent development of #MeToo followed film mogul, Harvey Weinstein, being accused of sexual misconduct in 2017. See https://www.9news.com.au/world/harvey-weinstein-suspended-from-own-company-amid-sexual-harassment-claims/ee82a798-e115-43c7-ab8a-f2462240893b (accessed September 13, 2019).
2. The key topics are discussed in an article by Monica Anderson and Skye Toor (2018), "How Social Media Users Have Discussed Sexual Harassment since #MeToo Went Viral", Pew Research Center, at https://www.pewresearch.org/fact-tank/2018/10/11/how-social-media-users-have-discussed-sexual-harassment-since-metoo-went-viral/ (accessed November 14, 2019).
3. A 2018 article published in the *New York Times*, "#MeToo Brought Down 201 Powerful Men. Nearly Half of Their Replacements Are Women" by Audrey Carlsen, Maya Salam, Claire Cain Miller, Denise Lu, Ash Ngu, Jugal K. Patel and Zach Wichter, states that since #MeToo at least "200 Prominent Men have Lost their Jobs after Public Allegations of Sexual Harassment". The article is available at https://www.nytimes.com/interactive/2018/10/23/us/metoo-replacements.html (accessed November 18, 2019).
4. We also acknowledge that such issues may also pertain to the treatment of male sector workers. However, in contrast to the numbers of males that have lost positions as noted above, only three females were noted as also losing their jobs in the report by Audrey Carlsen, Maya Salam, Claire Cain Miller, Denise Lu, Ash Ngu, Jugal K. Patel and Zach Wichter at https://www.nytimes.com/interactive/2018/10/23/us/metoo-replacements.html (accessed November 18, 2019).
5. This panel – *Sexual Misconduct in the Music Industry* (SXSW, 2018a) – comprised Beth Martinez (Danger Village PR) (Panel Moderator), and Andrea Domanick (West Coast Editor, Noisey), Peggy Hogan (Art Not Love Records) and Caitlin White (Editorial Director of Music, Uproxx). A recording of the panel discussion was reviewed at https://schedule.sxsw.com/2018/events/PP70021 (accessed August 31, 2018).
6. The second industry panel – *#TimesUp: Turning the Hashtag into Action in a Structureless Music Industry* (SXSW, 2018b) – comprised Jenna Gauio (Vydia VP Product Management and Marketing) (Panel Moderator), and Emma White (Artist), Mary Lambert (Artist) and Emily Hackett (Artist). A YouTube recording of the panel discussion was reviewed at https://www.youtube.com/watch?v=vJgTGqzEdTs (accessed September 3, 2018).
7. This is reported in an interview with one of the 'Time's Up' writers, Kalie Shorr, with Lauren Tingle, "Kalie Shorr Talks 'Time's Up' by Song Suffragettes: Twenty-three Rising Artists Featured on Empowerment Anthem", http://www.cmt.com/news/1790413/kalie-shorr-talks-times-up-by-song-suffragettes/ (accessed September 3, 2018).
8. 'Time's Up' was recorded by the Song Suffragettes and can be accessed at *Song Suffragettes – Time's Up*, published January 18, 2018, https://www.youtube.com/watch?v=shv3V37wNXE (accessed September 3, 2018). The "Time's Up" movement was established in 2017 to advocate for women's rights. See https://timesupnow.org/about/our-staff/ (accessed May 31, 2020).
9. This is from an interview with one of the 'Time's Up' writers, Kalie Shorr, with Lauren Tingle, "Kalie Shorr Talks 'Time's Up' by Song Suffragettes: Twenty-three Rising Artists Featured on Empowerment Anthem", http://www.cmt.com/news/1790413/kalie-shorr-talks-times-up-by-song-suffragettes/ (accessed September 3, 2018).

10. This is reported by Zanda Wilson (2018) in "Isabella Manfredi of The Preatures Talks #MeToo and Sexual Misconduct in the Music Industry on QandA", *The Music Network*, https://themusicnetwork.com/isabella-mandredi-of-the-preatures-discussed-sexual-misconduct-in-the-music-industry-on-qanda/ (accessed August 15, 2018).
11. Vicki Gordon (a leading Australian industry figure) was quoted in an article by Katie Booth (2017), "Women 'Chronically Disadvantaged' in the Australian Music Industry: Fixing Gender-based Inequality in the Music Industry", *The University of Sydney News*, https://sydney.edu.au/news-opinion/news/2017/07/31/women-chronically-disadvantaged-in-the-australian-music-industry.html (accessed February 15, 2018).
12. This is reported in an article by Andrea Domanick (2018), "The Dollars and Desperation Silencing #MeToo in Music", https://noisey.vice.com/en_us/article/9kzex7/inside-music-industry-sexual-misconduct-harassment-problem-and-metoo (accessed September 3, 2018).
13. This is quoted in a *New Statesman* article by Kate Mossman (2018), "Lily Allen: Why #MeToo Hasn't Hit the Music Industry", https://www.newstatesman.com/2018/05/lily-allen-why-metoo-hasnt-hit-music-industry (accessed September 3, 2018).
14. The study was funded by and conducted in collaboration with Entertainment Assist.
15. This study was commissioned by an independent music charity Help Musicians UK.
16. This is quoted in the article by Kate Mossman (2018), "Lily Allen: Why #MeToo Hasn't Hit the Music Industry", https://www.newstatesman.com/2018/05/lily-allen-why-metoo-hasnt-hit-music-industry (accessed September 3, 2018).
17. This information is reported in a *Billboard* article by Danielle Bacher (2016), "The Saga of Kesha, Dr. Luke and a Mother's Fight: 'He Almost Destroyed Us' (Exclusive)", https://www.billboard.com/articles/news/magazine-feature/6980931/kesha-dr-luke-battle-inside-story-mom-pebe-sebert-interview-exclusive (accessed September 4, 2018).
18. Rick Altman is an Emeritus Professor and is distinguished from *Nashville*'s director, Robert Altman, in this discussion by the use of his Christian name. See Rick Altman, https://clas.uiowa.edu/cinematic-arts/people/rick-altman.
19. This was a politically heightened time which included the Watergate scandal, America's involvement in the Vietnam War and the impeachment of President Nixon.
20. Often underpinning the film's comedic elements are image and hype examples including the merchandising by former Pop! bandmate Colin Thompson (Scott Porter) and his "Whiff of Colin" cologne and Cora's car number plate of "CORA 1".
21. Prince-Bythewood talked about her motivation for writing the film in an interview published by ScreenSlam (2014a), "Beyond the Lights: Director Gina Prince-Bythewood Official Movie Interview", published November 14, 2014, https://www.youtube.com/watch?v=YafQ1wzltxE (accessed January 16, 2018). In this interview Prince-Bythewood discussed her love of hip-hop/R&B but also of her concern over the expectation of hypersexualized female artists.
22. This is reported by Ashley Velez (2014) in "5 Cool Facts You Didn't Know about 'Beyond the Lights'", USC Annenberg School for Communication and Journalism, http://www.neontommy.com/news/2014/11/5-cool-facts-you-didn-t-know-about-beyond-lights.html (accessed May 31, 2020).
23. This quotation is from an interview published by ScreenSlam (2014a) when Prince-Bythewood discusses her writing processes, "Beyond the Lights: Director Gina Prince-Bythewood Official Movie Interview", published November 14, 2014, https://www.youtube.com/watch?v=YafQ1wzltxE (accessed January 16, 2018).

24. This quotation is featured in an interview with Prince-Bythewood and host Rian Johnson (2015), "Beyond the Lights Q&A with Gina Prince-Bythewood | BFI", published on November 18, 2015, https://www.youtube.com/watch?v=sj5UIHVBYa4 (accessed January 19, 2018).
25. Noni's character is biracial; her mother is white. The use of 'Blackbird' is therefore multilayered; it signifies oppression and aligns with Noni's ongoing struggles.
26. *Beyond The Lights - Official Trailer*, published by Beyond the Lights on August 8, 2014, https://www.youtube.com/watch?v=1rvgJ2WbDsc (accessed January 19, 2018).
27. This is discussed in an interview published by ScreenSlam (2014b), "Beyond the Lights: Gugu Mbatha-Raw 'Noni' Official Movie Interview", published November 14, 2014, https://www.youtube.com/watch?v=LDP8Y_TvCFo (accessed January 16, 2018).
28. The quotation occurs in a ScreenSlam (2014a) interview where Prince-Bythewood discusses her preparation of Mbatha-Raw for the role of Noni, "Beyond the Lights: Director Gina Prince-Bythewood Official Movie Interview", published November 14, 2014, https://www.youtube.com/watch?v=YafQ1wzltxE (accessed January 16, 2018).
29. Here, Mbatha-Raw discusses her preparation for playing Noni. It is quoted from an interview published by ScreenSlam (2014b), "Beyond the Lights: Gugu Mbatha-Raw 'Noni' Official Movie Interview", published on November 14, 2014, https://www.youtube.com/watch?v=LDP8Y_TvCFo (accessed January 16, 2018).
30. The call and response tradition emanates from African and African-American vocal traditions including work songs and field hollers, and subsequently was heard in blues and gospel musics. See "Blues" by Elijah Wald (2012) in *Grove Music Online*, https://www-oxfordmusiconline-com.simsrad.net.ocs.mq.edu.au/grovemusic/view/10.1093/gmo/9781561592630.001.0001/omo-9781561592630-e-1002223858?rskey=3eoYee&result=2 (accessed June 9, 2020).

References

Altman, R. (1991) "24-Track Narrative? Robert Altman's *Nashville*". *Cinémas* 1/3: 102–125.

Baskin, R. and H. Gibson (1975) '200 Years'. *Nashville Soundtrack*. USA: Lions Gate Music Co. (ASCAP), Landscape Music Co. (BMI), Silvery Moon Music (ASCAP), Plumbago Publishing Co. (BMI).

Cardullo, R. J. (1976) "The Space in the Distance: A Study of Altman's 'Nashville'". *Literature/Film Quarterly* 4/4: 313–24.

Cooper, R., A. Coles and S. Hanna-Osbourne (2017) *Skipping a Beat: Assessing the State of Gender Equality in the Australian Music Industry*. The University of Sydney, Business School, https://www.agec.org.au/wp-content/uploads/2018/09/Skipping-a-Beat-Assuring-the-Value-of-Gender-Equality-in-the-Australin-Music-Industry-2017.pdf (accessed December 18, 2018).

DATA USA (2016) *Sound Recording Industries: Diversity*, https://datausa.io/profile/naics/5122/#gender (accessed September 4, 2018).

Diffrient, D. S. (2017) "Backup Singers, Celebrity Culture, and Civil Rights: Racializing Space and Spatializing Race in *20 Feet from Stardom*". *Black Cinema: The New Series* 8/2: 25–49.

Golden, A. (2001) "Ethics in the Music Business and its Impact on Popular Music, Society and Culture". *Working Paper Series 5/2001*. Victoria University of Technology, Victoria School of Management, http://vuir.vu.edu.au/188/1/wp5_2001_golden.pdf (accessed August 14, 2018).

Gordon, E. E. (1999) "All about Audiation and Musical Aptitudes: Edwin E. Gordon Discusses Using Audiation and Music Aptitudes as Teaching Tools to Allow Students to Reach their Full Music Potential". *Music Educators Journal* 86/2: 41–44.

Gray, D. E. (2009) "Dispatches from the Frontline: The 1981 Brixton Riots and the Restructuring of Black British Identity". Master of Arts Thesis, University of Maryland, Baltimore.

Gross, S. A. and G. Musgrave (2016) *Can Music Make You Sick? Music and Depression: A Study into the Incidence of Musicians' Mental Health*. London: MusicTank Publishing, University of Westminster. https://www.helpmusicians.org.uk/assets/publications/files/can_music_make_you_sick_part_1-_pilot_survey_report_2019.pdf (accessed May 31, 2020).

Hughes, D. (2015) "Technological Pitch Correction: Controversy, Contexts, and Considerations". *Journal of Singing* 71/5: 587–94.

Hughes, D., M. Evans, G. Morrow and S. Keith (2016) *The New Music Industries: Disruption and Discovery*. London: Palgrave Macmillan.

Kloman, H. and L. Michaels (1983) "'A Foolish Optimist': Interview with Robert Altman" [Introduction by V. W. Wexman]. *Film Criticism* 7/3: 20–28.

Neville, M. (2013) *20 Feet from Stardom* [DVD]. Transmission Films. A Gil Frieson and Tremelo Production.

Nixon, R. (1974) "Remarks at the Grand Old Opry House, Nashville, Tennessee, March 16, 1974". In *The Public Papers of the Presidents of the United States: Richard Nixon* [January 1 to August 9, 1974], 279–82. Washington, DC: United States Government Printing Office. https://www.govinfo.gov/app/collection/ppp/president-37_Nixon,%20Richard%20M./1974/01%21A%21January%201%20to%20August%209%2C%201974 (accessed September 13, 2019).

Rush, J. (1990) "Who's in on the Joke: Parody as Hybridized Narrative Discourse". *Quarterly Review of Film and Video* 12/1-2: 5–12.

UK Music (2017) *UK Music Diversity Survey Results: UK Music Diversity Taskforce – Workforce Diversity Survey Results 2016*. https://www.ukmusic.org/news/uk-music-diversity-taskforce-workforce-diversity-survey-results-2016 (accessed May 31, 2020).

van den Eynde, J., A. Fisher and C. Sonn (2016) *Working in the Australian Entertainment Industry: Final Report*. Melbourne, Victoria: Victoria University. https://static1.squarespace.com/static/584a0c86cd0f68ddbfffdcea/t/587ed93e3e00be6f0d145fe0/1486006488652/Working%B1in%B1the%B1Australian%B1Entertainment%B1Industry_Final%B1Report_Oct16.pdf (accessed May 31, 2020).

8 Trailer Trash or Inspired Vocalization?

Song as Promotion and Aesthetic Object in Cinematic Previews

James Deaville and Agnes Malkinson

Introduction

Since its first appearance in 1912 (Kernan, 2004: 27), the film trailer has developed into one of the most popular and durable cinematic paratexts. Marc Weinstock, president of worldwide marketing for Sony Pictures, cites the results of exit surveys when he notes that "trailers are the most influential driver of audience interest – generating 50 percent, compared with 30 percent for TV spots".[1] On YouTube, surfers looked at and listened to 1 billion trailers during the first three quarters of 2013.[2] For *The Avengers*' first trailer, released in early March 2012, a record 13.7 million people accessed the trailer in 24 hours on iTunes.[3] And Hollywood studios spend about $3.5 billion annually on advertising, most of which is invested in trailers.[4] For such a ubiquitous and popular cultural object, the dearth of academic research into its production, construction and reception is remarkable – this chapter endeavours to fill that gap through presenting one aspect of its audiovisual appeal to audiences, both in general terms and in case studies.

Song in trailers occupies an interesting position as it at once conveys aesthetic substance and purveys a commercial product. While music in trailers can at times replicate cinematic functions, the constraints and objectives of the trailer mean that music functions differently in this context (Deaville and Malkinson, 2014). The intimate link to an explicitly profit-driven industry often obscures the aesthetic value of heavily commodified art forms, like trailers. Art objects that are overtly commercial carry the stigma that they forego artistic integrity in order to maximize revenues. Arguably, the element most capable of engaging audiences, affecting meaning and creating allure, crucial to the commercial and aesthetic success of trailers, is music, and one of its manifestations, the sung song.

Trailers

Lisa Kernan defines the film trailer as "a brief film text that usually displays images from a specific feature film while asserting its excellence, created for the purpose of projecting in theatres to promote a film's theatrical release" (Kernan, 2004: 1). Although a standard description in the secondary literature (Veits, 2014: 17–18; Ortega, 2007: 131), Kernan's omits the aspect that some scholars regard as the most decisive for trailer narrative: its sonic dimension.[5] Moreover, here she privileges the trailer's promotional function over the aesthetic considerations behind this "brief film text", a position likewise reflected in the growing academic literature about paratexts. To be fair to Kernan, she does elsewhere argue that "trailers are a form of advertising and a unique form of narrative film exhibition, wherein promotional discourse as well as narrative pleasure are conjoined" (Kernan, 2004: 1). However, she does not develop the argument about narrative pleasure, while the work of Keith M. Johnston explores it in detail, establishing analytical parameters for approaching trailers as aesthetic objects:

> As an innovative short film format, trailers are complex layered texts that can be analyzed in themselves, for what they say, for how they communicate and position studio-, star-, technology-, and genre-specific messages. They are more than windows into film reception or to the wider world of feature publicity materials (Johnston, 2009: 9).

As a result of these considerations, we will define the cinematic trailer as a short film of aesthetic value and promotional function that presents a narrative constructed from moving images, graphics, dialogue, sounds and music, in association with an upcoming film. We argue that trailers possess artistic value in and of themselves, conveying aesthetic substance while purveying a commercial product in a binary ontology. One must approach them from both perspectives in order to come to a fair appraisal of their qualities and functions.

Trailers, whether for films or other cultural artefacts, fall into the category of texts that Gérard Genette identified in 1987 as paratexts (Genette, 1997), and which Thomas Doherty has called "the satellite debris orbiting and radiating out from the core text".[6] Genette was working with literary paratexts, but the following description can also apply to cinematic previews: "the paratext is neither on the interior nor on the exterior: It is both; it is on the threshold; and it is on this very site that we must study it" (Genette, quoted in Macksey, 1997: xvii). Whether the dust jackets and cover illustrations of books or the trailers and posters for films, the paratext occupies a vital "in-between" position within the realm of textuality, making present a corresponding and antecedent text (Genette, 1997: 77). Genette demarcates two types of paratexts: the epitext that is external to the text and the peritext that is internal to it – trailers are epitextual to a film, while title sequences bear a peritextual function. Fred Greene, writing in *Movie Trailers 101*, may feel that "the title sequence, despite its proximity to the feature, has greater formal variation and experimental possibility [than] the trailer, [which] given its function, is more constrained",[7] yet the epitext of the trailer is an "entranceway paratext" (Gray, 2010: 35), the public's first point of contact with a film. Trailers also have the potential for greater narrative freedom since they occupy a time and space other than those of the film text itself. Nevertheless, both categories of paratexts confirm Gray's speculation that "much of the textuality that exists in the world is paratext-driven" (Gray, 2010: 46). And in the world of the trailer, it is not necessary to consume the text in order to experience aesthetic pleasure in the paratext.

Still, trailer studios would be remiss if their products did not entice the audience to attend a cinematic showing, in other words, did not translate into box-office receipts. Considering the film industry's huge investment in advertising, expectations for the promotional success of these "mini-movies" runs high, which is one reason why film studios spend so much on individual previews and provide film footage to multiple trailer firms,[8] ultimately picking the one the studio considers to be most effective or combining the multiple submissions into one "Frankenstein trailer" (Marich, 2013: 31). Researchers from diverse fields of study, including marketing and psychology, have attempted to determine which aspect(s) of a trailer are most compelling. Already in 1985, well before film scholars discovered trailers and other film paratexts as suitable topics for investigation, a team of academics conducted an experiment on theatre-goers, which demonstrated how film previews influenced the strength of audience expectations in the realms of suspense, suffering, violence and romance (Eastman et al., 1985). Since then social scientists have explored the diverse appeals exploited by trailer-makers to generate adequate audience interest in coming attractions to ensure eventual attendance (Finsterwalder et al., 2012). The focus of these studies has remained grounded in the trailer's visual narrative, however, to the exclusion of the dimensions of sound and music.

One empirical investigation that does significantly invoke music's role was undertaken by a team of marketing researchers and published in 2012[9] (Finsterwalder et al., 2012). Surveying a group of twelve commerce students, they discovered that "all but one of the participants indicate that music plays a pivotal role in creating the overall mood and tone of the trailer, thus drawing the viewer into the storyline of the trailer without being consciously aware of it" (Finsterwalder et al., 2012: 592). They also found that "music engenders a strong emotional response when it corresponds with the visual elements of the trailer",[10] and "incorporating elements of the music from a prominent composer/singer into the trailer may influence expectations and entice more consumers to go and watch the film" (Finsterwalder et al., 2012: 593).

Trailer director Mark Woollen succinctly summarizes these observations when he notes that "trailers are all about rhythm, pacing, and feeling... Sometimes 70,

80 percent of the job [making trailers] can be trying to find that perfect piece [of music]".[11] Trailer editor Mike Flanagan similarly establishes that music is essential for setting "the tone of a trailer", to the extent that he begins work on it by finding "a piece of music that fits [his] 'story'".[12] He also argues that well-chosen trailer music can cover up or smooth over flaws and furnish the audience with valuable information about a film.

Voice

According to Graham F. Welch,

> here are two constellations of [vocal production] that have the greatest socio-cultural significance, categorized as speech and singing. However, there is potential (and actual) overlap between the two, because both sets of behaviours are generated from the same anatomical and physiological structures and... are shaped by cultural experience (Welch, 2005: 239).

Youngmoo E. Kim and Brian Whitman suggest that "our auditory physiology and perceptual apparatus has [sic] evolved to a high level of sensitivity to the human voice... No other instrument exhibits the [comparable] amount of physical variation" (Kim and Whitman, 2002: 17). For instance, Yipeng Li and DeLiang Wang found in their study that individuals have the ability to easily identify the voice of another human amongst musical accompaniment and interfering sounds in monaural recordings (Li and Wang, 2007). Even upon a single hearing and with little training, humans have the capacity to recognize the singing voice of a particular individual in disparate musical contexts (Kim and Whitman, 2002: 17). This heightened sensitivity to vocal production is of course useful for marketing strategists – the voice represents an auditory medium that is at once acknowledged by an audience and has the capacity to convey semantic, affectual and associative meaning.

The human voice is a central feature in many marketing campaigns. The primary message is presented through vocalizations, like descriptive speech, dramatization and singing, and it often employs a combination of these approaches. Thus some brands exploit the voice in sonic logos, like the iconic commercial company signoff "By Mennen", which cleverly corresponds musical rhythm and pitch to the phrase's natural speech stresses and intonation. For the purpose of branding, the sung jingle – a practice carried into the present from the early days of sound advertising – has proven itself as an effective marketing device, acting as a brand's "musical catchphrase", like in McDonalds' 'I'm lovin' it' campaign launched in 2003. The voice is also used to convey a brand's slogan, like L'Oréal's "Because You're Worth it". Popular songs that feature sung lyrics or melody are also often featured in various audiovisual marketing materials, these texts typically serving a cross-promotional purpose, i.e., when two or more products are marketed simultaneously to the profit of both (Shada, 2008; Belch and Belch, 2014; Picard, 2014). In the marketing of film, some form of vocalization is usually present, and if absent, is so to create a particular effect.

These practices draw upon empirically established research: many studies have shown that the parameters of the voice influence the reception of an advertisement's message and impression of the brand (Gélinas-Chebat et al., 1996; Chattopadhyay et al., 2003; Oakes and North, 2011). For instance, the rate of speech, the amount of words spoken within a specific timeframe, can have an effect on the auditor's perception of the speaker and message. According to David B. Buller and R. Kelly Aune, an increased speech rate is more effective in the persuasion of a listening audience (Buller and Aune, 1992). Voice pitch is also linked to hormone production cycles in women, and it has been demonstrated that higher female voices communicate sexual appeal, whereas lower pitched male voices give the impression that the speaker wields power and authority (Pipitone and Gallup Jr, 2008; Borkowska and Pawlowski, 2011). Emotional expression carried through the voice has also been widely explored – most notably by Theo Van Leeuwen in his study of pitch contour and variation (Leeuwen, 1999) – emphasizing the musicality of the spoken voice (Titze, 1994; Scherer, 1995). These findings on the manipulation of vocal attributes collectively serve to highlight that much more information is communicated to an audience than merely the linguistic content of a message.

In conversation, voice actors speak freely about the approach that is taken to vocal performances for film trailers. In an interview from 2013, Hal Douglas, an iconic commercial voice artist featured in such trailers as *Con Air* (1997), *Men in Black* (1997), *What Women Want* (2000) and *Cloudy with a Chance of Meatballs* (2009) describes how he manipulates his voice for certain effects:

> the sound that I often use is a difficult range to hear because it blends in with the band. If I'm reading copy, it's a problem, usually I will automatically raise my pitch, bring it up into my mouth more and out of my throat... I don't like the sound of it, but it cuts through the mix... [lowers voice] if I speak down here, then you lose some of the flavour of the words, they don't have the clarity. If you want clarity, you can start biting, get mean with it.[13]

Michel Chion distinguishes between uses of the spoken voice in cinema, identified as "theatrical", "textual" and "emanation" speech. Theatrical speech is perceived as being spoken by the onscreen characters – it serves a "dramatic, psychological, informative, and affective function" (Chion, 1994: 171). As the most common use of the human voice in cinema, theatrical speech often is the centre of the action, but holds no power over the film world, unlike textual speech. Textual speech "acts upon the images... an archaic power: the pure and original pleasure of transforming the world through language" (Chion, 1994: 173), and most commonly occurs in the form of narration or voice-over. Both theatrical and textual speech relies on the clarity of the spoken word, and in addition to their relative functions in cinema, on semantic understanding of language. Emanation speech refers to character vocalizations that are not fully understood by the audience through distortion or decentring in relation to a film's other elements.[14] This use of voice in cinema shifts the focus from the meaning of spoken content to the acoustic properties of the voice (Chion, 1994: 172–83).

In his discussion on the role of popular music in creating emotion in film, Murray Smith draws on Chion's vocal distinctions and extends "theatrical" and "emanation" speech to the singing voice in popular music.[15] Smith asserts that lyrics often have theatrical significance in popular songs, depending on genre. In other contexts, especially when the singing voice is displaced or not clear, "the vocals register a human presence and expressivity, but not through language as such" (Smith, 2006). He also argues that in some cases popular song lyrics will have the effect of "narrativizing" the onscreen images, providing the possibility for an enriched or alternative reading.

In his book *The Sounds of Commerce: Marketing Popular Film Music*, Jeff Smith identifies the popular song in cinema as not only serving a promotional function, but also "a way of establishing mood and setting, and… a commentary on the film's characters and action" (Smith, 1998: 155). In film trailers, promotional elements are integrated with narrative form, a derivation of cinematic conventions, and the result is that which likewise capitalizes on the singing voice in popular song. For instance, the trailer for the 2013 film *The Campaign* features the song 'Taking Care of Business' by Bachman-Turner Overdrive (BTO; Randy Bachman, 1973), but for much of its duration the music is obscured by dialogue (emanation). When foregrounded, the lyrics reinforce the narrative, as the first 35 seconds present a montage of a politician working hard on the campaign trail (theatrical).

In *Audio-Vision*, Chion describes what he labels "materializing sound indices", or "MSIs".[16] The term "refers to any aspect of a sound which reflects with more or less precision the material nature of its source and the concrete history of its production" (Chion, 1994: 114). A sound can contain none or an infinite number of MSIs, depending on the nature of its production or manipulation. They provide the listener with information about the source of the sound, the substance, the manner in which it was produced, and the environment in which it occurred. A lack of MSIs provides very little information, leading to an impression of the ethereal or symbolic. The unevenness of a sound as it progresses, as well as "accidents" made during its production, contribute to the perception of materiality. Even the out-of-tuneness of a voice within an ensemble will draw the curiosity of the ear and foreground its production (for an example, see the discussion of *The Hangover* below). Chion continues:

> In many musical traditions perfection is defined by an absence of MSIs. The musician's or singer's goal is to purify the voice or instrument sound of all noises of breathing, scratching, or any other adventitious friction or vibration linked to producing the musical tone. Other musical cultures strive for the opposite: the "perfect" instrumental or vocal performance enriches the sound with supplementary noises, which bring out rather than dissimulate the material origin of the sound (Chion, 1994: 114–15).

In summation, the materiality of the singing voice contributes to the communication of genre for marketing purposes, with the capacity to elicit aural curiosity and draw the ear, while adding diversity to the soundtrack of a trailer text.

Trailer Song and Promotion

Promotion

The trailer involves a complex integration of promotional rhetoric and creative practice which has resulted in an audiovisual medium that has continuously developed in a tradition that spans over a century. Promotional strategies are implemented through a constellation of appeal practices that are creatively and carefully realized in a wide range of audiovisual elements.

Campaigns of the 1950s and 60s brought increasing diversity in the way song was used in film promotion. Largely out of fashion since the rise of high-concept cinema in the mid-1970s, title songs were at the height of popularity during this time period and the industry was able to exploit them to maximize its profitability. Major songs of this period from films like *Breakfast at Tiffany's* (Blake Edwards, 1961), *What's New Pussycat?* (Clive Donner, 1965) and *The Graduate* (Mike Nichols, 1967) were recorded many times by different singing groups and artists in order both to promote the film through the dissemination of the song(s) and to maximize licensing profits. 'Moon River' (Henry Mancini and Johnny Mercer, 1960) was released in 27 different versions within a year of its production (Smith, 1998: 61), which resulted in significant licensing profits. According to Smith, a successful timeline for song release in relation to film premiere was established: songs were to be disseminated four to six weeks before the film release in order to maximize profits (Smith, 1998: 63). Record executives, producers and composers collaborated on a film's score to determine its commerciability (Smith, 1998: 62–63), such considerations inevitably impacting music for trailers.

This is evidenced in the trailer for *The Graduate*, which features Simon and Garfunkel songs 'The Sound of Silence' (Paul Simon, 1964), 'Scarborough Fair' and the commissioned 'Mrs. Robinson' (Paul Simon, 1967).[17] Though only partially complete by the final cut of the film, 'Mrs. Robinson' earned widespread commercial success. More recently, the trailer entitled 'Dream' for the film *Maleficent* (Robert Stromberg, 2014), a variant of the original Disney film *Sleeping Beauty* from 1959, features the song 'Once Upon a Dream' (Pyotor Ilyich Tchaikovsky adapted by George Bruns; Jack Lawrence and Sammy Fain, 1959) that was first released in the original film. The cover is performed by Lana Del Rey and reached moderate peak positions on pop single charts in the U.S.[18] Critics commented on the "haunting performance",[19] and the radio effect of Del Rey's vocals lent to the singer's "moody and low key" image.[20] Not only an object of intertextual interest, Disney's release of Del Rey's version represents a continuation of the company's practice of contracting well-known or rising vocal artists to perform songs featured in their films, including 'Colors of the Wind' (Alan Menken and Stephen Schwartz, 1995) sung by Vanessa Williams for *Pocahontas* (Mike Gabriel and Eric Goldberg, 1995) and 'Reflection' (Matthew Wilder and David Zippel, 1998) performed by Christina Aguilera for *Mulan* (Barry Cook and Tony Bancroft, 1998).

Aesthetics
Richard Dyer's study *In the Space of a Song: The Uses of Song in Film* adopts the perspective that songs take up space and time in film (Dyer, 2012). He elaborates on this by remarking how "music itself is a spatial as well as a temporal art, perceptually and also literally" (Dyer, 2012: 25), and applies that observation to cinematic song on the one hand through the identification of convergent or divergent screen time and music/song time (for example, film song can make diegetic time seem to stand still). On the other hand, "song is physically produced somewhere" and it takes up space (Dyer, 2012: 25–26). These temporal and spatial parameters necessitate a cinematic diegesis in order for their full effect to be realized, for in the "trailer-verse" everything is compressed, including our sense of time: there cinematic hours are measured by minutes, and minutes by seconds. This altered temporality with its narrative condensation means that trailer song must occupy a different aesthetic position than its counterpart in feature film (including the musical). And song in trailers also arguably inhabits a more constricted space than that afforded by cinematic fulsomeness.

Such use of the human voice in cinematic previews of course serves a promotional end (see below), but as a site of narrative pleasure, trailer song:

1. exploits and manipulates (in the case of parody) audience familiarity with the music from other contexts;
2. appeals to a more specific audience through its genre-based status in relation to the diegesis;
3. narrativizes (and thus helps to explain and contextualize) onscreen images; and
4. adds another layer of vocal narration – whether theatrical or emanational – to the trailer text.

Functionality of Trailer Song

The singing voice in trailers performs different functions depending on its relationship to the diegesis. While it can replicate cinematic functions, serving non-diegetically as an element of the soundtrack, diegetically as a performance, or infra-diegetically as supernatural presence, trailer song nevertheless differs from that in film by at once conveying aesthetic substance and purveying a commercial product.

Diegetic singing performances in trailers are found most commonly in the trailers for the comedy genre, often foregrounding a comedic act (Deaville and Malkinson, 2014). In these contexts the voice is presented as "raw", giving the impression that little to no post-production has been applied to mitigate perceived imperfections in the recorded voice, such as poor intonation, off-rhythm, and cracks or breaks in the delivery. According to Chion, as discussed above, these qualities lend a materiality to the voice and foreground vocal production.

For example, in the official trailer for *The Hangover* (2009), Mike Tyson sings along to Phil Collins' 'In the Air Tonight' (1980) out of time and off-pitch,[21] rendering his performance comical as it is juxtaposed with the mixed and mastered studio version underneath his voice. This approach to the diegetic singing voice in comedy trailers lends an immediacy or improvisatory quality to the voice, assuming fidelity to live performance, but is in fact often just as manipulated. In the first official trailer to *The Dictator* (Larry Charles, 2012), Sacha Baron Cohen's character is introduced with four seconds of diegetic singing. The vocal performance adopts phonemes that are similar to the Arabic language, but in this combination they are nothing but nonsensical utterances, as pointed out by the character himself.

Both of these examples displace language and bring the materiality of the voice to the forefront of the listener's ear, operating more as emanation rather than semantic singing. This treatment of diegetic singing in trailers positions the advertised film firmly in the comedy genre, whereby it captures the attention of audiences that have a preference for that particular genre.

The dominant source of non-diegetic singing in the trailer is the popular song that forms the underscore, while occasionally emerging to the foreground in transitional passages or to emphasize action. This singing also serves a structuring function, unlike diegetic and infra-diegetic singing that instead lend affect or colour to the trailer. Lyrics in non-diegetic singing can support, ironicize, or be displaced by the dialogue and the trailer's narrative. In comedy, divergent popular-song style types from differing time periods provide a foundation for a broad field of audience identifications. In contrast, other or hybrid genres use a single popular song throughout, which transitions between the background and foreground, the vocals driving the foregrounded sections.

The term "infra-diegetic" refers to the space a sound occupies between the diegetic and non-diegetic realms in film. Whether the source of the sound or voice emanates from inside or outside of the filmic world is not clear to the audience. Music is often deployed infra-diegetically in horror and science fiction cinema to convey a sense of confusion, distress or disorientation as the audience strains to place the cause of the sound, usually in contexts where supernatural or unearthly presence or altered mental states are invoked.[22] This treatment of sound is common in horror genre trailers, and is especially notable in its application to the singing voice.

For example, in the trailer for the 2010 remake of *Nightmare on Elm Street* (Samuel Bayer, 2010), children sing the infamous minor-third warning tune for Freddy Krueger ("one two he's coming for you, three four better lock your door, five six grab your crucifix…"). Playing children are visualized onscreen prior to the singing; though they have no connection to the trailer narrative, their presence functions as "narrative lure". According to Matt Hills, "the acousmêtre plays a significant role in promotional paratexts; official trailers repeatedly feature monstrous sounds without televisually revealing the fantastic" (Hills, 2011: 28).

Uses of Trailer Song

The most common occurrence of trailer song is the recognizable popular song presented in excerpt. Here genre determines the number of songs used, for in comedy the trailer could feature up to five distinct numbers, while horror normally presents none except in cases of diegetic or infra-diegetic vocalities that parody the mundane or acousmatize the supernatural. The particular mix of song excerpts reflects not only genre distinctions but also a temporal spread, often within one and the same trailer, in order to cast the widest promotional net possible. This practice is particularly evident in comedy – the trailer for *Ted* (Seth MacFarlane, 2012), for example, prominently features Harry Nilsson's theme song 'Best Friend' (1969) from the television comedy series *The Courtship of Eddie's Father* (1969–1972), alongside 'How You Like Me Now' by The Heavy (2009). The trailer's deployment of 'Best Friend' serves a dual function, appealing to audience members who might recall the show while exploiting its traditional media association with father-son bonding (here, representing John's attachment to Ted). Multiple song excerpts predominate in genres that do not rely heavily upon sound effects, in comparison with horror and action-adventure, each of which features a distinctive mix of sounds.

The most exceptional use of trailer song occurs when it extends over the entire preview text or a major portion thereof, either continuously or intermittently. Such strategic deployment elevates the song to a higher level of narrativity, both framing and interpreting the images while maintaining its own musical and semantic meanings. When used, the practice typically inhabits the action/science fiction genre, like in the trailer to the *Edge of Tomorrow* where an accompanied, vocoder-synthesized male voice intones the phrase 'This Is Not the End'

(Johnny McDaid, 2013) at strategic points throughout the narrative, framing and grounding dialogue and sound effects. Quite similar is the vocoder realization of Johann Johannsson's 'The Sun's Gone Dim' in the 2011 trailer to *Battle: Los Angeles* (Jonathan Liebesman, 2011), only it plays continuously as other sounds are progressively introduced to the mix. More limited use of the recurring or extended unifying song occurs in trailers to *The Dark Knight Rises* (Christopher Nolan, 2012) (a boy singing the U.S. national anthem) and *Where the Wild Things Are* (Spike Jonze, 2009) ('Wake Up' by Arcade Fire).

Although not technically song, wordless choral vocables (non-semantic vocalization) figure especially in action-film trailers on mythological or epic topics and in fantasy trailers. In derivation from Chion, Murray Smith identifies this non-linguistic emanational use of voice as registering "a human presence and expressivity", as indicated above. However, in many occurrences it specifically references a supernatural, inhuman presence, such as in trailers to fantasy films *Maleficent*, *Harry Potter and the Half Blood Prince* (David Yates, 2009) and *The Lord of the Rings: The Two Towers* (Peter Jackson, 2002).[23] A cliché both in film and trailer, such vocalizations can transport the audience into a timeless realm, beyond language. It also conveys a sense of awe and wonder and – as human expression – directly appeals to the senses.

Trailer song in a language unintelligible to the audience may likewise function non-semantically, but it represents a different set of meanings, recognized by Chion as a separate "technique of relativizing speech". Perhaps most notably, recent Western filmed portrayals of armed conflict in the Middle East have spawned trailers that exploit chanting in Arabic, in an orientalizing attempt to situate and authenticate the drama. These trailers include *Black Hawk Down*, *The Hurt Locker*, *Incendies* and *The Kingdom*, while the rhythmic chanting of prisoners in *The Dark Knight Rises* invokes a more primal association of "relativized speech" beyond language.

Case Studies

A closer study of trailers selected from the genres of comedy and action/science fiction reveals how the strategies, practices and devices described above function in specific paratexts. Song fulfils its purpose quite differently in the *Hangover* movies (Todd Phillips, 2009; 2011; 2013) and *The Edge of Tomorrow* (Doug Liman, 2014), on the one hand heightening comedic effect, on the other hauntingly providing structure and meaning for the narrative. And yet in both examples, the use of song self-reflexively draws our attention and foregrounds the human element in the respective story.

The Hangover (2009), The Hangover Part II (2011), The Hangover Part III (2013)
The Hangover franchise consists of three films that centre on the amnesiatic adventures of five friends. The trailers for these films exhibit similar treatment of music and sound: despite having been produced by different trailer companies, a clear attempt at sonic branding is employed to present a coherent narrative trajectory among them. Musically, the trailers each include songs by the rock band Wolfmother and feature at least one excerpt from a hip-hop song that involves both rapping and a lyrical chorus. These songs serve a cross-promotional function as they are often current releases by highly successful artists, including Rihanna, Jay-Z and Kanye West. Furthermore, the choruses are often foregrounded, drawing attention to the lyrical vocalization and "hook" of the song. Most notably, the use of the diegetic singing voice is featured in each campaign, both in full-length trailers and even in many of the significantly shorter and more compressed television spot advertisements.

Diegetic singing is a common feature among the marketing campaigns for each instalment in the trilogy. In the official trailer for the first film, *The Hangover*, Mike Tyson makes a cameo appearance singing 'In the Air Tonight' by Phil Collins (Stilwell, 2005), out of tune and out of time, lending a "raw" materiality to his performance. Clearly drawing on the notoriety of Tyson, the sonic spectacle of his singing is markedly humorous because of his degraded professional reputation, the well-known dated song and Tyson's amateurish screen performance.

In a striking use of the incongruity of sonic materiality with onscreen image, the first trailer for the final film of the trilogy opens with the beautiful acousmatized singing of Gounod's 'Ave Maria'. The voice is quickly de-acousmatized to reveal that the vocal artist is actually the erratic Alan character, who is central to the franchise narrative. The disjuncture of voice and body and unexpected revelation is a common trope in comedy film, and here firmly positions *The Hangover Part III* within the comedic tradition. This particular use of the singing voice also extends the threads of sonic branding that characterize the marketing of these films.

Edge of Tomorrow (2014)
The first trailer for *Edge of Tomorrow* (2'33") interweaves two narrative strands, warfare with aliens and a temporal loop. Aliens have defeated earth's forces; Major William Cage (played by Tom Cruise) finds himself caught in a time loop, wherein he is killed again and again, but each time around he learns ever more about combating the aliens even as he teams up with Special Forces warrior Rita Vrataski (Emily Blunt). Created by Wild Card Creative Advertising, the trailer presents the potential audience member with considerable action footage as supported by appropriate sound effects, as well as the star appeal of Cruise and Blunt (exploited in frequent close-ups), dialogue between the two actors and Cruise's opening narration. The fragmented narrative clearly establishes the war and the time loop,

but leaves open such questions as the ultimate means of resolution, the reason for the temporal disturbance and even the nature of the aliens.

The trailer's music does not specifically address those issues; however, it does work with the images to reinforce believability for both the time loop and the possibility of a favorable outcome, through the repeated lyrics "this is not the end". Not only the words, but the full texture of Johnny McDaid's song 'This Is Not the End' recurs throughout the preview, in keeping with the concept of the time loop. McDaid, a member of the band Snow Patrol who was commissioned to write the song for the film, recorded a six-minute version of the track under the project name Fieldwork, in a single released at the end of 2013.[24] Wild Card subsequently edited the track to serve the trailer, resulting in the soundscape of an accompanied, vocoder-synthesized male voice intoning the words at strategic points throughout the trailer narrative. Thereby the song frames and grounds the other aural elements of dialogue and sound effects, as well as the narrative of the moving images, affording it a crucial structuring role.

Needless to say, the song's hollow, futuristic timbre makes it appropriate for the genre of science-fiction and for this particular story, deployed both to support and to suggest an alternative to the unfolding visual and sonic narrative. Its calmness and initial lack of percussion – in contradistinction to typical soundtracks to action/adventure trailers – has led several YouTube commenters to identify the style as ambient, although others suggested influences from Daft Punk and Depeche Mode.[25] Above all, the commenting public tied *Edge of Tomorrow*'s music with its vocoder, slow tempo and melodic style to that for *Battle: Los Angeles*, 'The Sun's Gone Dim' by Johann Johannsson, as already suggested.

Taking a closer look at the use of 'This Is Not the End', we can observe how the six-minute track's musical sequence is roughly followed in the trailer. The opening is dominated by the ascending three-note theme and the vocal phrase that takes over in the middle, to end with the song's third motif before the final montage where McDaid's closing half-step idea dominates. There are moments when the music is supplanted by dialogue, sound effects or even silence, yet for each section the original track's music fits so well that the analyst wonders whether the trailer was cut to the edited song. The five-note 'This Is Not the End' recurs five times, perhaps not coincidentally three times linked to graphics: with the promotional title for the director and the individual titles for Cruise and Blunt. Of course, once the song's sonority is established, it becomes less necessary to restate the vocal line for the audience to experience both the "circularity" and the promise of McDaid's music. The words not only suggest the narrative of temporal repetition, but of an outcome that may be favourable.

In fact, the sonic realm becomes increasingly complex as the trailer progresses, with a military-style beat entering at midpoint, attempting to efface the muted optimism. All the while the sound effects fulfil a similar function –

they provide the realistic sounds of lost combat, and consistently rise in pitch and intensity whenever invoked. The song lyrics' final appearance occurs before the closing visual montage, which is accompanied by the half-step idea that enables the acceleration of images and concomitant increase of excitement. The trailer ends with a version of the opening three-note motif, bringing closure to the mini-epic, which demonstrates how musical means and promotional ends can be brought to work together through song, thereby creating an engaging audiovisual text.

Conclusion

Trailer song clearly functions differently from the uses of the singing voice in feature film, where a song will take up a comparatively small percentage of the running time. At once a marketing tool and audiovisual text for enjoyment, the film trailer exploits the sung song as a powerful means for the integration of promotional strategies with aesthetic experience. Instrumental music may continue to predominate in the underscores of cinematic previews, as a sonic marker of genre identity, a prime component of continuity and a key structuring device. However, the use of the human voice can contribute to the expression and diversity of the trailer soundscape, for example helping us to appreciate the caricature of Tyson in *The Hangover*, to enter into John's inner world in *Ted* and to believe in the time loop and the outcome of the feature-length *Edge of Tomorrow*. This balance of marketing strategy and artful production creates an aesthetic of allure that compels the listener-viewer and demonstrates how song contributes to the awakening of desire for and anticipation of the coming attraction.

About the Authors

Professor James Deaville is a musicologist specializing in music, composers and musical practices and institutions of the nineteenth and twentieth centuries, having published and spoken about such diverse topics as Franz Liszt, music criticism, television news music, African-American entertainers in turn-of-the-century Vienna and "fascist" Nordic composers during the Third Reich. He has published in the *Journal of the American Musicological Society*, *Journal of the Society for American Music*, *19th Century Music Review*, *Echo*, *Current Musicology*, *Hamburger Jahrbuch für Musikwissenschaft* and *Canadian University Music Review* (among others).

Agnes Malkinson is a PhD candidate in Communication and Media Studies at Carleton University, Canada. Her research area focuses on Canadian advertising history, advertising regulation, and audiovisual promotional media. She has previously worked and published in the areas of sound/music in film promotion and television advertising.

Notes

1. John Lopez, "Hollywood's Two Minute Auteurs", *Businessweek.com*, December 8, 2011, http://www.businessweek.com/magazine/hollywoods-twominute-auteurs-12082011.html (accessed April 15, 2017).
2. Scott Bowles, "After 100 Years, Movie Trailers Are Still Must-see Viewing", *USA Today*, January 6, 2014, http://www.usatoday.com/story/life/movies/2014/01/06/trailers-five-secrets/4034907 (accessed April 15, 2017).
3. Jordan Zakarin, "'The Avengers' New Trailer Claims Top iTunes Download Record", *The Hollywood Reporter*, March 2, 2012, http://www.hollywoodreporter.com/heat-vision/avengers-new-trailer-itunes-record-chris-evans-robert-downey-jr-296562 (accessed April 15, 2017).
4. Motion Picture Association of America (MPAA) statistics establish that in 2016, the industry earned $11.4 billion in box-office revenues in North America. http://www.mpaa.org/wp-content/uploads/2017/03/MPAA-Theatrical-Market-Statistics-2016_Final-1.pdf (accessed April 15, 2017).
5. See the introduction by Philip Powrie and Guido Heldt to a special issue of *Music, Sound, and the Moving Image* for a detailed discussion about the importance and function of music and sound in trailers (Powrie and Heldt, 2014).
6. Thomas Doherty, "The Paratext's the Thing", *The Chronicle Review of Higher Education*, January 6, 2014, http://chronicle.com/article/The-Paratexts-the-Thing/143761?cid=megamenu (accessed April 15, 2017).
7. Fred Greene, "The Title Sequence and the Trailer: Whether Peritext or Epitext, Almost Always More Interesting Than Their Feature!" *Movie Trailers 101*, April 5, 2012, http://www.movietrailers101.com/the-title-sequence-and-the-trailer-whether-peritext-or-epitext-almost-always-more-interesting-than-their-feature (accessed April 15, 2017).
8. A single trailer can cost anywhere from $30,000 to $100,000 (Lopez, 2011).
9. It is interesting to observe how the literature survey supports all of its claims with a bibliographic example other than that for music: "other film researchers focus on... the amount and appropriateness of music in the trailer" (Finsterwalder et al., 2012: 590).
10. Chion terms the salient moment in which the aural and visual meet a "synch point", "the place where the audiovisual 'arch' meets the ground before taking off again" (Chion, 1994: 58–62).
11. Jason Kehe and Kaite M. Palmer, "Secrets of a Trailer Guru: How This Guy Gets You to the Movies", *Wired.com*, June 18, 2013, https://www.wired.com/2013/06/online-trailers-mark-woollen (accessed April 15, 2017). Elsewhere Woollen states "I'd say music is 90 percent of the work we do; it establishes the rhythm..." (Lopez, 2011).
12. Mike Flanagan, "How to Edit a Trailer that Will Get Your Film Noticed", *microfilmmaker.com*, http://www.microfilmmaker.com/tipstrick/Issue14/Edit_Trl.html (accessed April 15, 2017).
13. Tom Jackman, "Hal Douglas, Renowned Voice-over Artist from Lovettsville, Leaves this World at 89", *The Washington Post*, March 17, 2014, http://www.washingtonpost.com/blogs/local/wp/2014/03/17/hal-douglas-renowned-voice-over-artist-from-lovettsville-leaves-this-world-at-89 (accessed April 15, 2017).
14. Chion devotes a chapter to this use of voice in Jean Vigo's *l'Atalante* (1934) in *Film: A Sound Art* (2009). Voices are displaced, layered and decentred, which results in a material aural effect.

15. Murray Smith, "The Sound Sentiment: Popular Music, Film, and Emotion", *16:9* 4/9 (November 2006), http://www.16-9.dk/2006-11/side11_inenglish.htm (accessed April 15, 2017).
16. Roland Barthes offers a different approach to materiality in vocal music in his essay "The Grain of the Voice" (Barthes, 1977).
17. In comparison with the other newly composed songs, 'Scarborough Fair' was a traditional British folk song recorded by Simon and Garfunkel for the film.
18. "Lana Del Rey – Chart History", *Billboard.com*, https://www.billboard.com/music/lana-del-rey/chart-history (accessed June 2, 2020).
19. Andrew Sims, "Lana Del Rey's 'Once Upon a Dream' Released – Listen!" *Hypable.com*, January 26, 2014, http://www.hypable.com/2014/01/26/lana-del-rey-maleficent-once-upon-a-dream/ (accessed April 15, 2017).
20. Scott Mendelson, "Lana Del Rey Covers 'Once Upon A Dream' for Angelina Jolie's 'Maleficent'", *Forbes*, January 26, 2014, http://www.forbes.com/sites/scottmendelson/2014/01/26/lana-del-ray-covers-once-upon-a-dream-in-new-trailer-for-angelina-jolies-malificent/ (accessed April 15, 2017).
21. This well-known song from 1981 would appeal to an audience familiar with Tyson's early successes from the late 1980s.
22. Philip Hayward uses the term "infradiegetic" to signify an agency whereby film sound falls between the "extra-narrative affective dimension of the film score… into the audiovisual, narrative and 'logical' coherence of the film's narrative world" (Hayward, 1997: 37). Although a variety of designations exist for the space between the diegetic and non-diegetic realms, Hayward's seems to correspond most closely to this common sonic trope of horror and science fiction trailer genres.
23. An early cinematic use of the wordless choir to evoke wonderment occurs in the titles to the film *The Wizard of Oz* (Victor Fleming, 1939).
24. The full version (without added visualizations) can be found on YouTube at https://www.youtube.com/watch?v=R9M6RB_WF_0 (accessed April 15, 2017).
25. "All Comments", YouTube, https://www.youtube.com/all_comments?v=32eywT-bQhQ (accessed April 15, 2017).

References

Barthes, R. (1977) "The Grain of the Voice". In *Image-Music-Text*, translated by S. Heath, 179–89. New York: Hill and Wang.
Belch, G. E. and M. A. Belch (2014) *Advertising and Promotion: An Integrated Marketing Communications Perspective*, 10th edn. New York: McGraw Hill.
Borkowska, B. and B. Pawlowski (2011) "Female Voice Frequency in the Context of Dominance and Attractiveness Perception". *Animal Behaviour* 82/1: 55–59.
Buller, D. B. and R. K. Aune (1992) "The Effects of Speech Rate Similarity on Compliance: Application of Communication Accommodation Theory". *Western Journal of Communication* 56/1: 37–53.
Chattopadhyay, A., D. W. Dahl, R. J. B. Ritchie and K. N. Shahin (2003) "Hearing Voices: The Impact of Announcer Speech Characteristics on Consumer Response to Broadcast Advertising". *Journal of Consumer Psychology* 13/3: 198–204.
Chion, M. (1994) *Audio-Vision: Sound on Screen*, edited by C. Gorbman. New York: Columbia University Press.
Chion, M. (2009) *Film: A Sound Art*, translated by C. Gorbman. New York: Columbia University Press.

Deaville, J. and A. Malkinson (2014) "A Laugh a Second? Music and Sound in Comedy Trailers". *Music, Sound, and the Moving Image* 8/2: 121–40.

Dyer, R. (2012) *In the Space of a Song: The Uses of Song in Film*. Abingdon, Oxon: Routledge.

Eastman, S. T., D. E. Bradbury and R. S. Nemes (1985) "Influences of Previews on Movie Viewers' Expectations". In *Current Research in Film: Audiences, Economics, and Law*, edited by B. Austin, 51–57. Norwood, NJ: Ablex Publishing.

Finsterwalder, J., V. Kuppelwieser and M. de Villiers (2012) "The Effects of Film Trailers on Shaping Consumer Expectations in the Entertainment Industry – A Qualitative Analysis". *Journal of Retailing and Consumer Services* 19: 589–95.

Gélinas-Chebat, C., J.-C. Chebat and A. Vaninsky (1996) "Voice and Advertising: Effects of Intonation and Intensity of Voice on Source Credibility, Attitudes toward the Advertised Service and the Intent to Buy". *Perceptual and Motor Skills* 83/1: 243–62.

Genette, G. (1997) *Paratexts: Thresholds of Interpretation*, translated by R. Macksey. Cambridge: Cambridge University Press.

Gray, J. (2010) *Show Sold Separately: Promos, Spoilers, and Other Media Paratexts*. New York: New York University Press.

Hayward, P. (1997) "Danger! Retro-Affectivity! The Cultural Career of the Theremin". *Convergence: The International Journal of Research into New Media Technologies* 3/4: 28–53.

Hills, M. (2011) "Listening from Behind the Sofa? The (un)Earthly Roles of Sound in BBC Wales' Doctor Who". *New Review of Film and TV Studies* 9/1: 28–41.

Johnston, K. J. (2009) *Coming Soon: Film Trailers and the Selling of Hollywood Technology*. Jefferson, NC: McFarland.

Kernan, L. (2004) *Coming Attractions: Reading American Movie Trailers*. Austin, TX: University of Texas Press.

Kim, Y. E. and B. Whitman (2002) "Singer Identification in Popular Music Recordings Using Voice Coding Features". *Proceedings of the 3rd International Conference on Music Information Retrieval* 13: 17.

Leeuwen, T. v. (1999) *Speech, Music, Sound*. New York: St. Martin's Press.

Li, Y. and D. Wang (2007), "Separation of Singing Voice from Music Accompaniment for Monaural Recordings". *IEEE Transactions on Audio, Speech, and Language Processing* 15/4: 1475–487.

Lopez, J. (2011) "Hollywood's Two-minute Auteurs". *Businessweek.com*. December 8. http://www.businessweek.com/magazine/hollywoods-twominute-auteurs-12082011.html (accessed April 15, 2017).

Macksey, R. (1997) "Foreword". In G. Genette, *Paratexts: Thresholds of Interpretation*, translated by R. Macksey, xi–xxii. Cambridge: Cambridge University Press.

Marich, R. (2013) *Marketing to Moviegoers: A Handbook of Strategies and Tactics*, 3rd edn. Carbondale, IL: Southern Illinois University Press.

Oakes, S. and A. C. North (2011) "The Impact of Narrator Age Congruity on Responses to a Radio Advertisement". *Journal of Marketing Communications* 17/3: 183–94.

Ortega, V. R. (2007) "Transnational Media Imaginaries: Cinema, Digital Technology and Uneven Globalization". PhD dissertation, Cinema Studies, New York University.

Picard, R. G., ed. (2014) *Media Product Portfolios: Issues in Management of Multiple Products and Services*. New York: Routledge.

Pipitone, R. N. and G. G. Gallup Jr (2008) "Women's Voice Attractiveness Varies across the Menstrual Cycle". *Evolution and Human Behavior* 29/4: 268–74.

Powrie, P. and G. Heldt (2014) "Introduction: Trailers, Titles, and End Credits". *Music, Sound, and the Moving Image* 8/2: 111–20.

Scherer, K. R. (1995) "Expression of Emotion in Voice and Music". *Journal of Voice* 9/3: 235–48.

Shada, A. L. (2008) "Cross Promotion and the Disney Channel: The Creation of a Community through Promotions". PhD dissertation, Bethel University, MN.

Smith, J. (1998) *The Sounds of Commerce: Marketing Popular Film Music*. New York: Columbia University Press.

Smith, M. (2006) "16:9 in English: The Sound of Sentiment: Popular Music, Film, and Emotion". *16:9 filmtidsskrift* 4/19. http://www.16-9.dk/2006-11/side11_inenglish.htm (accessed April 15, 2017).

Stilwell, R. J. (2005) "Clean Reading: The Problematics of 'In the Air Tonight' in *Risky Business*". In *Pop Fiction: The Song in Cinema*, edited by M. Caley and S. Lannin, 139–54. Bristol: Intellect Press.

Titze, I. R. (1994) *Principles of Voice Production*. Englewood Cliffs, NJ: Prentice Hall.

Veits, C. (2014) *Conflict Coverage Promotion: High Quality or High Concept? A Multimodal Analysis of Claims-making in Conflict Coverage Promotional Spots of Al Jazeera English and CNN International*. Hamburg: Anchor Academic Publishing.

Welch, G. F. (2005) "Singing as Communication". In *Musical Communication*, edited by D. Miell, R. A. R. MacDonald and D. J. Hargreaves, 239–60. New York: Oxford University Press.

9 'You've Got a Friend in Me':
Singing Voices in the Toy Story Films

Natalie Lewandowski and Penny Spirou

Introduction

Drawing on animation sound studies (Coyle, 2010), film sound theory (Chion, 1994; Doane, 1985), vocal analysis (McCoy, 2012) and star studies (Dyer, 2004), this chapter demonstrates that the voice has an integral function in the narratives of the first three *Toy Story* films. These three films are linked through the narrative focus on the toys' linear connection to the character of Andy.[1] The voice emotionally connects the audience with the lead characters, interacting with the narratives at hand, weaving a storyline that invites the audience to believe in the fictional world of "the toys". This chapter will focus on how the singing voice and vocal style of characters provide a narrative continuity which allows audiences to engage with the three *Toy Story* films regardless of the gaps between their release dates (1995, 1999 and 2010). This chapter argues that the songs, as performed by the characters, form a *mise en abyme* (story-within-a-story)[2] which provides further information and context for the films' toys.

A Story about Toys

Created by Pixar[3] films, the *Toy Story* series uses the singing voice as an aid to character development and narrative progression. *Toy Story* (John Lasseter, 1995) was the first computer-animated feature film (O'Steen, 2011: 25) with the following two films in the series, *Toy Story 2* (John Lasseter, Ash Brannon and Lee Unkrich, 1999), and *Toy Story 3* (Lee Unkrich, 2010), continuing in this production style. The *Toy Story* series uses the singing voice as protagonist through the inclusion of diegetic character songs; non-diegetic songs and singing aid the narrative through their lyrical content. The varied uses of the singing voice – as narrator, communicator and entertainer – emphasize the importance of continuity in character voice and musical theming (see Tables 1–3 for a listing of songs, placement and context). To maintain a consistent music theme, the *Toy Story* trilogy predominantly features composer Newman's work including his award-nominated song,[4] 'You've Got a

Friend in Me' (Randy Newman, 1995) which is the theme song carried throughout all three films. This continuity is also applied to character voices, with the same actors employed in each film to provide the voices of *Toy Story*'s lead animated characters, including Tom Hanks as Woody and Tim Allen as Buzz Lightyear.

The two core characters that feature in the first three *Toy Story* films are Woody the cowboy and Buzz Lightyear the space ranger (the protagonists). In addition, there are several support toy characters who feature in all the films. Included in this group are Mr Potato Head (Don Rickles), Slinky Dog (Jim Varney), Hamm the pig moneybox (John Ratzenberger) and Rex the green dinosaur (Wallace Shaw). Additionally, although not playing a major character role, John Morris voices Andy, the young boy who owns the toys, across the three films. The original film, *Toy Story*, tells the story of Woody the toy cowboy and his fellow toy friends who live in Andy's bedroom. The daily lives of the toys are disrupted when Andy receives a new space ranger toy for his birthday, the multi-functional and futuristic Buzz Lightyear. This new toy is convinced that he is, in fact, not a toy and this attitude adds to the jealousy and suspicion which his arrival has caused for former favourite Woody. Woody feels upstaged and manages to formulate a plan that eventuates in him and Buzz being isolated from the other toys. To add further drama to the narrative, this separation occurs as Andy and his family are moving house – thus making the journey back to be reunited with Andy, an experience in which they band together and become friends.

Toy Story 2 was released in 1999, four years after the initial *Toy Story* film. Following on the theme of a shared adventure, this second film sees Woody again being separated from the rest of the toys; however this time it is not his intention and results through an unfortunate garage sale accident. After being stolen from the garage sale by an evil toy shop owner and toy collector (Big Al, voiced by Wayne Knight), Woody is confronted with the knowledge that Big Al plans to sell him to a Japanese toy museum, separating him from his friends forever. Woody meets fellow toys, Jessie the cowgirl (voiced by Joan Cusack), Stinky Pete the Prospector (voiced by Kelsey Grammer) and Bullseye the horse (a silent character) at Big Al's apartment. These toys were all part of the *Woody's Roundup* cowboy television series, and together they form a valuable collection. As Woody discovers the history of *Woody's Roundup* together with his new friends, Jessie, Pete and Bullseye, his old friends back home frantically plot a mission to find Woody. Similar to the first film, the path to being reunited allows for further character development and action-packed scenes where Woody is forced to decide between his new and old friends. A happy ending ensues when Woody and some of his new Roundup friends come home to Andy's room together.

Toy Story 3 (2010) was released eleven years after *Toy Story 2*. The large gap between productions is not ignored in the fictional narrative with the diegetic passing of time being presented as yet another key toy separation moment. This time, the separation is for all the toys from their owner Andy who is now grown up and is packing for college. The toys are very concerned that Andy will not take them with him. However, they accidentally end up in a donation bag headed to the local early childhood centre, Sunnyside Daycare. After being donated, the toys are initially happy about their new home as opposed to gathering dust in college-bound Andy's room. Instead, they are going to be played with every day. However, this daydream is short-lived after Sunnyside Daycare toy baron, Lotso the scented bear (voiced by Ned Beatty) and his cronies decide that the new arrivals are better suited to the Caterpillar Room where very young children take less care when playing with them. An "us vs. them" drama ensues as Andy's toys collectively try and break Lotso's evil rule over Sunnyside Daycare. In a highly climactic scene where all the toys fear they will be destroyed at the local recycling plant, they finally find a way home by jumping on a pickup truck which drives them back to Andy's house. The end credits show that Sunnyside Daycare is being rebuilt as a friendlier place that is no longer subject to Lotso's dictatorship and is now run by the new Mattel management team of Barbie (voiced by Jodi Benson) and Ken (voiced by Michael Keaton).

As described above, each film has an antagonist, a character who holds them captive, preventing them from returning to their beloved owner, Andy. In the first film it is the young neighbour, Sid Phillips (voiced by Erik von Detten), who aims to strap a rocket to Buzz Lightyear in order to see him fly and eventually explode. In the second film it is Big Al who intends on taking Woody, along with new characters Jessie and Stinky Pete, to Japan to be displayed in a museum. Stinky Pete also plays a villainous role here, as he impedes Woody's return home when Buzz and the toys come to rescue him. In the third film, Lotso forces the toys to stay at Sunnyside Daycare, against their will. The toy antagonists have deep, foreboding, mature voices compared to Woody and Buzz who have lighter, casual vocal tones. These differences in pitch range tell the audience who the threatening characters are and who the safe and kind characters are that the audience aligns with (van Leeuwen, 2009: 427). Thus it can be inferred from van Leeuwen (2009) that the characters Woody, Buzz and friends are considered "harmless" and hence more approachable to the child-oriented audience, because of their naturally higher pitched voices. This was a key aspect in casting the lead character voices for the three films. According to *Toy Story* director, John Lasseter, Tim Allen sounded like an "everyday guy" (Paik, 2007: 87) allowing identification with the character Buzz Lightyear as an approachable hero. Similar traits were called on for the character of Woody (Paik, 2007: 87). Both Hanks[5] and Allen[6] have significant acting careers which enable them to be sonically recognizable to audiences and allows their star image to be further reflected in the animated characters of Woody and Buzz (Dyer, 2004: 3).

Believability of the characters' stories is the key to engaging with the diegesis of *Toy Story* for Lasseter. Due to this direction, the voice actors did not manipulate their voice in recording sessions. The use of their natural voice does not lead the film audience to question who is behind the voice of the character and allows for complete commitment in following the story. Of the three films, *Toy Story 3* was not directed by John Lasseter but was directed by the original film editor on *Toy Story* and the co-director on *Toy Story 2*, Lee Unkrich. However, despite the changes in director, all vocal character elements remain the same (McLean, 2011: 68). Similarly, the main vocal and music contributor, Randy Newman, also remains consistent across the three films (see Tables 1–3).

The Animated Voice

Animation films rely on music to enhance or underline the narrative (Hill, 1998: 165). In the case of the first three *Toy Story* films, the music aids in bringing the characters to life and allows the audience to empathize with what are otherwise "plastic" toys. While the narrative framework of some early animations is similar to that of musical genre films (Goldmark, 2002: 93), this is not the case with the *Toy Story* films. Rather, the *Toy Story* films follow a linear fictional narrative with few instances of characters breaking into song. There has been extensive scholarship regarding the animation methods and film productions of Disney which are outlined by Coyle and Fitzgerald (2010: 224) and demonstrate the considerable interest in animation production. However, little of the writing has a focus on music or the voice.

Although the notion of reality in cartoons and animation is far more flexible than in live-action film (Goldmark, 2002: 93), *Toy Story*'s use of the voice and song does not commonly feature characters spontaneously performing songs. This is atypical to other Disney animated musical films such as *The Lion King* (Roger Allers and Rob Minkoff, 1994) and *Pocahontas* (Mike Gabriel and Eric Goldberg, 1995). Coyle and Fitzgerald have discussed how Disney changed their style of music within animation akin to Broadway musicals. In doing so: "Disney was able to confirm its reach across the USA and revive its reputation as a force in animation and popular music by bringing the studio aesthetic of Hollywood together with the musical-theatre style of Broadway" (2010: 223).

This musical approach is not taken within the *Toy Story* series of films; however, despite this, character songs remain integral to the development of the narrative arc of each film. Meaning through song is created in scenes where montages indicate the passing of time, a character's backstory, or emphasize the inner emotions of particular toys. Voice and songs are used to "add value to narrative impact" (Coyle, 2010: 11) in animation film. *Toy Story* achieves this by aligning particular songs to characters, giving them an emotional backstory and encouraging empathy from audience members by "leap[ing] out of the screen and into the viewer's imagination" (Coyle, 2009: 3). This is particularly important for the young viewer and the notion of character believability.

This sonic signature in the *Toy Story* series is the song 'You've Got a Friend in Me' composed by Randy Newman and performed by Newman and various artists over the series. The manner in which this song is used falls within the classic Disney style use of music, where the soundtrack is purely used to reinforce the narrative (Wells, 2010: 41). Furthermore, the lyrics for each song within the series, be they specifically composed for the series or licensed pre-recorded songs (notably in *Toy Story 3*), are "important carrier[s] of rhetoric... communicating [the] film's themes" (Ward, 2002: 86–87). The song 'You've Got a Friend in Me' in particular anchors the narrative across all three films. The audience's familiarity with the track further enhances the links of friendship between characters across the series despite changes and disruptions to their environment and various emotional upheavals. The song therefore is linked with key friendship developments within the films. For example, towards the end of *Toy Story*, 'You've Got a Friend in Me' features two voices (Randy Newman and Lyle Lovett) instead of one (Randy Newman), demonstrating the new friendship between Buzz and Woody (see Table 1).

In order to assess varying vocalities, McCoy's outline of paired-adjectives (2012: 2–7) have been adapted and applied to each song. These contrasting adjectives were paired along a five-point continuum and include vocal characteristics such as bright to dark, twang to loft, forward to back, clear to breathy, clean to raspy, conversational to ringing, nasal to non-nasal, free to forced, and good diction to poor diction (2012: 8–14), together with short phrasing to sustained phrasing. Our analyses demonstrate how changes in vocal tone, phrasing and diction add to narrative progression. The analyses were conducted in conjunction with visual accompaniment and, as such, the additional characteristic of "synchronization to image" was added to reflect the close relationship with the corresponding image. The findings of the analyses are included in the discussion below.

'You've Got a Friend in Me'

Newman employs short and clear phrasing typical of songs sung for children, allowing ease of understanding and likeability. Specific words which are linked to emotion (including "love", "friend" and "destiny") are extended with longer phrasing to reinforce the message of friendship and relationships between the toys and their owner, Andy. Newman's clear diction is not forced, with the voice following the unconstrained and upbeat melody. Overall the voice is clearly synchronized to image, especially with respect to panning; when we first hear the song in *Toy Story*, the lyrics and vocals start right on cue when the opening title "Toy Story" comes up on the screen (00:01:34). However, there is no actual animated character singing the song within the diegesis and yet the clear synchronization between the opening title and lead melody of 'You've Got a Friend in Me' forms a clear link for

Table 1: *Toy Story* (1995) and the singing voice

Song	Start time	End time	Context	Performers	Credits	Narrative relationship
You've Got a Friend in Me	00:01:30	00:02:47	Non-diegetic	Randy Newman	Written and produced by Randy Newman	Opening credits, introduction to characters including Andy
Strange Things	00:18:56	00:20:50	Non-diegetic	Randy Newman	Written and produced by Randy Newman	Transition from Woody to Buzz Lightyear becoming Andy's favourite toy
I Will Go Sailing No More	00:45:00	00:46:36	Non-diegetic	Randy Newman	Written and produced by Randy Newman	Buzz discovers he is not a space ranger but a toy
Hakuna Matata	01:09:11	01:09:16	Diegetic	Nathan Lane, Ernie Sabella, Jason Weaver and Joseph Williams	Music by Elton John, lyrics by Tim Rice	Plays on radio in Andy's car while Woody and Buzz try to get on the moving truck
You've Got a Friend in Me	01:13:28	01:15:25	Non-diegetic	Randy Newman and Lyle Lovett	Written and produced by Randy Newman	End credits

the audience and the film series as the song itself is intertwined from this point forward. The same Newman rendition of 'You've Got a Friend in Me' is used in the opening credits of the Toy Story 3 film, synchronized to a montage of Andy growing up. The use of the same song in Toy Story 3 works to take the audience back to the world of the toys in the first film and released 15 years prior.

The scores of the first three *Toy Story* films are composed by Randy Newman. A well-known figure in the film music world, Newman scored five out of Pixar's first seven films (Paik, 2007: 107) and has received fourteen Academy Award nominations including a win in 2002 for 'If I Didn't Have You' from Pixar film, *Monsters Inc.* (Pete Docter, David Silverman and Lee Unkrich, 2001). Although Newman is certainly not the only person responsible for all the music within these *Toy Story* films, he is widely recognized as composing the core songs for each of the films. According to Winkler (1987), words and music need to interact to generate meaning. The lyrics are simple yet convey important meanings by leaving certain things unsaid (Winkler, 1987: 1–2). Newman's songs act as an extension of the lead characters within the films (Winkler, 1987: 16), especially Woody, Jessie and Buzz. Newman's songs form the *mise en abyme* within all three films (the story-within-a-story technique was initially employed to understand the phenomenon in literature and theatre [see White, 2001]). This is confirmed with the visual montages that accompany the songs. The montages closely follow the lyrics, often going back in time to show how the characters have come to be in the situation they are in. This linking of the songs and visual action, as a method of narrative continuity for the audience, allows emotional understanding of the characters' feelings in a short space of time.

When discussing their vision for the music and songs in *Toy Story*, producer Dana Anderson and director Lee Unkrich felt that the music and songs were a key element in determining the emotion and pacing of scenes (Unkrich, 2010). This is particularly obvious when listening to the upbeat music selected for the epilogue in *Toy Story 2*, which was used to "tie up dangling scenes" (Unkrich, 2010). The process of selecting an appropriate song for the final epilogue of *Toy Story 3* involved the team discussing how they wanted something with more energy than the original version of 'You've Got a Friend in Me', resulting in the song being performed by the band Gipsy Kings (Unkrich, 2010). This Spanish rendition of 'You've Got a Friend in Me' is complemented on screen with Buzz and Jesse dancing the paso doble (a Spanish dance inspired by bull fighting). The song has a faster tempo and the vocal delivery is notably more invigorated and upbeat than the original.

The expressive raspy vocals with strong diction are a characterizing feature of the Gipsy Kings and their broader catalogue of songs. 'You've Got a Friend in Me' is closely synchronized with the dance moves of Jessie and Buzz, an amusing romantic interlude, which leaves audiences on a high note as the end credits continue to roll. The mood created by the Gipsy Kings was intended by Unkrich who stated, "We wanted people to gather themselves… and reenergise and we think 'You've Got a Friend in Me' as performed by the Gipsy Kings is the perfect way to end the film" (Unkrich, 2010). The vocal quality of the Gipsy Kings works in two ways in this scene: to link back to Buzz Lightyear who appeared in the *Toy Story 3* narrative in "Spanish mode", and secondly, to reunite the toys in an upbeat finale, again exemplifying the strength of their friendships.

Songs as *mise en abyme*

The first three *Toy Story* films employ the use of both composed and pre-recorded music in order to develop narrative, explore the internal struggle of the characters and assist the audience in understanding their relationship to others. Disney films such as *Beauty and the Beast* (Gary Trousdale and Kirk Wise, 1991), *Aladdin* (Ron Clements and John Musker, 1992) and *The Lion King* (Roger Allers and Rob Minkoff, 1994) employed the musical film genre technique of characters breaking into song, mid-narrative. The *Toy Story* creators avoided this and opted to have other voices, beyond the characters, to illustrate emotion and narrative (Lasseter in Paik, 2007: 106). This is not the case for every instance as the characters do sing in *Toy Story 2* (Woody and Wheezy sing), see Table 2, but largely, the singing voices are external to the character voices in the three films. The songs therefore convey an internal monologue which is revealed to the audience. Similar to the musical film genre, the musical sequences in *Toy Story* explain complex emotions that cannot be adequately addressed through dialogue. The voices of characters and voices of singers are plausibly one and the same. For instance, 'You've Got a Friend in Me' sounds as though it could be Woody singing to Andy in the first film when considering timbre and delivery. This song is consistently played throughout all three films (in some way or another). However, there is a transformation and evolution of this one song within the three narratives. As discussed above, one of the core transformative elements is the singing voice as it changes from Randy Newman to Lyle Lovett to Tom Hanks to Robert Goulet and, in the third film, to the Gipsy Kings with Nicolas Reyes and Tonino Baliardo. The different voices suggest that the meaning behind the song can apply to different scenarios that the characters encounter and that different characters express the same sentiment in their actions. Through the lyrics,[7] it is clear that the core theme is friendship. The commitment to and support of friends is evident in all of the *Toy Story* films, as discussed in the narrative summaries above. As well as its appearance in each film, a consistency with 'You've Got a Friend in Me' is that in each film it appears at the conclusion, which is a common feature of animation films' theme songs (Koizumi, 2010: 69). By this understanding, 'You've Got a Friend in Me' is the *Toy Story* theme song.

Although 'You've Got a Friend in Me' is used twice within the first *Toy Story* film, each version is discernibly different, with the final version – played over the closing credits – involving two people singing a duet which reflects the strengthened friendship between Buzz and Woody. The varied styles of Newman and Lovett demonstrate the different characteristics of Buzz and Woody. There is no strong synchronization with image required, as the song is simply played over the end credits – the song's meaning is therefore neutral. Newman's vocality in this rendition has not altered significantly to that of the first solo rendition of the song heard at the start (opening credits) of the film. Lovett's voice complements Newman's with a slightly brighter tone, although still clear and with strong diction – the two characters are now having a vocal conversation within the constraints of the song. This implies that Buzz and Woody have put aside their differences and are now friends (conflict resolution in the classic narrative structure of the film) – the highlighted characteristics reflect the positive attitude of the two toys and the health of their friendship. Conversely, in Toy Story 2, Buzz and Woody's friendship is troubled as Woody decides to leave for Japan. As Woody tries to forget the friendships he has been forging with the other toys, the song, 'You've Got a Friend in Me' (Table 2), is heard diegetically, being sung by an onscreen television version of Woody in his own television show Woody's Roundup. This time the song is voiced by Tom Hanks, whose vocal characteristics and slower pace of delivery give a nostalgic feel.

This twangy country version of 'You've Got a Friend in Me' is pared back and accompanied only by acoustic guitar. We can see Woody watching his other self on screen as the lyrics of the song sink in. Hanks' raw vocality, with minimal accompaniment, provides reflection on the decision which Woody needs to make about whether he will stay with his friends or travel to Japan to be in a toy museum. The context of the song in this scene, together with Hanks' alternate vocality, takes both Woody and the audience back to recall the friendships that were made in the first Toy Story film. In this scene, the believability of Woody's character is enhanced due to Hanks not only being the character voice, but also the singing voice. As the narrative shifts, by the final sequence of Toy Story 2, we are reminded of the joy which the original version of 'You've Got a Friend in Me' was characterized. Aptly, it is no longer Hanks singing. Instead, Robert Goulet sings an upbeat jazz rendition of the song which illustrates a brassy and celebratory rendition of 'You've Got a Friend in Me'. The tone of the song is jovial, with Goulet's clear vocality convincing the audience that all is well again. The placement of characteristics on the analytical continuum is reflective of the jazz genre from which this rendition draws inspiration. The phrasing is relatively even, with sustained parts reflective of the ends of the chorus. The image is largely synchronized to Wheezy the penguin singing the song diegetically "live" to an audience of toys in Andy's room. This scene, accompanied by Goulet's vocality, demonstrates that it is not only Woody and

Buzz's friendship that has been saved, but also all of the other toys in Andy's room who have been reunited.

The vocals used in all the songs within *Toy Story* and *Toy Story 2* are not performed by the character voices, instead being sung by other musicians; however, the narrative arc and lyrics to the songs imply that these songs are being sung by the characters at hand. An example of this from the first *Toy Story* is when Woody begins to realize that he is being replaced by Buzz as Andy's favourite toy, mirrored in the song 'Strange Things' sung by Randy Newman. Newman's vocality in 'Strange Things' adapts to a more purposeful mode, which emphasizes the emotional changes Woody is undergoing through this song. With stronger diction, the topic of the song is reflective of Woody's emotion within the situation as he feels he is being replaced by Buzz as the favourite toy. The diction is punchier, as though the words "some new punk in a rocket!" (00:19:08) are being spat out with anger, an emotion that Woody is clearly feeling given his actions in the accompanying scene. The chorus features strained and elongated phrasing, with the word "strange" dragged out. Synchronization to image is also clearly linked to the lyrics in ways that demonstrate that even though the audience cannot clearly see someone singing on screen, the alignment to character is evident through the vocal delivery and the lyrics of the song.

An example of song lyrics adding believability to the characters by being intertwined with the narrative arc is the song 'I Will Go Sailing No More', also sung by Newman. This song plays when Buzz realizes that he is not a real space ranger and is, in fact, just a toy.[8] This song, although sung by Newman – whose voice has lent itself to Woody thus far – is reflective of the emotion that Buzz is feeling after discovering he is not a "real space ranger" but a "toy". There are moments where Buzz attempts to fly and prove everyone wrong and that, he is, indeed a space ranger. Here there is strong synchronization with the lyrics, emotion and image within the scene – although, again, the audience cannot see anyone singing the words. Newman employs a breathy vocal tone combined with a louder dynamic and sustained sections that highlight the emotional turmoil Buzz is feeling when he leaps from the top of a staircase and attempts to fly. Although the song is performed by Randy Newman, not Buzz (Tim Allen), the lyrics clearly act as a *mise en abyme* for Buzz. The vocals indicate that this is what Buzz is singing to the film audience. It is a crucial part in the discovery of his true identity as a toy and not a space ranger. This realization is difficult for Buzz to accept and a major turning point in his character and the narrative.

Newman's ability to mould his vocal characteristics to match the emotions of the characters on screen is again demonstrated in the upbeat song 'We Belong Together'. Despite this song being played over the closing credits of *Toy Story 3*, it still forms a narrative glue as the audience sees a glimpse into the new life which the toys will have at Sunnyside Daycare, thus giving a positive sense of closure.

The lyrics are clearly reflective of the new environment being represented at Sunnyside Daycare. The song is played over the end credits of the film alongside a small screen which shows a continuation of the narrative, highlighting the new life which the toys are experiencing both at the day care centre and with their new owner. Newman employs more sustained notes and phrases as well as an expressive raspier vocality reflecting the pop genre of the song.

The song 'When She Loved Me' in *Toy Story 2* is a strong example of *mise en abyme*. The visual montage that accompanies this track shows Jessie's past life with her owner, Emily. The song is not sung by Jessie, it is sung by Sarah McLachlan; however, the lyrics illustrate Jessie's feelings and emotions on being abandoned by her owner (see Table 2). The song provides an overview of her past, explaining her behaviours and personality in the present. The song, 'When She Loved Me' is an emotional ballad;[9] Lasseter felt the song was a more efficient and successful way of telling Jessie's story and aligning her relationship with her owner Emily with that of Andy and Woody (Lasseter in Paik, 2007: 152). The song conveys more emotion than dialogue could and reveals more about the character. The impact on the film audience is stronger as there is a deeper insight into the emotional struggle and history of the character. In the case of Jessie, 'When She Loved Me' reflects the experience of being a discarded toy who was once loved and cared for, like a childhood best friend (Lasseter in Paik, 2007: 154). The song plays over a montage flashback of Jessie and her owner, while the lyrics of the song narrate their relationship. In the montage, Jessie appears happy with her owner, as they spend a lot of time together and share many different life experiences. In the time lapse, it is clear that the owner has grown up and ultimately throws Jessie under her bed, never to be played with again. McLachlan's singing voice in 'When She Loved Me' is soft, melancholic and feminine, reflecting Jessie's longing for the lost friendship with her previous owner, Emily. McLachlan's vocality further emphasizes Jessie's feelings.

McLachlan's song is the only song within the *Toy Story* trilogy sung by a female vocalist. McLachlan's vocal tone is breathier than Newman's, with more sustained phrases that are synchronized to images reflecting the lyrics being sung. As with the emphasis on specific emotional words sung by Newman in 'You've Got a Friend in Me', McLachlan's diction is clearer on specific words such as "heart", "together", "loved" and "me". McLachlan's vocality changes and becomes more emphasized as the story, as told by the words, becomes sadder. However, overall her voice is bright and lyrical, which reflects the happy times that Jessie shared with her owner, Emily, in the synchronized montage.

Another *mise en abyme* is introduced in the song 'Woody's Roundup', which plays four times throughout *Toy Story 2*. The song is a television theme song for the fictional television show of the same name. The song is sung by Riders in the Sky. Sometimes referred to as a children's band, Riders in the Sky are a country/western music and comedy group. This song is repeated in the same style, three times within the film (at 00:22:17, 00:26:51 and 00:33:08) and thus is analysed only once here, although the continuum position of some characteristics do change when Bullseye the horse, Woody and Jessie jump on the deck and change the speed of the record playback with their dancing. This will not be analysed separately as it is the same track with altered playback. As Riders in the Sky are a music group with vocals being contributed by several members (often in unison), the vocal analysis is of the overall vocality rather than that of individual voices. Across all three times that the song is heard, the synchronization to image is attributed with the lyrics and context. This occurs either where the characters are interacting with the song being played through a diegetic television set or through a record player; the band singing the song is not seen. The extratextual appeal of Riders in the Sky and genre matching to Woody, the cowboy, reflect the popular television genre of the 1940s and 50s. 'Woody's Roundup' is a sonic representation of Woody's past identity and his possible future. Audible is the advertising jingle aspect of the song 'Woody's Roundup' as a separate music video was made for this song. This medley includes a slower country version of 'You've Got a Friend in Me', which brings Woody back to the reality of his current life with Andy and his friendship with the other toys (see Table 2). 'You've Got a Friend in Me' is of significance here as Woody comes to a realization that his identity does not match the Woody on television, working as the resolution of the narrative.

Toy Story 3 is the first film in the series that utilizes licensed popular music tracks (see Table 3). These are the songs 'Dream Weaver' (written and performed by Gary Wright, released in 1975) and 'Le Freak' (performed by Chic, written by Bernard Edwards and Nile Rodgers, released in 1978). The two tracks are played to further explicate the relationship between Barbie, and new character, Ken. 'Dream Weaver' reflects their immediate attraction when meeting for the first time, and 'Le Freak' shows Ken's comic abilities when parading his impressive wardrobe in front of Barbie. The use of popular music tracks in these scenes is for comic purposes. As these songs have been heard prior to the film, they are instantly identifiable and have connotations based on audience experience. In all three *Toy Story* films, there are no other tracks that are placed for a comic purpose until the final track of *Toy Story 3*, 'You've Got a Friend in Me', is sung in Spanish. The humour in this version of the song is understood as the tune has been heard throughout all three *Toy Story* films, making the theme song cohesive and fluid through the entire toy and audiences' shared experience.

Conclusion

The vocal characteristics outlined above illustrate how voice and song in animation are used to show shifts in emotion. Animation as a genre has greater emo-

Table 2: *Toy Story 2* (1999) and the singing voice

Song	Start time	End time	Context	Performers	Credits	Narrative relationship
Woody's Roundup	00:22:17	00:22:56	Diegetic	Riders in the Sky	Music and lyrics by Randy Newman	A VHS copy of an advertisement for 'Woody's Roundup' is played for Woody by Jessie, Bullseye and The Prospector
Woody's Roundup	00:26:51	00:27:24	Diegetic	Riders in the Sky	Music and lyrics by Randy Newman	Bullseye jumps onto a record player and starts the song. Woody and Jessie jump on and speed up/slow down the record as they run across it.
Woody's Roundup	00:33:08	00:33:36	Diegetic	Riders in the Sky	Music and lyrics by Randy Newman	Woody tries to get his arm back and the TV turns on. The song plays while Woody is returned to a glass cabinet and Al (the toy collector) finds the remote to turn the TV off.
When She Loved Me	00:46:40	00:49:17	Non-diegetic	Sarah McLachlan	Music and lyrics by Randy Newman	A montage of Jessie's life with her owner, Emily. The montage shows Emily playing with her; however as she grows older, she discards Jessie (leaving her under the bed and eventually leaving her as a donation to charity).

Table 2: *Toy Story 2* (1999) and the singing voice (cont.)

Song	Start time	End time	Context	Performers	Credits	Narrative relationship
You've Got a Friend in Me	01:03:47	01:04:38	Diegetic	Tom Hanks	Music and lyrics by Randy Newman	Woody looks up to the TV to see Woody, playing guitar in his own TV show, singing. Buzz, who has left him, can hear the song too. Woody scrubs the bottom of his shoe to reveal Andy's name and says "What am I doing?"
You've Got a Friend in Me	01:20:56	01:22:00	Diegetic	Robert Goulet	Music and lyrics by Randy Newman	Wheezy (the squeaking penguin) has been repaired and sings to celebrate. His voice is considerably deeper and the song is in 'big band style'. During the performance, Woody and Buzz pledge to be friends "for infinity and beyond". The barbies also feature as back-up singers.
Woody's Roundup	01:27:38	01:27:58	Non-diegetic	Riders in the Sky	Music and lyrics by Randy Newman	End credits

Table 3: *Toy Story 3* (2010) and the singing voice

Song	Start time	End time	Context	Performers	Credits	Narrative relationship
You've Got a Friend in Me	00:05:12	00:06:07	Non-diegetic	Randy Newman	Written and produced by Randy Newman	Montage of Andy growing up, playing with all of his toys, especially Woody (he is holding Woody the most). The song fades abruptly and the image fades to black. Andy has grown up and no longer plays with his toys, which star in his toy chest. He is now 17 years old.
Dream Weaver	00:22:27	00:22:46	Non-diegetic	Gary Wright	Written by Gary Wright	Ken and Barbie meet. The music signifies their instant attraction to each other.
Le Freak	00:59:13	00:59:38	Diegetic	Chic	Written by Bernard Edwards and Nile Rodgers	Ken models his outfits for Barbie (by her request)
We Belong Together	01:30:31	01:32:16	Non-diegetic	Randy Newman	Written by Randy Newman, produced by Mitchell Froom	End credits. Small screen continues story, where new toys are donated to the day care centre (including Emperor Zurg from *Toy Story 2*).
You've Got a Friend in Me (para Buzz Español)	01:33:33	01:35:46	Diegetic to non-diegetic	Gipsy Kings with Nicolas Reyes and Tonino Baliardo	Music and lyrics by Randy Newman, produced by Tonino Baliardo and Nicolas Reyes	Buzz Lightyear (who was accidentally programmed to 'Spanish mode' earlier in the film) dances the Paso Doble with Jessie when Bullseye turns the music on a CD player.

tional emphasis, due to its very process on synchronization and temporal elasticity (Chion, 1994: 62). As a result, the voice becomes an anchor for narrative believability, allowing the audience to relate to and empathize with the emotional struggles of what, in the *Toy Story* films, are related to largely plastic inanimate objects. The use of songs and specific vocal delivery styles in the *Toy Story* series of films enhances the believability of these animated characters. The voices within the films literally bring the characters to life as they are real-life recordings of actors' voices; however, perhaps more importantly, the songs elevate this to include the emotional upheavals of the individual characters. Although the use of Hollywood vocal actors certainly contributes to characterization and identification of specific toys within each film (Fitzgerald and Hayward, 2010: 172), it is the songs that form continuity between the films, specifically the repeated use of 'You've Got a Friend in Me'. The re-use and re-versioning of the song through the use of several different character voices and genre manipulations illustrates the importance of song in representing a continuing voice for otherwise "lifeless" animated characters. These songs are the *mise en abyme*, allowing audiences to have further insight into the characters' feelings. Rather than following the Disney musical genre formula of animated films, the *Toy Story* series demonstrates how the sonic techniques found on the soundtracks of live-action films work to voice the inner narratives of key protagonists.

About the Authors

Dr Natalie Lewandowski is a research collaborator, educator and consultant specializing in screen sound, public relations, media copyright, regional music and Australian contemporary art. With a background in marketing, communications and economics, Natalie's approach integrates industry insight with critical analysis, resulting in a holistic approach which involves key stakeholders. Recent research projects and publications include an edited volume on music, health and wellbeing; ethnographic studies of Australian regional live music scenes; and case studies on creators in the Australian and New Zealand film soundtrack industries.

Dr Penny Spirou is Student Learning Support Manager at AFTRS (Australian Film, Television & Radio School). Her research has been published in journals including *Comedy Studies*, *Celebrity Studies*, and *Studies in Australasian Cinema*. Most recently Penny has published book chapters in *Singing Death* (2017) and *Music in Comedy Television* (2017).

Notes

1. As such, this chapter is not concerned with the latest addition to the franchise, *Toy Story 4* (Josh Cooley, 2019).

2. Peleg (2004: 263–64) describes the definitions of *mise en abyme* in a variety of contexts including biblical research, literary and fine arts.
3. Pixar's animated repertoire of feature-films include: *A Bug's Life* (John Lasseter and Andrew Stanton, 1998), *Monsters Inc.* (Pete Docter, David Silverman and Lee Unkrich, 2001), *Finding Nemo* (Andrew Stanton and Lee Unkrich, 2003), *The Incredibles* (Brad Bird, 2004), *Cars* (John Lasseter and Joe Ranft, 2006), *Rataouille* (Brad Bird and Jan Pinkava, 2007), *WALL-E* (Andrew Stanton, 2008), *Up* (Pete Docter and Bob Peterson, 2009), *Cars 2* (John Lasseter and Brad Lewis, 2011) and more recently, *Planes* (Klay Hall, 2013).
4. 'You've Got a Friend in Me' was nominated for an Academy Award for Best Original Song in 1996 and Golden Globe Award for Best Original Song in 1995 but lost both to 'Colors of the Wind', featured in the Walt Disney feature animation, *Pocahontas* (Mike Gabriel and Eric Goldberg, 1995). This information can be accessed on the Official Academy Awards Database: http://awardsdatabase.oscars.org (accessed February 2, 2015).
5. Tom Hanks was cast in lead roles in *Sleepless in Seattle* (Nora Ephron, 1993), *Philadelphia* (Jonathan Demme, 1993), *Forrest Gump* (Robert Zemeckis, 1994) and *Apollo 13* (Ron Howard, 1995) in the lead-up to the release of the first *Toy Story* film.
6. Tim Allen is known for his role as Tim Taylor in the TV series, *Home Improvement* (1991–1999). He also starred in family films including *The Santa Clause* (John Pasquin, 1994), *Jungle 2 Jungle* (John Pasquin, 1997), *Christmas with the Kranks* (Joe Roth, 2004), and *The Shaggy Dog* (Brian Robbins, 2006) before and during the release of the *Toy Story* trilogy.
7. The lyrics to 'You've Got a Friend in Me' can be accessed here: http://www.disneyclips.com/lyrics/lyricstoy.html (accessed February 4, 2015).
8. The lyrics to 'I Will Go Sailing No More' can be accessed here: http://www.disneyclips.com/lyrics/lyricstoy3.html (accessed February 2, 2015).
9. The lyrics to 'When She Loved Me' can be accessed here: http://www.disneyclips.com/lyrics/lyricstoy4.html (accessed February 2, 2015).

References

Chion, M. (1994) *Audio-Vision: Sound and Screen*. New York: Columbia University Press.
Coyle, R. (2009) "Thwack! Hearing the Motion in Animation". *Animation Journal* 17: 3–6.
Coyle, R. (2010) *Drawn to Sound: Animation Film Music and Sonicity*. London: Equinox.
Coyle, R. and J. Fitzgerald (2010) "Disney Does Broadway: Musical Storytelling in *The Little Mermaid* and *The Lion King*". In *Drawn to Sound: Animation Film Music and Sonicity*, edited by R. Coyle, 223–48. London: Equinox.
Doane, M. A. (1985) "The Voice in the Cinema: The Articulation of Body and Space". In *Film Sound: Theory and Practice*, edited by E. Weis and J. Belton. New York: Columbia University Press.
Dyer, R. (2004) *Heavenly Bodies: Film Stars and Society* (2nd edn). London: BFI.
Fitzgerald, J. and P. Hayward (2010) "Resilient Appliances: Music, Sound, Image and Narrative in *The Brave Little Toaster*". In *Drawn to Sound: Animation Film Music and Sonicity*, edited by R. Coyle, 160–73. London: Equinox.
Goldmark, D. (2002) *Tunes for 'Toons: Music and the Hollywood Cartoon*. Berkeley and Los Angeles: University of California Press.
Hill, M. (1998) "Life in the Bush: The Orchestration of Nature in Australian Animated Feature Films". In *Screen Scores: Studies in Contemporary Australian Film Music*, edited by R. Coyle. Sydney: AFTRS Publishing.

Koizumi, K. (2010) "An Animated Partnership: Joe Hisaishi's Musical Contributions to Hayao Miyazaki's Films". In *Drawn to Sound: Animation Film Music and Sonicity*, edited by R. Coyle, 60–74. London: Equinox.
McCoy, S. (2012) *Your Voice: An Inside View* (2nd edn). Delaware, OH: self-published by Scott McCoy.
McLean, T. J. (2011) "Making of Toy Story 3". *Hollywood Reporter* 417/2: 68–71.
O'Steen, B. (2011) "Inside the World of the Pixar Editor". *CinemaEditor* 3/61: 25–26.
Paik, K. (2007) *To Infinity and Beyond! The Story of Pixar Animation Studios*. San Francisco: Chronicle Books.
Peleg, Y. (2004) "'Yet forty days, and Nineveh shall be overthrown' (Jonah 3.4): Two Readings (*shtei krie 'ot*) of the Book of Jonah". In *God's Word for our World Volume 1: Biblical Studies in Honor of Simon John De Vries*, edited by J. H. Ellens, D. L. Ellens, R. P. Knierim and I. Kalimi, 262–74. New York and London: T&T Clark International.
Unkrich, L. (2010) *Toy Story 3 DVD*. Disney Enterprises, Inc./Pixar Animation Studios, Buena Vista Home Entertainment Australia.
Van Leeuwen, J. (2009) "A Semiotics of the Voice". In *Sound and Music in Film and Visual Media*, edited by G. Harper, R. Doughty and J. Eisentraut, 425–37. New York and London: Continuum.
Ward, A. R. (2002) *Mouse Morality: The Rhetoric of Disney Animated Film*. Austin, TX: University of Texas Press.
Wells, P. (2010) "Halas & Batchelor's Sound Decisions: Musical Approaches in the British Context". In *Drawn to Sound: Animation Film Music and Sonicity*, edited by R. Coyle, 40–59. London: Equinox.
White, J. J. (2001) "The Semiotics of the *mise-en-abyme*". In *The Motivated Sign: Iconicity in Language and Literature 2*, edited by O. Fischer and M. Nänny, 29–54. Philadelphia: John Benjamins.
Winkler, P. (1987) "Randy Newman's Americana". *Popular Music* 7/1: 1–26.

10 The Singing Voice and its Use to Evoke Unease, Discomfort and Violence

Liz Giuffre and Mark Thorley

Music's place in evoking, creating and managing a range of audience responses in cinema has been widely explored (Chion, 1999; Lannin and Caley, 2005; Sonnenschein, 2001). Often, the film music considered includes the singing voice although the singing voice's place as a key feature of film music remains significantly underexplored as existing studies focus almost exclusively on the genre of the film musical. Given the fact that music discourse has long acknowledged that "the vocal line of most songs is the focal point that carries the weight of musical expression" (Moylan, 2002: 46), it is surprising that to date there has been less variety in the way the singing voice has been considered in cinema studies. As Chion argues, there is huge potential for the voice to be understood as a primary marker, and evoker, of dramatic expression (Chion, 1999).

This chapter explores the role of the singing voice in performance on screen as it is used to evoke unease, discomfort and even violence. We focus on the isolated power of the voice in a similar way to Chion's formulation of the "acousmêtre" (1999: 17–30) in relation to the voice on screen. Chion's acousmêtre considers the effect of the disembodied or body-less voice, and he calls the voice without a visualized body a "special being, a kind of talking and acting shadow" (1999: 21). This process of withholding and revealing the voice and its bodily source, as well as revealing unlikely voice and body combinations, is one that we argue can contribute to particularly violent cinematic effects. For Chion, there is a direct action associated with this use of the voice, with "the acousmêtre's powers" (1999: 23) tied to whether or not the audience is able to see the source of the voice on screen, and then, to what degree this revelation fits the rest of the story. Unlike the usually pleasant or happy use of the voice in, say, the musical, Chion suggests the voice as part of the acousmêtre "brings disequilibrium and tension" by virtue of "being in the screen and not, wandering the surface of the screen without entering it" (1999: 24). He directly links the voice and violence in this examination, notably with Fritz Lang's films *M* (1931) and

The Testament of Dr Mabuse (1933), Orson Welles' *The Magnificent Ambersons* (1942) and Alfred Hitchcock's *Psycho* (1960) (1999: 19–22).

Following Chion's lead, this chapter explores ways in which the singing voice can create a dissonance in a broader range of films. We argue that the singing voice can be used in performance even if it is not apparently coming from the character onscreen – the use of non-diegetic singing can become motivator, marker and enabler of dramatic action. Given the limited attention that the singing voice has had beyond the musical spectacle and performances of pleasantness, we propose two types of cross-purpose singing voice performances that identify connections between the singing voice and to evoke feelings of unease or violence: the use of individual singing voices and their relationship to control; and the use of communal singing and its relationship to competition and power. We use case study examples that are particularly well-known for their depiction of violence or unease, but revisit them to demonstrate the role the singing voice plays in creating this effect. We have also highlighted examples of the singing voice that may seem otherwise marginalized, or what Gorbman describes as "artless singing" in cinema and other screen media, where a character is expected to sing, but not necessarily perform to what may otherwise be considered to be a professional or pleasant standard (2011).

Moving beyond the "Pleasantness" of the Musical

Existing work exploring the singing voice in film tends to focus on the musical as a genre. Here, as "a genre of spectacles" (Cohan, 2002: 63), the singing voice is used to draw the audience in with virtuosic (if not highly unrealistic) staged performances. Usually accompanied by highly staged dance routines, the singing voice performed on screen in this context has become so common that it has become (for better and worse) a defining characteristic of the genre, such that "bursting into song on screen is both the delight and difficulty of the screen musical genre" (Wood, 2006: 306). Such negotiations result from the high expectations of the audience watching the singing voice performances, as the suspension of the narrative often accompanying the musical performance makes audiences less patient towards any other type of oversight. As Wood explains, "the moment where song takes over from speech… when treated with skill and finesse can seem like the most natural thing in the world, yet when carelessly done is jarring and comedic" (ibid.).

The spectacle of the singing voice was constructed in early musicals such that often, more than one performer was required to achieve the final screen effect. For example, the singing voice of Marni Nixon was considered an appropriate match for the visual appearance of Audrey Hepburn's Liza Doolittle in *My Fair Lady* (1964). This is a common example of the "practice of song dubbing in the Hollywood film musical" widespread for much of the genre's history (Siefert, 1995:

44). Such instances, where an "ideal" singing voice was chosen to accompany an "ideal" visual performance, creates what Frith calls a "Body Electric", a process started with the mediation of the voice via radio and recording where "people became accustomed, *for the first time ever*, to hearing a voice without a body" (1995: 6, original emphasis).

Building on Barthes' famous connection between the body and voice as the "grain", with "the materiality of the body speaking its mother tongue" (2005: 182), Frith acknowledges the power of the body/voice signification process in explaining how audiences of radio, then later film and television, might be in danger of being without a grain, or without "the voice as it sings, the hand as it writes, the limb as it performs" (Barthes, 2005: 188). Frith explains how the audience and producers of mediated music work "assign bodies" to singing voices and "imagine their physical production" based on cultural and contextual expectation (Frith, 1995: 6), given that often we are unable to see/hear or have a clear connection with the body once the singing voice is mediated. Although Frith acknowledges that in everyday practice, as well as in popular music (and by extension, film and television), "voices can change over time" (ibid.), he maintains that "the voice and how it is used (as well as words and how they are used) becomes a measure of someone's truthfulness" (1995: 7), ultimately contributing to the development of "the vocal personality" (1995: 8).

The singing voice's link to the film character or "someone's truthfulness" is a concept that has often been considered in relatively simple emotional expressions that characterize the musical (most commonly, heteronormative love). However, it can equally allow for the development of threats, violence and discomfort. As we will demonstrate, the use of the singing voice in diegetic and non-diegetic forms, as leitmotif and as marker of physical and character-built space, can be observed in a variety of ways beyond the musical in order to explore often quite unpleasant motivations and actions. This approach also allows us to explore the production of the singing voice beyond the mere appearance of its connection with the actor on screen, taking into account effects, manipulations and other features of the recorded voice.

Uncomfortable, Unspectacular and Violent Voices

Film scholarship concerned with the singing voice beyond the musical does exist, but it is relatively rare. Gorbman offers the term "artless singing" (2011: 157) as a way to identify and explore a form of singing voice that is not virtuosic or a spectacle on its own. Instead, it is a larger part of what "happens in a fiction film when characters sing – not in the patently artificial, artful song performances that we normally call musical numbers, but in moments that are construed and perceived as integral parts of the 'realistic' diegetic world" (2011: 157). In contrast to classic Hollywood performances of the singing voice which feature characters "singing prettily" (Dyer, 2012: 114), Gorbman argues that instead, the artless singing voice appears in many different forms and contexts, noting that "motives for singing in movies are almost as numerous as motives for talking" (Gorbman, 2011: 158). Gorbman's category is an attempt to discuss a type of film event that she argues "falls through the disciplinary cracks" between film and music studies (2011: 157), and unlike the narrative disruption of the traditional musical where the singing voice creates its own spectacle, "artless singing lies somewhere between speech and music" (ibid.).

Gorbman's analysis of artless singing in film acknowledges the range of the voice that may include "imperfections" such as "breathiness, faltering and quavering, false notes, singing out of comfortable range, pauses, forgotten or mistaken lyrics" (2011: 159). While such features may be considered undesirable in the context of the traditional musical, in the context of artless singing these are reoriented so as to "equate amateurishness with authenticity" and represent a form of "natural and sincere expression of character" (2011: 159). This isolation of relative vulnerability and uniqueness displayed through the actor's vocal performance, and their display of a sometimes imperfect singing voice, is what Gorbman calls "a key way of evoking character, subjectivity, and interrelationships, and accordingly deserves as much critical attention as does film dialogue or camerawork and editing" (2011: 170).

Prior to Gorbman's definition of artless singing, another notable exploration of non-specialist singing is McLean's work on gender, voice and character in film noir (1993). McLean argues for the uniqueness of the singing voice as a dramatic device yet argues its distinction from other dramatic tools, noting that "we lack a precise theoretical terminology with which to describe the way music and musical numbers function outside of the musical genre" (1993: 12). McLean references Rita Hayworth's performance of strong female characters in film noir as a way to demonstrate how the singing voice "produces a space in which performance can be read as resistance" (ibid.) in the genres beyond the musical, and concludes by appealing to future film scholars to explore ways of "looking at music and performance [in films]... that transcend the musical genre" (ibid.).

Since McLean's work, there has been little sustained work on the singing voice in these broader genre categories. Connections between gender, embodied character and cross-genre/era film have been explored by Greene (2009), who presents a broadly feminist exploration tied to the vocal performances present in films *Singin' in the Rain* (Gene Kelly and Stanley Donen, 1952), *Mulholland Drive* (David Lynch, 2001), *Blue Velvet* (David Lynch, 1986) and *Citizen Kane* (Orson Welles, 1941). In *How The West Was Sung: Music in the Westerns of John Ford*, Kalinak (2007) explores the singing voice and character development in genre, including examples of singing used to develop the place of the other, such as the "Indian" in early cowboy films (2007: 73). Beyond film, iconic writer and television drama pioneer Dennis Potter's use of singing in television drama has been acknowledged "as a means of disrupting and disorientating viewer expectations" (Mundy, 2006: 60). Here the singing voice of popular musicians, mimed rather than performed by actors, was able to provide a sonic and visual counterpoint that "established the importance of popular song as a dramatic device capable of delivering a range of complex effects including 'emotional reclamation'" (ibid.).

Some of the most concentrated and prominent use of popular music in violent contexts (particularly that of distinctive vocal music beyond a soundtrack score) appears in Quentin Tarantino films. Tarantino's audio/visual stylization of violence with *Reservoir Dogs* (1992) became "a defining moment for both Hollywood ultraviolence and the role of the song in cinema" (Coulthard, 2009: 1), and his subsequent films have built on this style focusing on the "up-tempo and pop nature of the songs... [with] an emphasis on hip, retro nostalgia, and temporal dislocation (songs are rarely contemporaneous with the film's date of production or diegetic action)" (2009: 2). Coulthard argues that Tarantino films feature "a dominance of song over the sounds associated with physical brutality and violence" (ibid.); however, interestingly, her analysis pays little specific attention to the singing voice in the songs used in his films. She does note the way "lyrics in song become in this way another instance of dialogue" (2009: 5), yet there remains much to acknowledge about the delivery of the singing voice in these cases and its effect.

For example, Coulthard makes reference to a Dusty Springfield vocal appearance as featured in *Pulp Fiction* (Quentin Tarantino, 1994) (Coulthard, 2009: 3), though in her analysis there is no development of the distinctive sonic code of this singing voice as it impacts the scene (ibid.). Such an omission misses a key nuance in popular music's effectiveness: the grain of the voice and the connection between a singer and the song being performed carries much of the semiotic weight for the final sonic experience. If we listen and watch the scene again where 'Son of a Preacher Man' (John Hurley and Ronnie Wilkins, 1968) sounds as a prelude to Mia Wallace (Uma Thurman) and Vince Vega (John Travolta) having a "date", Springfield's voice is not just any voice in the mix, but a recognizably gendered and culturally stylized performance. Her singing voice is as breathy as actress Uma Thurman's delivery of her lines, crooned and produced by the pop track in a comparable way to the actress Thurman's delivery of Mia Wallace's lines as they appear broadcast over the house intercom in the scene. As such, the violence that is being sonically underpinned is not just rhythmic or generically "pop", but also noticeably featuring a female sound. This scene is not violent in itself but is situated within a context of clear threat (and previous demonstrations) of male-dominated violence (the threat that Vega will be killed if he sleeps with Wallace). Here, then, Tarantino uses a female singing voice in a nuanced way, to develop the character of Wallace and her relationship to Vega – the audience is left knowing that Vega, who is employed as security for Wallace, is actually under threat from her.

Violence, Discomfort and Control – the Singing Voice and its Relationship to Character and Action

Tarantino films are perhaps the most famous examples of popular music and violence in contemporary Western cinema, and the above example demonstrates that there is another layer of meaning that can be uncovered by focusing on the singing voice in these films. Moving beyond Tarantino, we now explore some other prominent examples of films which use popular music to create a sense of violence or unease. Again, we are building on the existing literature listed above to offer new ways to consider the relationship between the singing voice, character and action.

The films explored here represent a range of eras and include films that are notorious for their use of music in relation to violence, but have yet to be examined in terms of the singing voice's presence in this construction of meaning and identity. To do this, we propose the following categories or group types for appearances of the singing voice in films that develop power relations and control, negotiating violence. Our focus on the singing voice, particularly where iconic popular musicians are clearly featured, acknowledges the semiotic power of the singing voice as a distinct communicator of meaning. The singing voice in film, as in popular music generally, draws on "the individuality of each singer and the uniqueness of every voice" (Hughes, 2013: 13) in order to engage film audiences.

Type 1: Singing Presence/Absence as it Links to a Character's Ability to Perform Violence

Prior to Tarantino's work, popular music has also been replayed, re-voiced and evoked in films featuring violent acts. Perhaps most famous was Stanley Kubrick's sonically stylized work in *A Clockwork Orange* (1971), a film that uses quite specific approaches to music and singing in its depiction of the themes of delinquency, psychiatry and dystopia set in London sometime in the future. While music is central to the film generally (particularly with the central character Alex DeLarge's [Malcolm McDowell] love of Beethoven), there are three iconic scenes from the film which rely on diegetic singing on screen. All of these feature violence and the singing voice as a method of eliciting a response from characters on screen and from the audience. The first, where a tramp is singing 'Molly Malone' whilst drunk, provokes protagonist DeLarge to actively object to him singing the "songs of his forefathers", following this with a violent assault. The singing works directly as a trigger to a violent response in DeLarge (and similarly, for his followers as they also join in). In the second such scene, a woman is singing an excerpt from Beethoven's Ninth Symphony in the milk bar to which Dim (one of DeLarge's followers) blows a raspberry as a show of his lack of appreciation. DeLarge's response is to hit Dim with his stick. His violent response therefore reinforces his view that the performance of Beethoven should be respected and listened to. Finally, in the third scene to feature singing, DeLarge performs 'Singin' in the Rain' (Arthur Freed and Nacio Herb Brown, 1929) whilst raping Mary Alexander. His singing is punctuated and certain notes emphasized by kicking Mary Alexander's husband and assaulting her without disturbing the phrasing of the song.

This scene, which has been widely referenced in broader film scholarship, uses the singing voice to directly engage violence and punctuate it, demonstrating DeLarge's control of the soundtrack, and furthermore providing an outward display of the apparent enjoyment he has in inflicting this pain on another person. In each of the cases, the singing voice develops the character of DeLarge in the film, but is also directly linked to assertions of power and the character's ability to perform violence. In the first and second examples, singing works as a direct provocation, with another character's voice directly drawing DeLarge's character to act violently. However, in the first two cases the singing stops once the violence begins – the other characters literally have their voices silenced. By the third example, DeLarge starts to sing himself as he begins his violent rampage, with the performance of the singing voice and the body connected directly. This sequence of engagements between the characters, proximity and the singing voice is carefully manipulated in the film to create a cumulative process of audience engagement, and by the third time that DeLarge appears as the singer himself, the association between violent actions and his character is so strong that the threat of DeLarge's actions is almost as frightening as the violent act itself.

Following Kubrick and the rise of Tarantino, violent stories such as Mary Harron's development of *American Psycho* (2000) have also used the singing voice to develop character. The film follows Patrick Bateman (Christian Bale), a wealthy young finance professional in 1980s New York who goes on an almost comedic murdering spree. Initially a written text that used popular song and violence in tandem, in the adaptation to film, Harron allowed for the discussion of specific singing voices as well as the performance of these to be part of the lead up to, and execution of, key violent acts by protagonist Bateman. So, while the use of non-diegetic music in the film is relatively straightforward and, in general, works with (rather than in counterpoint) to visual elements, the presence of the singing voice seemingly allows Bateman to perform violent acts.

The connection made between Bateman's character and the singing voice of another (existing and well-known) performer is developed later in the film as Bateman's character chooses music to accompany his acts of extreme violence. Before his first murder he asks his victim, Paul Allen, "You like Huey Lewis and the News?" before discussing nuances of the recording including comments about its general production ("the whole album has a clear crisp sound and a new sheen of professionalism that really gives the songs a big boost"). As he moves from preparing his murder weapon (an axe) to killing the man, 'Hip to be Square' plays and Huey Lewis' voice is heard in the overall soundscape. While there has been previous academic commentary about this scene and Bateman's action of "philosophizing pop song" (Kooijman and Laine, 2003: 50) in the prelude to violent acts, what is missing is attention to what the sound of the voice (as a threat, and then a reality) actually achieves. Here the voice acts as a way to communicate Bateman's mood to the audience as an apparent calm after the storm – having talked about his preference about this song and that particular vocal performance before performing the murder, now the audience (and Bateman, supposedly) are both in close enough proximity to the Lewis singing voice to hear it directly. Like Tarantino's use of seemingly mundane or disconnected music set against the severity of the violence visually depicted, here the singing voice is in some ways sonically at odds with what would diegetically be likely in the scene. However, it adds a level of commentary and provides finality to that particular section. Bateman's build up to the murder of Allen is much longer than the act of killing him, and discussion of the singing voice is comparable to the actual (recorded) singing voice performance heard, yet the anticipation of the voice (and the violence) is what makes the final performance of each so arresting. The singing voice eventually replaces the onscreen sound and though we see Bateman panting, we only hear the voice of Huey Lewis' performance, a performance that is relatively reserved and clearly stylized with a 1980s production aesthetic. The male singer uses a slight vocal distortion with the delivery of the key lyric "it's hip to be square", though overall, there is still a clear sonic sterility and artificiality in reflection of the clinical manner in which Bateman approaches violence. Just as Bateman prepares himself for violence by wearing a raincoat so as to avoid actually "getting dirty", the vocal performance is sanitized within the expectations of a mainstream popular music aesthetic.

The singing voice's absence later in the film can actually be understood as stunting Bateman's ability to kill, starting with a scene where an instrumental (or vocally absent) version of the 'Greatest Love of All' (Michael Masser and Linda Creed, 1977) plays while Bateman takes longer before becoming violent. Significantly, the two "failed" attempts at murder do not involve Bateman controlling the sung music. In one, he fails to bring himself to murder work colleague Luis Carruthers in a restaurant toilet (perhaps because he cannot control what music the restaurant plays). In another, he cannot bring himself to murder his secretary with the nail gun he holds unseen behind her head despite it being in his own apartment where he could choose the music. Lastly, in the closing scenes, when he goes on an uncharacteristically random killing spree, the violence is accompanied by non-diegetic (rather than Bateman's choice of) music.

Though Bateman does not himself "sing", his choice of the singing voice in his actions is nevertheless highly significant in its relationship with the violence. Fundamentally, the singing voice in the popular music chosen is used as a device to help move him towards the violence he desires. His choice of sung music is shown and heard during successful murder scenes to demonstrate the character's control and to potentially express through the song what he cannot otherwise express. This expression is metaphoric and stylized rather than lyrically direct; the 1980s style of production is highly polished, tightly controlled and pre-dates the more organic styles of performance and production which emerged subsequently. Furthermore, it is interesting to note that the sung music used is all male vocal based. Though he "features" Whitney Houston in his discussion of the 'Greatest Love of All' prior to a murder, we do not hear her version – instead, it is an orchestral and vocally absent performance. Largely though, the lyrics, performance and themes of the chosen music form a counterpoint to the violence.

More recent examples of this use of diegetic and non-diegetic singing to develop character and its proximity to violence and unease come with *Silver Linings Playbook* (2012) and *American Hustle* (2013), each directed by David O. Russell. Neither of these films offers much more variety in tone and genre than *American Psycho* and *Clockwork Orange* (mixing crime, drama and comedy), yet each also relies on the development of feelings of unease, discomfort and some elements of violence to engage their audiences. In *American Hustle*, music is used in the film diegetically and non-diegetically, with a mixture of popular music songs. However, the example which is most powerful, complex and of note here, is the singing voice as it is used by one of the protagonists' wives, Rosalyn (Jennifer Lawrence), when she performs a rendition of 'Live and Let Die' (Paul McCartney and Linda McCartney, 1973). The scene initially starts with Rosalyn in a restaurant with mafia-member Pete Musane (Jack Huston), through whom she has effectively informed to the mafia about her husband. After pleading with Musane to let her husband live, we see Irving being led into her car as the lines of 'Live and Let Die' begin non-diegetically. The song continues as we see her go home and then she begins to sing along with the backing vocal line of the Wings original song with the lyrics "You know you did, you know you did, you know you did". Rosalyn's onscreen singing voice then forms a virtual duet with Paul McCartney's famous recording as the scene then cuts between Rosalyn singing along with the song, and Irving being driven off between two mafia members. In the instrumental section, she is seen to dance and clean in one strange "performance" act, with McCartney's voice (and by implication, her husband) now also silenced. With this depiction of the singing voice, one very specific to the scene and one removed, famous and distant, we are able to gain an insight into Rosalyn's character. The doubling of the voice aligns to Rosalyn's character being at once personally affected by what is happening to her husband as well as her removal from the actual action and eventual fate of her husband.

Overall, the choice of song suggests the anticipation of violence because the viewer is aware from Rosalyn's actions that Irving is in danger. The violence is unseen as the scene relies more heavily on suggestion underpinned by Rosalyn's singing performance of 'Live and Let Die'. The lyrics in particular are highly resonant with her sentiment – that is, Irving must die such that she can go on living.

Type 2: Singing Together – Vocal Competition and Power Struggles

Communal singing, or the presence of multiple singing voices, can perform a different function to individual or featured performances. Just as a single or featured singing voice can develop a key character or motivation, group singing can offer a variety of character types and positions, and by extension, competing agendas. The effect of group singing or experiences of communal singing has been expressly linked to mood by music psychologists (Unwin and Kenny, 2002; Gick, 2011), and here we explore the particular effect of groups of singing voices and their role in narrative film development. Again, the emphasis is on the creation of feelings of relative unease, deployment of power and competition.

An iconic example of different types of group singing voices is featured in Alfred Hitchcock's *The Birds* (1963). Generally known for its pioneering sound design (Wierzbicki, 2008), the film famously features a series of attacks by birds focused firstly on lead character Melanie Daniels and then on a variety of other characters in the film. Much has been written on the sonic production of the bird sounds throughout the film, but we argue here that the use of the singing voice in the film is also designed to propel the film's suspenseful narrative tension.

There are two key occasions where diegetic music performance is used. The first is when Melanie Daniels performs Debussy's 'Deux Arabesques' in the Brenner's house. The second time, explored here, is the scene where the birds prepare to attack the children in the school. In this scene, Daniels waits on a bench outside the school (having been dispatched to collect Cathy Brenner from school). As the birds gather behind Daniels (unseen by her), the sound of children performing a version of 'Risseldy Rosseldy' (an old American folksong with additional stanzas written for the scene by Evan Hunter) can be heard in the school. As the birds gather, the song and performance seems monotonous and foreboding, thus building the tension. There is no sound of the birds, just the sound of children singing. As Daniels enters the school, the sound of the singing becomes more intimate as performers and listener are put into the same acoustic space.

There are a number of key aspects to this example of singing used in the film to manage feelings of unease, discomfort and violence. Firstly, there is the difference between the "bird song" (if it can, indeed, be called that), and that of the children heard throughout the film. The bird song is electronic, jarring and angular (deliberately different to natural bird song) and while it is recognizable as bird song, it is nevertheless disturbing in its sonority. While the bird song thus reflects a predatory instinct, the children's singing reflects innocence and vulnerability. Secondly, in the school scene, Daniels only hears the children singing and does not see (or hear) the birds (the audience sees the birds gathering). Interestingly, the children's singing seems to have temporarily silenced the birds' usual "song". As such, the viewer is invited to interpret the singing performance differently to Daniels. While Daniels is blissfully unaware, the audience is held in suspense and tension, feeling further unease that the main character does not share their insight. Thirdly, the choice of song and performance has some key characteristics. The song itself has quite short stanzas and so just as the listener thinks it is coming to an end (and some sort of release will be achieved), it starts all over again. This serves to build the tension even more (particularly in the context of Daniels still being unaware). The high-pitched children's voices are also reflective of weakness (Sonnenschein, 2001), reflecting susceptibility and fragility. Additionally, although the intention is that they sing in unison, this is not achieved particularly well with deviations in pitch and timing. This serves to give the impression that while they may seem to be united against any threat, in fact they can easily be split up and thus are not particularly effective in defending themselves against the birds. This auditory sense is reproduced visually later on when individual children fail to keep up with the main group and get picked off by the birds.

Communal singing is used in a similar way in the highly violent *Dirty Harry* (Don Siegel, 1971). Set in San Francisco, the film follows Detective Harry Callahan's (Clint Eastwood) pursuit of sociopath murderer Scorpio (Andy Robinson). Callahan is portrayed as effective but violent, ignoring orders whether from his superiors or the City Mayor. Scorpio is similarly violent, but is, at times, portrayed as a victim often of Callagan's (and the system's) disregard for boundaries. In terms of overall sound design, the film's setting in the urban location of San Francisco is reflected and explored through the film's score written by Lalo Schifrin. The music is jazz-tinged with lush strings and vocals underpinned by a funk-grounded rhythm section, percussion, brass and synthesizer. Each violent scene is anticipated with music which often starts with eerie and weird sound effects, with tempo building towards, for example, a shooting.

Of most note here is the singing scene where Scorpio hijacks the school bus. When Scorpio jumps on the bus, he initially whispers to the driver "Hear me, old hag. Drive or I'll decorate this bus with your brains" before more loudly saying "Just get started, I'll tell you where". He then turns happily to the children saying "Alright, let's have some fun now" before inviting them to suggest a song to sing. Although a number of arms are raised, he singles out a small girl, who after some encouragement starts the first line of 'Old Macdonald Had a Farm' which the rest of the bus join in on enthusiastically with the next "E-I-E-I-O" line. This use of singing is unusual within the rest of the soundscape of the film, already indicating a change is about to occur for the audience. A boy at the back of the bus conducts enthusiastically, before singing the line "and on that farm he had some ducks" which cuts to the petrified driver's face. As the lines "quack quack here and a quack quack there" are heard, the bus is seen disappearing into the distance across a bridge. After an interluding scene involving the Mayor, Callahan and a telephone conversation, the bus scene is re-introduced. The sound of the children singing in the bus is mixed with traffic noise and the noise of the bus itself (though the singing is given unrealistic prominence given the visual perspective). The sound of the singing fades as the bus enters a tunnel and then upon emerging, the children are being compelled to sing "Row, row, row your boat" with less convincing enthusiasm than before. The boy at the back (previously conducting enthusiastically) puts his hand up and asks where they are going, to which Scorpio replies they are going to the ice-cream factory but anyone who doesn't want to go can get off. When two boys put their hands up, the boy who previously conducted (and now wants to go home to his mother) is struck on the head. Scorpio shouts for the children to sing, and turns back to the bus and restarts "Row, row, row your boat". As the children become too frightened to even join in, he compels them with further lines such as "Are you sick, are you sick, what is it?" and "I'm gonna kill all your mothers". Becoming increasingly irate, the lines "merrily merrily, merrily, merrily" are too high pitched for Scorpio and he struggles to even sing them.

There are some key concepts in this example of the children's voices and performance in evoking unease, discomfort and violence. Firstly, the singing in the film has greater impact by being in such stark contrast to the music in the rest of the film. Where Schifrin's score is lush and controlled, the singing performance is gritty, disturbing, unexpected and real. Secondly, the nature of the children's voices is significant (just as it is in *The Birds*). Their voices are pure and reflect innocence, while the high pitch reflects weakness and vulnerability (particularly in contrast to Scorpio's own singing as a power indicator). Thirdly, the manner in which communal singing is used by Scorpio is particularly disturbing in its discord between what the audience knows and what the children know. The initial innocence and willingness to join in (particularly with the girl starting the song and the boy conducting) quickly becomes an enforced compulsion to sing. The threat (and actual use) of violence then becomes part of that compulsion, such that the innocent performance becomes a forced act. Lastly, Scorpio's own performance brings its own disturbing element. His performance becomes increasingly angry, and at one point he cannot reach the high notes such is his inability to control the performance.

The Singing Voice's Effect on Character, Relationships and the Audience

The examples discussed above demonstrate how the central characters who use singing do so to administer control or intimidation. Feelings of discomfort and unease are evoked when the central character goes beyond the compulsion to just listen by forcing other characters to take an active part in the experience. To some extent, *American Psycho* takes this path, as those who are about to experience violence seem to need to share Bateman's in-depth appreciation of the recorded performance. Similarly, in *American Hustle*, Rosalyn Irving's son Danny has to watch her performance of 'Live and Let Die' even though it seems (in the eyes of the audience) to be an extremely disturbing spectacle. The most extreme example is obviously *Dirty Harry* where the initial willingness of the children to sing turns to compulsion with verbal abuse and physical violence being used to make them sing. This seems a particularly disturbing scenario given the innocence of the children and their previous happy-go-lucky approach to the situation. The compulsion to take part in the singing performance is therefore a violent act in itself, in its forcing of an individual to use their body in a manner which they would not necessarily wish to do at that point in time. Fundamental to the examples discussed is the performance itself, and there are a number of characteristics therein which relate to the evoked response such as pitch, texture, production style and artful (or artless) performances. Furthermore, the fact that many of the violent protagonists in these examples are comfortable in using singing as part of violence (singing is usually associated with pleasure) is disturbing.

This chapter has explored how feelings of discomfort, unease and violence can be evoked by the use of the singing voice in film. Having done so, it is clearly important to draw some key conclusions into how particular performances, songs and characters (to name just some aspects) elicit such responses. The singing performance, whether in an overly violent film or one with some disturbing or uneasy scenes, needs to be considered within the overall "sonic context" of the film – that is to say, what else happens in the rest of the film in terms of sound design, music choice and so on. For example, *The Birds* is an extremely quiet film and so the single diegetic singing performance has more impact and thus greater potential to elicit a response unique to that scene. Similarly, with *Dirty Harry*, the children's performance is in stark contrast to the lush, controlled and complex Lalo Schifrin soundtrack. In its gritty, panicked delivery, it stands out as an auditory experience totally unlike the rest of the film. Finally, in hybrid films like *American Hustle*, the use of the singing voice provides a sonic prompt for the swift change of character that happens throughout the film; where visual cues may only provide a hint at genre or narrative, sonic markers like the nuanced singing voice confirm the developing relationship and effect of character in relation to the story. Therefore, the more incongruent the singing performance is within the overall sonic context of the film, the more potential it has to elicit a response unique to that scene.

About the Authors

Dr Liz Giuffre is a Senior Lecturer in Communication at the University of Technology Sydney. She also regularly works in the national independent arts press as a journalist and commentator, including work as the regular contributing editor for *Metro* magazine, a regular contributor to *Critical Studies in Television*, and columnist for *The Conversation*.

Dr Mark Thorley's research centres on the creative industries, with particular emphasis on the role of technology. This work draws upon his background as a classically-trained musician, technologist and entrepreneur. His is a past Director of the Music Producers' Guild in the UK, and a Senior Fellow of the Higher Education Academy.

References

Barthes, R. (1977/2005) *Image, Music, Text: Essays Selected and Translated by Stephen Heath*. London: Fontana.
Chion, M. (1999) *The Voice in Cinema*. New York: Columbia University Press.
Cohan, S. (2002) "Gendered Spectacles". In *Hollywood Musicals: The Film Reader*, edited by S. Cohan, 63–66. London and New York: Routledge.
Coulthard, L. (2009) "Tarantino, Popular Music and New Hollywood Ultraviolence". *Music and the Moving Image* 2/2: 1–6.
Dyer, R. (2012) *In the Space of a Song: The Uses of Song in Film*. Abingdon, Oxon: Routledge.
Frith, S. (1995) "The Body Electric". *Critical Quarterly* 37/2: 1–10.
Gick, M. L. (2011) "Singing, Health and Well-being: A Health Psychologist's Review". *Psychomusicology: Music, Mind & Brain* 21/1-2: 1–32.
Gorbman, C. (2011) "Artless Singing". *Music, Sound & the Moving Image* 5/2: 157–71.
Greene, L. (2009) "Speaking, Singing, Screaming: Controlling the Female Voice in American Cinema". *The Soundtrack* 2/1: 63–76.
Hughes, D. (2013) "An Encultured Identity: Individuality, Expressivity and the Singing-self". *Australian Voice* 15: 13–19.
Kalinak, K. M. (2007) *How the West Was Sung: Music in the Westerns of John Ford*. California: University of California Press.
Kooijman, J. and T. Laine (2003) "American Psycho: A Double Portrait of Serial Yuppie Patrick Bateman". *Post Script* 22/3: 46–53.
Lannin, S. and M. Caley (2005) *Pop Fiction*. Bristol, UK: Intellect.
McLean, A. (1993) "'It's Only That I Do What I Love and Love What I Do': *Film Noir* and the Musical Woman". *Cinema Journal* 33/1: 3–16.
Moylan, W. (2002) *The Art of Recording: Understanding and Crafting the Mix*. Studio City, Los Angeles, CA: Focal Press.
Mundy, J. (2006) "Singing Detected: Blackpool and the Strange Case of the Missing Musical Drama". *Journal of British Cinema and Television* 3/1: 9–71.
Siefert, M. (1995) "Image/Music/Voice: Song Dubbing in Hollywood Musicals". *Journal of Communication* 45/2: 44–64.
Sonnenschein, D. (2001) *Sound Design: The Expressive Power of Music, Voice, and Sound Effects in Cinema*. Studio City, CA: Michael Wiese.

Unwin, M. M. and D. T. Kenny (2002) "The Effects of Group Singing on Mood". *Psychology of Music* 30/2: 175–85.

Wierzbicki, J. (2008) "Shrieks, Flutters, and Vocal Curtains: Electronic Sound/Electronic Music in Hitchcock's *The Birds*". *Music and the Moving Image* 1/2: 10–36.

Wood, G. (2008) "Why Do They Start to Sing and Dance All of a Sudden? Examining the Film Musical". In *The Cambridge Companion to the Musical (Second Edition)*, edited by W. Everett and P. Laird, 305–324. Cambridge: Cambridge University Press.

11 The Female Singing Voice:
Gospel, Blues, Epic Stories and Animation

Anne Power

Introduction

The emphasis on story in animated film is part of its appeal. As Ebert (1998: E5) wrote: "[Animation] is pure story, character, movement and form, without the distractions of reality or the biographical baggage of the actors". There is, in Coyle's words, the ability in animation to "order the world depicted in film in a different way – one that references and simulates 'reality' and yet surpasses it, presenting scenarios that we recognize as simultaneously other and the same" (Coyle, 2010: 5). This chapter sets out to critically evaluate the ways in which the female voice contributes to story in two animated films, *Hercules* (music by Alan Menken) and *Sita Sings the Blues* (music by composers including Harry Akst and Grant Clarke; Sam Coslow; Roy Turk and Fred Ahlert; Oscar Levant, Billy Rose and Mort Dixon; Romberg and Hammerstein II). While animated films have had substantial critiques, this chapter does not enter the debate that feminists have had with Disney films (Do Rozario, 2004; Ross, 2004; Tanner et al., 2003; Towbin et al., 2008; Wiersma, 2001). It acknowledges but does not enter the debate about the Forum on Hindu Awakening caused by protesting about *Sita Sings the Blues* (Tripathi, 2011). Instead, this chapter looks at the vocal performances that help to advance the story and even define a character's personality (Adamson, 1974).

When sound technology changed the film world, animated films embraced that change, from its earliest days using the spoken and sung voices of leading actors and singers to "voice" the characters they featured (Cooke, 2008). The focus here is on two musical genres in which female voices have been prominent in conveying emotional content, both pain and joy. Those idiomatic vocal ornaments – upward scoops or chromatic inflections – emerge in the performances of the female singers in the chosen animated films, emphasizing humorous and dramatic moments. This chapter looks at the juxtaposition of "the distinctive identifiable sound" (Cusic, 2002: 53) of gospel and blues with mythology grounded in ancient Greek and ancient Indian traditions, to provide a different lens on those stories. It commences with an analysis of the plots, with some background on the singers in the films before going on to explore the inter-connected visual and musical influences on the viewer-character relationship, critically evaluating especially the compositional elements that produce emotion in music. The chapter concludes with a discussion of what can make music memorable, with particular reference to the films analysed throughout.

The Plots – Part One

Hercules (Ron Clements and John Musker) is a 1997 animated musical fantasy film produced by Walt Disney Feature Animation. Disney animated musicals are intentionally life-affirming, with stories of hope and love overcoming adversity (Halfyard, 2010). This film is an epic story based on the legendary Greek hero, Hercules, the son of Zeus in Greek mythology. The story follows Hercules' birth; the kidnapping of Hercules as a baby by the followers of Hades, god of the Underworld; Hercules' discovery that he is the son of Zeus but no longer a god; his battle with the Hydra; his falling in love with Megara; his battle with the Titans and his decision to stay living on earth. Throughout these events, the assembled Muses function as a chorus, providing commentary on the story and allowing a period of time to elapse. In the animated film *Hercules*, the chorus consists of five female characters, the Muses of epic poetry, history, comedy, dance and tragedy. They are shown as African American women who sing in a gospel style. The singers of these roles are Lillias White, whose career on Broadway has spanned over thirty years; Vaneese Thomas whose heritage is Memphis soul, rhythm and blues (R&B) as well as gospel; Roz Ryan, another singer with a thirty-year Broadway career as a singer and comedienne; LaChanze, whose career has equally featured singing and dancing; and Cheryl Freeman, a singing actress and producer.

The Plots – Part Two

Sita Sings the Blues (Nina Paley) is a 2009 independent (indie) film based on the Ramayana epic,[1] told from Sita's perspective. Cutting across the epic story is a contemporary tale of a love affair that is breaking up. The film was directed, written, produced, designed and animated by Nina Paley. She used existing songs and a commissioned score to create an integrated aural and visual production. Paley commissioned original music from Todd Michaelson for the parts of the film where three shadow puppets tell the story of Rama and Sita. The ten songs that characterize Sita in the film are compiled from recordings that Annette Hanshaw made. Hanshaw was a singer in the late 1920s and early 1930s "jazz age",[2] using improvisation and swing rhythm. When she recorded for Columbia in the 1930s, she sang with some of the greatest musicians of the day: brass players Red Nichols and Miff Mole, pianist Adrian Rollini, jazz violinist Joe Venuti, guitarist Eddie Lang, clarinettist Benny Goodman, and the band leading Dorsey Brothers.

The story commences when Rama is banished from his kingdom for fourteen years and Sita accompanies him into the forest. The second part of the story occurs when Rama tracks a golden deer, leaving Sita alone in their forest hut and at the mercy of the marauding rival king Ravana. Sita sings of Rama and the lyric "I'll be so true to him he'll never doubt me" is painfully ironic, given Rama's suspicions later in the story. While the clarinet takes a solo, Ravana abducts Sita and she weeps bitter tears. While imprisoned in Ravana's kingdom, Sita's singing about "weepin'" reveals her sorry state. In response, Rama assembles the monkey warriors to go to save Sita.

Her joy is short-lived as Rama suspects Sita's conduct while in captivity and she goes through a trial by fire. When Rama and Sita are reconciled, there seems to be promise of a happy ending. Yet there is another twist in the tale as Rama banishes Sita because of doubts raised again by one of his subjects. Sita, pregnant with Rama's sons, is abandoned in the forest and reflects on happier times. When Rama comes back to the forest to claim his sons, Sita makes a decision to return to the womb of mother Earth.

These brief synopses of the stories prepare for the following section about the role of visual and musical influences in creating a viewer-character relationship.

Inter-connected Visual and Musical Influences in the Films

Visual and musical influences work together to affect the viewer-character relationship in animated films. Colour, lighting and design will be considered for the ways they create mood and have an impact on the viewer. Jazz ornamentation and improvisation, both rhythmically and melodically, will be considered for the ways that they invite the listener to experience emotions of joy or pain, expressing both the singer's voice and the composer's voice (Frith, 2008; Rischar, 2004). Animation is audio-visual by nature and consists of "separate images combined with continuous sound" (Brophy, 1991: 74). It operates through the "application of sound to the impression of movement in the image track" (Coyle, 2010: 10). Wells (2010) adds that sound in animation extends beyond the narrative and acts to articulate the metaphorical meaning of the animated story. In considering the layers of meaning, it is significant that these songs are socially and historically located (Toynbee, 2000). This is true both of the gospel sound that the Muses perform in *Hercules* and the distinctive "jazz age" sound of Annette Hanshaw in *Sita Sings the Blues*.

Hercules: Visual and Musical Factors

Elicitation of mood, according to Douglass and Harnden (1996), comes from the combination of a number of discrete elements including: colour, texture, design (use of line, mass and pattern), lighting, camera framing, camera angles and movement and lens focal length (74). Two of the visual factors that will be in focus here are colour and lighting. Colour affects mood by colour temperature (the spectrum of warm to cool colours) and colour saturation (domination by either warm or cool colours); for example, visual frames dominated by warm colours can suggest richness or physical warmth while frames dominated by cool colours can suggest coldness and cruelty (Douglass and Harnden, 1996). The appearance of the Muses in *Hercules* for their number 'The Gospel Truth' (Alan Menken and David Zippel, 1997) changes the colour saturation from shady blue-greys to the warm brown and yellow clay of the traditional Grecian urn. The Muses, with the tallest in the middle, are perched in the decorative oval design sitting under the rim of the urn. As they transform the border pattern into a staircase so they can descend from the vase, the colour changes to soft roses and purples, suggesting the coloured lenses in the lights of a cabaret setting, that soften the white of the Muses' flowing gowns. Purple is a colour that suggests the leadership of the gods and, in this context, the Muses are their town criers. With different lyrics about Hercules' heroism, the gowns are again flooded with colour from purple to yellow, with an occasional splash of jewel colour in sapphire blue and emerald green.

The Muses sing in the style of gospel music, borrowing the aspect of praise in that genre. According to Wald (2003), the term "gospel music" for the name of a genre circulated around 1938. The genre represented an adaptation of the music and performance styles of African American Pentecostal churches for secular entertainment, thus re-signifying gospel as popular music. The early musical styles that influenced gospel were blues, jazz, white hymnody, black hymnody and spirituals (Wise, 2004: 360). Moore (2002) also acknowledges the deep linkage of gospel and blues. Contemporary gospel vocal components include bluesy vocal runs, rhythm and blues (R&B) style vocal passages with some high belting, highly melismatic vocal passages, and substantial use of higher range and falsetto. The "gospelizing" of songs "applies African American music aesthetics including flatted notes, altered rhythmic pulses and pentatonic scales" (Robinson-Martin, 2009: 596). Moreover, Wald affirms that cultural critics today take gospel's hybridity for granted, linking it to a long and productive tradition of sonic boundary-crossing that lies at the root of all African American music (Wald, 2003: 391). The gospel sound in *Hercules* is inflected by Memphis soul, a shimmering, sultry style, featuring a driving beat on the drums. There is also influence from R&B that developed from and incorporated gospel and soul music. Composer Alan Menken had written a Broadway musical called *Leap of Faith* in 1992 in which the style was flavoured with the sounds of gospel. It is no surprise, then, that the score for Hercules "owns" the gospel style.

There are three ensembles that are the focus of this discussion: 'The Gospel Truth'; 'I Won't Say I'm In Love'; and 'A Star Is Born' (Menken, 1997). In the opening ensemble 'The Gospel Truth', there is an opportunity to provide the background to the story. Menken, in interview, talks of his goals as a composer for film and of the importance of the audience understanding the genre of the song: "Is there a compelling song moment here? What is the conceit of the song? Is it funny? Do we get it because it's ironic and funny? Or is it touching?" (Menken, 2011). In 'The Gospel Truth', individual singers share the opening verse. They sing about Zeus "taming the globe" and state that: "Though, honey, it may seem imposs'ble, That's the gospel truth". Then the group breaks into a solo call and response from the other singers. To intensify the sound, the group is answered by one singer with shouts.

In *Hercules*, the five singers often sing the penultimate chord and, before resolving to the final chord, they indulge in a long melismatic cadenza that at times is traded off among the singers. This is an authoritative ending, strong and intense. Gospel music by its nature is used to express charismatic states of emotion and belief; it is composed to express and convey those heightened emotions through quick tempos, rhythmic patterns and loud dynamics that rely on the singer's ability to breathe rapidly and "ecstatically" (Sellers, 2009). Gospel has a strong emphasis on the words. Much of the singing style is adapted to convey the text, and emphasizes sharp, often percussive consonants.

A little later in the story, the Muses become the back-up singers for the woman Megara with whom Hercules falls in love. In the song 'I Won't Say I'm In Love' (Alan Menken and David Zippel, 1997), the Muses first appear as statues in evening light with their gowns in purple shadows. Their role in this song sees them scatting "shoo doop, oooh", and not interfering. Then, abandoning any pretence at "cool", they collectively try to convince Megara that she is in love: "He's the earth and heaven to you, Try to keep it hidden, Honey, we can see right through you, Girl". In this section where they sing in harmony, the colour changes to rose and the position of the Muses changes to graduated heights from shortest to tallest, undulating and swaying viewed from the back and then again front-on. In the second verse, they move to hold up the temple's pediment (an element of Greek architecture) as they stand on columns. Again, the colour changes to rose and as the group dance becomes more energetic, there is the possibility that the shortest Muse will fall off her column. The humour does not change the sense that the Muses are positioned as knowledgeable in reading human emotions and translators of what they see for the viewer. In the final part of the song, the Muses are seen as sculptured heads on pedestals while they sing, "she won't say 'in love'" and when they return to their original statue poses, they end with "sha la la la, la la" and a deep sigh.

In the finale, the Muses sing 'A Star Is Born' (Alan Menken and David Zippel, 1997), the title words used as a motif that becomes the group response to an individual singer's call, as Hercules' "star" is set in the sky: "Gonna shout it from the mountaintops, A star is born... Honey, hit us with a halleluia, The kid came shining through, Girl". This foot-tapping finale is driven by the Muses, in their light gowns under rose and purple light again, until they jump back onto the urn. All of their appearances suggest richness, wit, undulating movement and warmth. Additionally, lighting contributes to the mood of scenes. The Muses are presented in this final song with a strong hot backlight presenting them in silhouette. Frames shot with this lighting technique suggest the warmth and glamour of the Muses.

Sita Sings the Blues: Visual and Musical Factors

Colour and textural detail in *Sita Sings the Blues* is a way of focusing on and identifying characters, as they are typically portrayed in the Ramayana epic. Rama is always blue and his blue skin symbolizes the infinite expanse of the blue sky, the ocean and the purity of the gods. He is shown bare chested and wearing a saffron dhoti (a traditional wrap around cloth). Sita is shown with an hourglass, voluptuous figure and with curling dark hair. Her rose-coloured choli (top) and skirt contrast with the "blue for boys" colour for Rama, according to the animator in interview (Lal, 2009).

The crafting of images to existing music, rather than music to images, can be successful and fit key moments in the story, as happens in *Sita Sings the Blues*. The ten songs (Sita Cue Sheet, 2009) are: 'Here We Are' (Harry Warren and Gus Khan, 1929); 'What Wouldn't I Do For That Man' (Jay Gorney and E. Y. Harburg, 1929); 'Daddy Won't You Please Come Home' (Sam Coslow, 1929); 'Who's That Knockin' At My Door' (Seymour Simons and Gus Khan, 1927); 'Mean To Me' (Fred E. Ahlert and Roy Turk, 1929); 'If You Want The Rainbow, You Must Have the Rain' (Oscar Levant, Billy Rose and Mort Dixon, 1928); 'Moanin' Low' (Ralph Ranger and Howard Dietz, 1929); 'Am I Blue' (Harry Akst and Grant Clarke, 1929); 'Lover Come Back To Me' (Sigmund Romberg and Oscar Hammerstein II, 1929); and 'I've Got a Feelin' I'm Fallin'' (Harry Link, Fats Waller and Billy Rose, 1929). The selection of the songs is consequently focused on the narrative.

The first song, 'Here We Are', expresses happiness. The vocal tone reflects cheerfulness and warmth and accompanies the animated images of Rama and Sita strolling through the forest. Muted trumpet, trombone and clarinet alternate to answer the short vocal phrases. The song occurs after Rama has been banished from his kingdom for fourteen years. Sita accompanies him into the forest and the lyrics that rhyme having no "bankful" with "still thankful" are zanily appropriate, expressing contentment with an ordinary life. The backgrounds are the Indian palace silhouettes, from which Rama and Sita depart, and subsequently the forest through which they make their way. This is vector art created and animated in Flash. The style is sometimes referred to as "paper-doll style" animation within Flash. The characters are made up of the body pieces (head, torso, upper arm, lower arm, hand and so on) that are hinged from one pose to another (as opposed to Keyframe animation that can use head rotations or body rotations and more complex posing). The animator layers the background to give it depth. Instead of just using a flat image of a background, she has the rows of trees moving at different speeds to give the illusion of depth. The rain of flowers as Rama and Sita are alone precedes another series of effects where both synchronized birds and purple-horned demons (rakshasas), which have been desecrating the ritual fires of the wise men, are despatched by Rama's arrows. Design and colour create interesting sensations of time and space. The singer Annette Hanshaw's gentle use of slides and vocal improvisation at the end of the song are crowned by her trademark "that's all" as she signs off.

There are nine other songs, six of which will be discussed in detail. The story unfolds when Rama leaves the hut, where he and Sita are living, to hunt in the forest. While Sita is alone, many-headed Ravana sneaks up. He is shown with a set of golden turban-like crowns, driving a chariot and heading off with Sita into the sunset. In 'Daddy Won't You Please Come Home', the setting is Ravana's palace where Sita is held captive. Musically, it emphasizes a yearning quality by building ascending arpeggio figures in the melody line that outline the tonic ninth chord (at "night after night"), straining upward and then falling away. As the song moves to its statement "I'm so lonesome", there are semibreve notes decorated by the singer with jazz ornamentation (mordents). Trumpet, clarinet and tenor saxophone take alternate solos to lead into a reprise. The harmonies, along with the singer's sliding articulation, are typical of the sophistication brought to the blues in the 1920s and 30s (Stroman and Michael, 1990). The blues is an emotional response and Palmer states: "The battering that the human spirit takes when it strains to ascend towards its true purpose: this is the subject matter of the blues" (Palmer, 1976: 55–56). A quirky visual feature of the song is a tap dancing moon on top of the walled garden. The monkey god, Hanuman (Rama's helper, shown as blue) listens to Sita playing clarinet. The song is her message to Rama, to be sent via his helper. When Hanuman delivers the message, Rama immediately summons the monkey warriors to rescue Sita.

In the song 'Who's That Knockin' At My Door?' where Rama comes to save Sita from Ravana, the mood is upbeat with Sita's lyric "I just had a sort of feeling this morning, Something good was gonna happen today". She vocally decorates long notes with jazz ornamentation intensifying the emotion of excitement. The interlude continues the rhythmic playfulness in the short subdivisions of the beat: "It can't be the mailman, the coalman, the iceman, they've been here today… If my sweetie's there outside, my arms and heart are open wide". An extended break gives the army time to attack. Rama bursts through the door and numbers of demons are shown falling in the face of Rama's arrows. The words "chop", "bash" and "whomp" are shown in lurid green, yellow and orange as the armies fight. As the song continues, flights of spears, bits of armour and eventually the many heads of Ravana are seen flying above the wall which guards Sita. The reprise of the interlude while the monkey warriors lay waste to Ravana's followers comically contrasts Sita's joy with the decimated Ravana and his army. The animated figures exemplify the typical content of the blues: "In their articulation of desire and joy... the blues songs acknowledged that the singers lived in their bodies and in the world that surrounded them... the very foundation of subjectivity" (Antelyes, 1994: 217).

Nevertheless, when Rama frees Sita, he rejects her as his wife. The song 'Mean To Me' shows her by day and night, with only Hanuman the monkey god for company. The progression that dominates 'Mean To Me' is a melodic sequence, richly harmonized with chromatic 7th and 9th chords and coming to rest on an appoggiatura on "sighing". The structure is simple with eight bars repeated. As Oliver (1960) wrote, "In the blues were to be found... the triumphs and miseries that were shared by all, yet private to one" (p. 32). Sita's suffering through Rama's "mean" behaviour is presented as an aspect of universal experience. In the instrumental break, a monkey band is shown on a raised dais, while Rama builds a pyre for Sita's trial by fire. The enduring image is of orange flames with Sita in the centre still singing and fantasizing about Rama and everything that has happened to her.

A stylized arrangement of grey clouds and a sun which registers surprise provide the images for the next part of the story. Sita is shown beside a lake, picking pink lotus blooms. Then with Rama and Hanuman, she is shown flying on a huge bird and looking out to the rainbow that guides them back to Rama's palace. However, another twist to her story takes place when Sita, now pregnant, is turned out from Rama's palace. The sun looks very bemused, the moon sheds tears and Rama turns an icy shoulder. Sita is driven by Rama's brother into the forest, up mountains and across the river.

While she waits to deliver her two sons, Sita sings 'Am I Blue'. Significantly, she is pictured blue – not Rama's sky blue but a deep midnight blue. When her sons are born, they emerge with the sky-blue colour of their father. The music of 'Am I Blue' commences with a simple melodic device of increasing the leaping interval from a fifth to a sixth and then a seventh, and using the flattened VIth chord to lead to the dominant 7th and tonic. The second half of the song, emphasizing contrast with the past, modulates to the dominant's relative minor and includes an attractive jazz violin solo. When the first eight-bar melody returns it appears in the accompaniment with a counter melody for the singer. The words rise and fall in the natural way that you would speak them (Roberts, 1972). As the song continues, there is increased improvisation on the melody, exploring higher pitches. This change is in response to the change in the lyrics and the emotion of the song.

Once again pictured in a forest hut, Sita's song is 'Lover Come Back To Me' and the images are of Sita, imagining herself in a castle tower and being rescued by Rama. The song depicts Sita grieving for the absence of her lover. It has become a standard that jazz artists are still re-interpreting. In the middle minor key section the text emphasizes loneliness, with the aching pain and emptiness of the song spiralling upwards in the song without resolution. Visually the change in colour temperature is shown by the change from the rain of brightly coloured flowers, when Sita and Rama were first walking together through the forest, to the shadowy browns and greys of dead leaves. Even the return to the original tonality, with some up-tempo jazz rhythms, brings no relief.

'I've Got a Feelin' I'm Fallin'' explores chromaticism freely in the melody as well as the chordal progression. The musical improvisations accumulate in the finale of this last song. The melody intentionally suggests being free from tonal conventions. Carol Oja (2000) has called this "jazz age" period of the 1920s a marketplace for modernism, where audiences were receptive to diminished and augmented chords that provided the sensations of harmonic tension and release. In the accompaniment, players move in and out of improvised solos. When Sita calls on Mother Earth to take her back, lightning flashes, light beams shine upward from a hidden crater and the Mother Earth goddess emerges as a translucent white figure to whom Sita runs. Quaintly, Sita's body undulations are now upside down as she falls down into her future state. In the instrumental break, Mother Earth dances, waving multiple arms and then, at the end of the song, she and Sita disappear behind the hills.

Conclusion

In both gospel and some forms of blues, female vocalists have taken a prominent role. However, it is the unexpected juxtaposition of elements when these genres are explored in the chosen films that make for memorability. It takes a quirky imagination to pair gospel singing with the Greek myth that is being retold in the *Hercules* story, especially when combined with the swaying movements of gospel singers. The combination makes for a new and somewhat surprising impact. The movements are musically emphasized by the idiomatic vocal ornamentation of slides and scoops. The female voices command attention. They can convey the story powerfully, with shouts and high belting; and they can convince characters to follow their hearts, with empathetic humming and scatting.

The female singers in *Hercules* not only contribute glamour and humour but also an authoritative presence. They provide a link with the artistry of the Grecian period in representing ceramic decoration; and they read the emotions of the characters for the viewer. They capture what Allen (1987) calls the sound, style and spirit of gospel music. The core elements of the sound include specific scales, flatted notes and many varieties of melodic and textual improvisation. The style is stamped by the way the core elements are used, whether in melismas, humming, scatting or melodic alterations of the melody. The music stays in the memory as a result of the level of emotion and energy of the performance, shown in the rhythmic intensity of the music and the vibrant treatment of words.

In *Sita* the quality of Hanshaw's voice makes a memorable contribution to the film. Her interactions with the jazz musicians in the tracks selected for the film demonstrate the musical ability she acquired in radio broadcasting. She understood her role in the band and shared the limelight with instrumental soloists. Tommy Dorsey is reported to have said of her that she was a musician's singer (Werner, 2000). Hanshaw was a capable pianist and could accompany herself, so it can be assumed that her knowledge of chords allowed her the theoretical basis on which to vocally improvise. The range of the songs discussed above is very similar, with the lowest note of all being a Bb3 (B-flat below middle C), and the highest an E5, a tenth above middle C. This mezzo range allows the singer to sound warm and entertaining. In commenting on film voices, Turk (1994) refers to the 1930s "American public's and, more precisely, the American male public's ambivalence towards the trained female voice" (104). By contrast, Hanshaw sings with markedly less classical vocal production, to which untrained female vocalists could relate. It is this direct quality that enables the Ramayana to speak in a fresh way. The improvisations, both rhythmic and textual, emphasize the lyrics about love, happiness, loss and pain. What is noteworthy is the emotional quality of the music enmeshed with the animated story.

An important factor here is that Hanshaw's recording technique using the technology of the microphone did not require powerful projection. With amplification, a singer could be heard above a band "without having to operate close to full volume and indeed could still project close to a whisper" (Johnson, 2000: 93). Yet Toynbee makes the point that "for all its apparent restraint, crooning *is* a projective technique... to reach forward by means of the technical apparatus to the individuated ear lobes of a mass audience listening at home on radio or phonograph" (2000: 77). This was the ability that Hanshaw possessed. She seems to deliver her lyrics as if to one other person through the medium of the recording. In a sense, the microphone shaped her singing style. Remarkably, she sang only between late 1926 and early 1934. In that time she mastered the recording technique that enabled her to communicate effectively with her audience. The power in this female vocalizing lies in the intimacy of the voice. The vocal ornamentation, whether rhythmically playful or harmonically inventive, emphasizes the song's mood and the story content.

In these two films, the singers have followed in long-standing traditions of two rich musical genres. Collectively or as a solo, they perform many functions, at one time revealing the inner thoughts of characters and at another defining a character's personality. Over all this, the female vocalists provide music that is integral to the impact of the chosen films. Whether the sound is heavy gospel belt or intimate improvisation, it is the female vocal that makes the music and film memorable.

About the Author
Anne Power is Associate Professor in the School of Education and Centre for Educational Research at Western Sydney University. Her research interests include music education, research methods, and leadership qualities that emerge through service learning. Her work with service learning and disadvantaged students, especially in First Nations communities, converges with themes of creativity. Anne has written on contemporary Australian opera, on approaches to singing in snapshots of Australian contexts, on developing a pedagogy for the voice across the K-10 curriculum, and she is an advocate for care of the voice in music education.

Notes
1. The *Ramayana* is a Sanskrit epic poem, regarded as one of the great works of both Indian literature and Hindu literature. With a focus on the duties of relationships, it tells the story of Rama (a manifestation of the Hindu supreme-god Vishnu), whose wife Sita is abducted by Ravana, the king of Lanka (present-day Sri Lanka). The main purpose of the story is to demonstrate the path of right living (dharma) for all creatures (see Narayan, 2012).
2. The "Jazz Age" was a term coined by F. Scott Fitzgerald, for his *Tales of the Jazz Age*, a title he decided on in 1922 and it was a feature of the 1920s, ending with the Great Depression (see West, 2002).

References

Adamson, L. (1974) "Suspended Animation". In *Film Theory and Criticism: Introductory Readings*, edited by G. Mast and M. Cohen, 391–400. New York: Oxford University Press.

Allen, R. (1987) "Singing in the Spirit: Ethnography of Gospel Performance in New York City's African American Church Community". Doctoral dissertation, University of Pennsylvania, cited in T. Robinson-Brown (2009) "Performance Styles and Musical Characteristics of Black Gospel Music". *Journal of Singing* 65/5: 595–99.

Antelyes, P. (1994) "Red Hot Mamas: Bessie Smith, Sophie Tucker and the Ethnic Maternal Voice in American Popular Song". In *Embodied Voices*, edited by L. C. Dunn and N. A. Jones, 212–29. Cambridge: Cambridge University Press.

Brophy, P. (1991) "The Animation of Sound". In *The Illusion of Life: Essays on Animation*, edited by A. Cholodenko, 67–112. Sydney: Power Publications.

Cooke, M. (2008) *A History of Film Music*. Cambridge: Cambridge University Press.

Coyle, R., ed. (2010) *Drawn to Sound: Animation Film Music and Sonicity*. London: Equinox.

Cusic, D. (2002) "The Development of Gospel Music". In *The Cambridge Companion to Blues and Gospel Music*, edited by A. Moore, 44–60. Cambridge: Cambridge University Press.

Do Rozario (2004) "The Princess and the Magic Kingdom: Beyond Nostalgia, the Function of the Disney Princess". *Women's Studies in Communication* 27/1: 34–59.

Douglass, J. and G. Harnden (1996) *The Art of Technique: An Aesthetic Approach to Film and Video Production*. Boston: Allyn & Bacon.

Ebert, R. (1998). "*Mulan* Captures Best of Disney Magic". *Albuquerque Journal* (June): E5.

Frith, S. (2008) "The Voice as a Musical Instrument". In *Music, Words and Voice: A Reader*, edited by M. Clayton, 65–71. Manchester, UK: Manchester University Press.

Halfyard, J. (2010) "Everybody Scream". In *Drawn to Sound: Animation Film Music and Sonicity*, edited by R. Coyle, 25–39. London: Equinox.

Johnson, B. (2000) *The Inaudible Music: Jazz, Gender and Australian Modernity*. Sydney: Currency Press.

Lal, M. (2009) "Malashri Lal in Conversation with Nina Paley". http://insearchofsita.blogspot.com.au/2009/12/malashri-lal-in-conversation-with-nina.html

Menken, Alan [interview] (2011) "Tangled, Movies Scores, Musicals, Enchanted 2, Snow Queen and more". Simon Brew (interviewer). http://www.denofgeek.com/movies/725326/alan_menken_interview_tangled_movie_scores_musicals_enchanted_2_snow_queen_and_more.html (accessed January 2, 2014).

Moore, A. (2002) "Surveying the Field: Our Knowledge of Blues and Gospel Music". In *The Cambridge Companion to Blues and Gospel Music*, edited by A. Moore, 1–12. Cambridge: Cambridge University Press.

Narayan, R. K., ed. (2012) *The Ramayana*. New York: Penguin Classics.

Oja, C. (2000) *Making Music Modern: New York in the 1920s*. London: Oxford University Press.

Oliver, P. (1960) *The Meaning of the Blues*. New York: Collier Books.

Palmer, T. (1976) *All You Need Is Love: The Story of Popular Music*. London: Weidenfeld & Nicolson.

Rischar, R. (2004) "A Vision of Love: An Etiquette of Vocal Ornamentation in African American Popular Ballads of the Early 1990s". *American Music* 22/3: 407–443.

Roberts, J. Storm (1972) *Black Music of Two Worlds*. Michigan: Praeger.

Robinson-Martin, T. (2009) "Performance Styles and Musical Characteristics of Black Gospel Music". *Journal of Singing* 65/5: 595–99.

Ross, D. (2004) "Escape from Wonderland: Disney and the Female Imagination". *Marvels and Tales* 18/1: 53–66.

Sellers, C. (2009) "'I Sing Because I'm Free': Developing a Systematic Vocal Pedagogy for the Modern Gospel Singer". Unpublished Doctor of Musical Arts Thesis, Ohio State University. https://etd.ohiolink.edu/!etd.send_file?accession=osu1249920108&disposition=inline (accessed May 28, 2020).

Sita Cue Sheet (2009) https://www.sitasingstheblues.com/license.html#cue-sheet (accessed May 28, 2020).

Stroman, S. and R. Michael (1990) *Creative Jazz Education*. London: Stainer and Bell.

Tanner, L., S. Haddock, T. Schindler Zimmerman and L. Lund (2003) "Images of Couples and Families in Disney Feature-length Animated Films". *American Journal of Family Therapy* 31: 355–73.

Towbin, A., S. Haddock, T. Schindler Zimmerman, L. Lund and L. Tanner (2008) "Images of Gender, Race, Age and Sexual Orientation in Disney Feature-length Animated Films". *Journal of Feminist Family Therapy* 15/4: 19–44.

Toynbee, J. (2000) *Making Popular Music: Musicians, Creativity and Institutions*. London: Arnold.

Tripathi, S. (2011) "Sita Sings the Blues: Film Causes a Stir in Queens". http://www.thedailybeast.com/articles/2011/07/24/sita-sings-the-blues-hindu-film-causes-a-stir-in-queens.html#url=/articles/2011/07/24/sita-sings-the-blues-hindu-film-causes-a-stir-in-queens.html (accessed January 8, 2014).

Turk, E. (1994) "Deriding the Voice of Jeanette McDonald: Notes on Psychoanalysis and the American Film Musical". In *Embodied Voices*, edited by L. C. Dunn and N. A. Jones, 103–119. Cambridge: Cambridge University Press.

Wald, G. (2003) "From Spirituals to Swing: Sister Rosetta Tharpe and Gospel Crossover". *American Quarterly* 55/3: 387–416.

Wells, P. (2010) "Halas and Batchelor's Sound Decisions: Musical Approaches in the British Context". In *Drawn to Sound: Animation Film Music and Sonicity*, edited by R. Coyle, 40–59. London: Equinox.

Werner, J. (2000) "Annette Hanshaw". http://annettehanshaw.tripod.com/page1.htm (accessed January 8, 2014).

West, J., ed. (2002) *F. Scott Fitzgerald Tales of the Jazz Age*. Cambridge: Cambridge University Press.

Wiersma, B. A. (2001) "The Gendered World of Disney: A Content Analysis of Gender Themes in Full-length Animated Disney Feature Films". Doctoral dissertation, South Dakota State University. *Dissertation Abstracts International, A: The Humanities and Social Sciences* 61/12: A4973.

Wise, R. (2004) *Defining African American Gospel Music by Tracing its Historical and Musical Development from 1900 to 2000*. Columbus, OH: Raise Publishing.

12 From Despicable to Happy:
Animated Vocality in the Evolution of Felonius Gru

Veronica Stewart and Diane Hughes

Introduction

In contrast to more traditional filmic song inclusions, the synchronization of singer-songwriter works presents a form of authorship in which a particular artist's vocality may be clearly evident. The following discussion focuses on situating such "vocality" in relation to animated characters and storylines. It specifically explores the "animated vocality" and creative processes of Pharrell Williams in the *Despicable Me* film series. The research draws on several analyses including song content, vocal nuances, musical stylisms, mediating technologies and related media interviews. Throughout the discussion, the interrelatedness of vocality (vocal, musical and mediated characteristics) and artistic identity is detailed through a purposively developed vocality framework which enables the communicative effect of animated vocality to be analysed and explored.

The chapter begins by introducing the concepts of vocality, originality in song and related filmic intelligibility. We then discuss the relevance of vocality in film before defining the term, *animated vocality*. This term underpins the development of the framework used to analyse the vocality of artist, Pharrell Williams, in the film series of *Despicable Me* (Chris Renaud and Pierre Coffin, 2010), *Despicable Me 2* (Chris Renaud and Pierre Coffin, 2013) and *Despicable Me 3* (Pierre Coffin and Kyle Balda, 2017). The discussion concludes with the ways in which animated singer vocality may heighten emotional expression and provide insight into character ideation and traits, and associated narrative.

Theorizing Vocality

In a broad sense, *vocality* may be defined as vocal expression that encompasses vocal utterances and sounds. These may include the idiosyncratic nuances, prosodic components and musical proclivities of a particular singer. However, vocality also expands the concept of "vocalization"[1] in its inclusion of other aspects such as enculturation and acculturation (Hughes, 2013; 2014). In a discussion on vocality and identity, Meizel (2011) reasons that vocality encompasses "all of the physiological, psychoacoustic, and socio-political dynamics that impact our perception of ourselves and each other" (267). It can therefore be argued that a singer's vocality is representative of the individual singer and includes sociocultural contexts, personal experiences and artistic intent. Because of the multiplicity of influences that inform a particular vocality, and as the voice is physically embodied, vocality is both intrapersonally responsive and emotive. As such, vocality can also be used to encompass and frame "metaphor and meaning, style and content, idea and performance" (Meizel, 2011: 269). Furthermore, vocality connects singing and song by linking "music in language to language in music" (Feld et al., 2004: 328).

In an article situating context-dependent choral vocality, Tongson (2011) initially discusses the pursuit and portrayal of "a so-called pure vocality" (230) that, in reality television, relates to "the fantasy of an amateur voice without studio trappings, a voice with raw, unbridled talent" (ibid.). Here, Tongson alludes to the appeal and recognition of the acoustic sonic properties and capabilities of the individual singer. Interestingly, in her subsequent discussion on choral vocality, Tongson incorporates the relevance of echo and "its institutional associations – to schools, churches, and other sites...as [settings] for collective vocal virtuosity" (2011: 231). While not discounting the relevance of collaboration within this vocality, the function of echo to the singing collective serves as a mediating factor. Facilitated by hard, reflective surfaces in reverberant spaces, such echo aids auditory perception of both the individual and the collective within the shared experience of communal singing. Vocality may therefore be extended to include the context in which it is engaged or through which it is mediated as both impact on how the singing voice is realized or heard.

In relation to the singer-songwriter vocality, communicative capability is inclusive of the individualized creative process and the realization of original musical works. Contemporary singer-songwriters encompass stylistic and identifying traits that include elements of tonality, musicality, vocal skill, personal characteristics and associated image. Such vocality is well suited to signifying character traits in film. It is also malleable in delivering narrative and associated characterization through uniquely and purposively composed songs.

Additionally, developments in popular culture musics[2] (Hughes, 2010) have led to myriad ways in which songs may be created and disseminated. The democratization of technologies (Hughes et al., 2016: 1–16) affords contemporary singer-songwriters with a range of instrumental choices, music production techniques and vocal processes (effects and treatments). These technologies may be used to inform and influence creative practices and outcomes (Hughes, 2015; Hughes and Evans, 2018). Discussion of a contemporary vocality must therefore also consider the mediated singing voice in which technology is utilized to achieve both filmic intelligibility and a resultant aesthetic. A range of technologies has the capability to afford "mediating modalities" (Burnard, 2012: 223) and the ensuing potential to impact the ways in which an overall vocality may be realized and heard.

Cumulatively, and for this discussion, vocality is not delimited by the acoustic voice and its properties. Furthermore, in instances where the artist is also the creator of the musical work/song, there is potential for intrapersonal connectivity and heightened communicative capability. In this context, it is relevant to consider Chion's concept of *vococentrism* (Chion, 1994: 5–6) in which voice is highlighted in film through its recording, resultant intelligibility and effective delivery. The commissioning of a particular singer-songwriter for film reflects vococentrism through its potential for vocal, along with creative and artistic, prominence. Vocality in this discussion is therefore presented as a complex performative construct of the singing voice inclusive of personal, vocal, musical, lyrical, creative and mediated markers. Such concepts function as "perceptual markers for deeply intertwined ideas about music and identity" (Meizel, 2011: 267).

Animated Vocality

The potential for vocality to align with narrative and character is vast. In the context of spoken voice and animation, actors are selected for traits that will facilitate the realization of character. Devoid of other aspects of direct human communication and associated performativity, such as gesture, body movement and facial expressions, actors in animation portray characters solely through the voice. While there is arguably a difference between the audible dimensions of character and the singing voice, the latter is capable of communicating beyond spoken capabilities. As Frith (1998) asserts, singing enables "two different sorts of meaning-making" (187) through its musical and lyrical components. Furthermore, the singing voice provides a uniquely musical, emotive and relatable dimension. As such, it is well suited for use in film in ways that may underpin or complement character, and/or express narrative through diegetic and non-diegetic inclusions. Equally, and as Moore (2001) states, it is the allure of the singing voice that is "the primary link between the artist and the listener, being the instrument shared by both" (Moore, 2001: 185). Frith (1998) extends the concept of relatable performativity by including audience centric responses such as "singing along, moving our throat and chest muscles appropriately – but also emotionally and psychologically, taking on (in fantasy) *the vocal personality*" (Frith, 1998: 198; original emphasis) of what is being sung.

It is the notion of "vocal personality" that directly correlates to vocality in animation. Coyle and Fitzgerald (2010) discussed the use of "generic [Broadway] techniques" (223) and highlighted the relevance of song as a focal point that "[brings] the studio aesthetic of Hollywood together with the musical-theatre style of Broadway" (ibid.). In doing so, Coyle and Fitzgerald emphasized the use of Broadway, musical theatre influenced songs and vocal delivery featured in *The Little Mermaid*

(Ron Clements and John Musker, 1989) particularly in relation to 'Part of Your World' (Howard Ashman and Alan Menken, 1989):

> As well as moving the story forward, the catchy songs contribute in a significant way to the emotional and narrative flow of the movie... All aspects of the music are driven by the lyrics, and the melody... The vocal delivery is theatrical and yearning, including extensive rubato, and alternates between singing and half-spoken delivery (Coyle and Fitzgerald, 2010: 230).

It is therefore through musical theatre styled songs, with their respective musical and expressive devices, that both singer and character vocalities can be combined in animation.

Aside from the potential commercial interests of assigning a popular singer-songwriter to a particular film, aligning the vocality of a singer-songwriter with a film's context, characterization and intent warrants consideration. Typically, the synchronization of existing songs may be an easier option for animated film. However, the inclusion of crafted songs promotes the creative ethos and originality of the animated score. The vococentric-animated production may be extended to include musical components that align with a particular artist vocality. The emotive vocality of the singer-songwriter can be responsive to or influenced by enhancing or complementing a character/narrative (see Figure 1). In this way, the transition from artist to animated vocality requires an influenced, partially adapted or modified, mediated vocality.

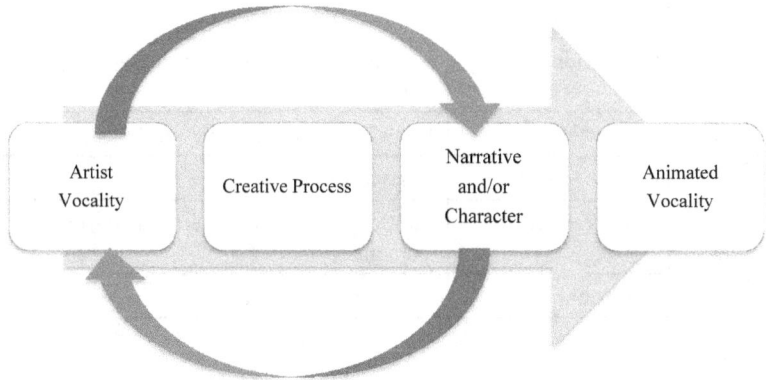

Figure 1: From artist to animated vocality

Framing and Analysing Animated Vocality

For analytical purposes, the framework outlined in Table 1 is used to determine the ways that vocality may be evident and utilized through the creation and synchronization of original songs in animated film. The framework draws on the concept of the "perceptual markers" (Meizel, 2011: 267) that are evident through the singing voice. This concept is developed here to include vocal, musical and mediated markers; the latter encompasses identified character and/or narrative markers used in animation. Table 1 offers a range of components that are contextually aligned to their associated markers.

Table 1: Animated vocality framework

Context	Markers	Components
Vocal	Timbre	Vocal tone, quality and individual expression
	Registration	Use of distinct vocal registers (such as chest or head registration[3]), or a blending of both
	Range	Extensive or limited; tessitura
	Nuances	Individual characteristics, sounds or utterances
	Expression	Dynamics (volume), phrasing and emotive elements
	Lyrics	Lyrical content (such as personal, relational or representative)
	Prosody	Spoken elements, metre and rhyme
Musical	Style	Nuances
	Accompaniment	Instrumentation
	Expression	Tempo; dynamics; song key
Mediated	Process(es)	Collaboration; influences
	Production	Vocal processing; technologies; effects; diegetic/non-diegetic
	Aesthetic	Resultant production and spatial qualities
	Artistic intent	Creative aim(s)
	Characterization	Additional or different persona and/or "personality"
	Narration	Elements of storytelling

The *Despicable Me* Film Series

Despicable Me (2010), *Despicable Me 2* (2013) and *Despicable Me 3* (2017) is a series of animated films produced by Illumination Entertainment and distributed by Universal Pictures. The first two films were directed by Chris Renaud and Pierre Coffin; the third film was directed by Pierre Coffin and Kyle Balda. *Despicable Me* (2010) traces the softening of the "super-villain" and protagonist Felonius Gru (or Gru) through the introduction and subsequent adoption of three orphaned children – Margo, Edith and Agnes. The second film, *Despicable Me 2* (2013), further explores the themes of finding love and prioritizing family relationships. The film depicts Gru's relationship with secret agent, Lucy Wilde, which develops alongside Gru's protection of his adoptive daughters from the film's antagonist, El Macho. The third film, *Despicable Me 3* (2017), extends the concept of family through the introduction of Gru's long lost brother, Dru. Gru's evolution and reform is strengthened by themes of family connection and a supposed retirement from villainhood.[4]

A focus on voice played a significant role in the development of Gru's initial characterization. Steve Carell, cast as the spoken voice of Gru, devised a distinct vocal accent and spoken vocality for the role. Producer, Chris Meledandri, explained that in the development of Gru's spoken voice Carell observed that "great villains in movies have really memorable voices so [Carell] started to play with different vocal approaches that involved accents".[5] In this way, the spoken vocality influenced the characterization of Gru. In *Despicable Me 3* (2017), Carell was also tasked with acting the voice of Gru's brother, Dru.[6] Vococentric elements were further highlighted throughout the film series by the vocality of Pharrell Williams in the creation and performance of original songs.[7]

Pharrell Williams

Pharrell Williams, commonly known by the mononym, Pharrell, is a multi-disciplinary contemporary artist. He is known primarily for his singing, songwriting and music production.[8] In order to frame Williams' particular vocality, the following section discusses his vocality in relation to both his artistry and songwriting. The analysis includes vocal, musical and mediated markers that include pop, jazz, R&B and hip-hop influences. The section concludes with an introduction to Williams' animated vocality.

Vocal, Musical and Mediated Contexts

Williams' primary musical context is in the creation and production of upbeat songs/music. An analysis of his recordings reveals a distinct vocal signature, and stylistic nuances with inherent hip-hop and jazz influences. In an interview on his creative practice, Williams noted that his childhood musical influences included Earth, Wind and Fire, Michael Jackson and Stevie Wonder.[9] Additional musical influences were identified in relation to his exposure to different types of chords and jazz voicings: "As a kid I grew up on major 7ths and minor 7ths and all those, you know, sophisticated jazz chords and groovy at the time too. So that made me pretty much always appreciate that type of chord".[10] Vocally, Williams' singing showcases a range of influences and enculturation. His particular aesthetic includes a generally high pitched, light higher range, sung over R&B, soul, pop and hip-hop music production. This can be heard in songs such as 'Frontin' (Pharrell Williams, Chad Hugo and Shawn Carter, 2003) and 'Angel' (Pharrell Williams, 2006). Both songs showcase Williams' typical vocal signature in which he combines rhythmic/rapping sensibilities with singing. Both songs engage melodic lines that are well paced, and combine harmonies and answering phrases; yet, at times Williams' phrasing is almost speech-like in delivery. At other times, he uses melodic and fast singing evident in the use of vocal ornamentation.[11] Utilizing the vocality framework introduced earlier, a synopsis of Williams' vocality is offered in Table 2.

Table 2: Vocality framework: Pharrell Williams

Context	Markers	Components
Vocal	Timbre	Usually light
	Registration	Uses both upper and lower registration, with some spoken elements
	Range	Extensive vocal range that includes lower range through to higher range
	Nuances	Singing is often delivered in the upper range; rhythmic patterns evident
	Expression	Often with short phrasing as opposed to long, sustained sounds/phrases
	Lyrics	Interpretative; expressive
	Prosody	Spoken elements, percussive rhythmic voice use
Musical	Style	Hip-hop, urban music, some rock and jazz influences
	Accompaniment	Mostly music production; beats
	Expression	Mostly upbeat or fast paced; energetic
Mediated	Process(es)	Individual; collaborative
	Production	Vocal processing; effects
	Aesthetic	Balance of vocals and musical instrumentation
	Artistic intent	Artistry that includes singing, songwriting, music production

Williams' Animated Vocality
An analysis of Pharrell Williams' involvement in the *Despicable Me* films provides insight into the synergies of Williams' vocality with the additional mediated areas of characterization and narrative. Throughout the synchronization of his songs, Williams' distinctive vocality is evident. All films feature songs written by Wil-

liams including: 'Despicable Me' (2010), 'Fun, Fun, Fun' (2010), 'Prettiest Girls' (2010), 'Just a Cloud Away' (2013), 'Happy' (2013), 'There's Something Special' (2017) and 'Doowit' (2017). These songs were selected and analysed for discussion due to the encompassed vocality and the evolution of Gru. For the purpose of this chapter, the songs discussed are a combination of filmic versions as well as the complementary songs as heard in each film's respective soundtrack. Each song version (underscore and film soundtrack) is identical except where noted. Film cues (00:00:00) are provided and refer to movie scenes underscored by the songs discussed; song cues (00:00) refer to the soundtrack album version.

Despicable Me (Renaud and Coffin, 2010)
The Villain
In *Despicable Me*, the protagonist, Gru, is introduced almost as Williams' singing voice is audible (00:03:15–00:05:34).[12] Here, Gru is walking through a park (00:03:15) as whistling is heard in a derivative melodic form of the movie theme track 'Despicable Me' (Williams, 2010). Gru proceeds to enter a local café in quest of his morning coffee, only to find himself annoyed by the customer line up (see Figure 2). When Gru enters the café (00:04:01), Williams' voice is heard, singing the first few lines of 'Despicable Me'. The lyrics of the song's hook (00:04:01–00:04:23) are reflective of Gru's "cranky" mood. The melodic line is sung as a single note rhythmically, repetitively and assertively on each syllable. The vocal context is subdued and speech-like which is particularly evident during slightly spoken sighs (00:04:21; 00:05:21; 00:05:32). There is a clear combination of simple voiced (sung) and unvoiced (whistling and sigh) sounds, which have been carefully crafted to underscore the narrative. Williams reportedly claimed that he had "never made a song about having a bad day and being in a super bad mood"[13] and perhaps this is reflected in Williams' intentional use of a distinctive and almost monotonal lower vocal register. The vocal and musical context of the verse uses a repetitive melody that is effected (for example, at 00:29–00:49). The verses are sung with straight tone (for example, at 00:34–00:41). Interestingly, and as the song progresses, Williams is joined by a "choir" of higher pitched voices of children singing the hook in a similar, ambivalent manner (for example, at 00:49–01:10).

According to the movie's producer, Chris Meledandri, Gru is "a sarcastic, sometimes nasty, curmudgeonly super villain".[14] During a montage where Gru reminisces about his childhood (00:53:36–00:53:54), the negative influences of Gru's mother, who failed to provide him with attention and affection, become apparent. This is despite Gru's desperate attempts to show his mother a string of clever ideas and inventions. The children's chorus described above also complements the childhood Gru as the younger voices add to the sense of innocence that Gru displayed as a child. They also provide a stark contrast to the sounds and actions associated with "villainy".[15]

'Despicable Me' was produced and written as the theme track of the movie (and the film franchise). Its lyrical content constantly refers to the film and narrative, and the hook is featured in its original format and is used as underscore. An instrumental version of 'Despicable Me', devoid of the voice, is also used as source music that links or "foreshadows" (Coyle, 2004: 95) later scenes. As the song was produced as the theme track, it could be further argued that the song, including its lyrical content and atypical Williams vocality, signifies a specific treatment and vocal aesthetic. This could be, as Coyle describes, an "associative" (2004: 96) connection. In this context, Coyle (ibid.) discussed that "for some audiences, the artist performing a song may have particular associations that can be used in the context of the film" (2004: 96). Using a known artist and appropriations of a particular song also serve to familiarize viewers "for specific scenes or sequences and the film as a whole" (2004: 96). This is not only apparent within the film itself, but also extends to the mediated context of film promotion and marketing. Meledandri explained that the "subversive tone"[16] of the *Despicable Me* franchise was "one of the reasons we were able to attract somebody as extraordinary as Pharrell".[17] Here, the essence of Gru's character allowed for an exploration of villainhood which was mirrored by the eclectic influences in Williams' creative works, his extensive vocal abilities and his animated vocality.

Figure 2: Screenshots of scenes underscored by the song 'Despicable Me' (Williams, 2010)

A Change in Gru
As the narrative unfolds, Gru's softer side becomes evident in his transition to being a happy, loving and doting father. To show this progression, several songs were created with a focus on joy, happiness and fun such as 'Fun, Fun, Fun' (Williams, 2010; for example, at 00:47:01) and 'Prettiest Girls' (Williams, 2010; for example, at 00:56:17). The song 'Fun, Fun, Fun' (Williams, 2010) takes on a pivotal moment in *Despicable Me* when Gru brings his soon to be daughters, albeit quite hesitantly,

to "Super Silly Fun Land". This is a theme park where Gru initially intends to leave the girls behind on a ride and rid himself of his responsibilities. As the sequence progresses from Gru's hesitation to scenes of emerging family connection (see Figure 3), Williams' usual vocality becomes evident through his high range, playful and melodic singing voice in 'Fun, Fun, Fun'. Gru is forced to stay close to the girls and, when the youngest daughter Agnes finds herself in an unfair mishap against a stallholder, Gru steps in to defend her and his transformation from heartless villain to loving father begins to unfold. Later in the film, Gru loses a potential lead for work and confesses to his staff of minions[18] that he may no longer be able to employ them. Gru's daughters then enter the scene with their piggy bank and offer their savings. A montage depicting Gru, his daughters and his mother is shown as Williams' voice is heard singing 'Prettiest Girls' that references his final transition into fatherhood.

Figure 3: Screenshots of scenes underscored by the song 'Fun, Fun, Fun' (Williams, 2010)

Despicable Me 2 (Renaud and Coffin, 2013)

It is interesting to note that segments of both 'Despicable Me' and 'Fun, Fun, Fun' (Williams, 2010) from *Despicable Me* (Renaud and Coffin, 2010) were also used in the second film, *Despicable Me 2* (Renaud and Coffin, 2013). This aids cohesiveness and correlates to the scenes of "villainhood" and mystery, and of childhood. Gru's narrative broadens to include a wife and mother for his children. This contemporaneously unfolds alongside the theme of falling in love. These themes are signified by the songs 'Just a Cloud Away' (Williams, 2013) and 'Happy' (Williams, 2013); songs that encompass and cement the theme of love, relationships and family. 'Just a Cloud Away' is heard when Gru's eldest daughter, Margot, meets a young boy, Antonio, and falls in love for the first time (00:41:24–00:42:26).[19] Interestingly, this is positioned just after Gru's daughters meet Lucy Wilde, his work partner, also for the first time. Gru's youngest daughter immediately teases Gru, and the themes of love and love interests become evident. These are supported by the "young love" context and the longing for love and family portrayed through the eyes of children. The musical context of 'Just a Cloud Away' is quick, upbeat and bright, with a lyrical pattern over a heartbeat-like bassline. The first and second verses feature a vocal call and response pattern in which Williams showcases an interesting switch between a lower vocal range and a higher/falsetto range. The chorus also utilizes this register shift. This vocal registration signifies the developing relationships which are additionally supported by repeated lyrics (00:19–00:34).

After Gru's failed attempt to date another woman, Gru receives a goodnight kiss on his cheek from Lucy Wilde. It is in this scene that the theme track for *Despicable Me 2*, 'Happy', is first heard. This song is significant as it encompasses Gru's conversion and falling in love. In a montage that depicts Gru as the opposite of his earlier, grumpier self as seen in the opening scenes of *Despicable Me* (see Figure 2), Gru is now seen dancing along the street, helping ducks cross a road and joining his community (00:54:10–00:55:18) (see Figure 4). The song is upbeat and, much like Williams' typical vocal signature, his vocality is evident in his upper range singing, and his playful, bright and energetic, 'Happy' performance. The lyrics highlight Gru's changing nature. Similar to 'Just a Cloud Away', the use of a call and response pattern is evident in the chorus. The word "happy" in each phrase is extended to underscore and harmonize with the response segment of each line. In the bridge section, Williams sings in a rhythmic and repetitive way. This is heard along with unvoiced sounds such as improvisational and speech-like utterances in the background. The word "happy" is sung by a higher voice, and slowly builds with the layering of vocal harmonies. The use of clapping, vocal sounds and percussive instruments underscores a montage of Gru dancing and engaging with his community. There is evidence of musically rhythmic diegetic sounds that include a hand clap (see still #1, Figure 4, 00:54:37) and percussive drumming (see still #2, Figure 4, 00:54:57–00:55:01). In the first example, Gru is seen giving a stranger a high-five synchronized hand clap; in the second example, he engages with a group of synchronized street drummers.

Despicable Me 3 (Coffin and Balda, 2017)

The third film in the series focuses on the opposing traits of criminality versus honour. It also features a deepening family connection between Gru, Lucy Wilde and their three adopted daughters. It is interesting to note that the song 'Despicable Me' as synchronized in the introductions of *Despicable Me* and *Despicable Me 2* is excluded in the introductory scenes of *Despicable Me 3*. Instead, the song underscores a brief scene (00:08:24–00:09:09) in which Gru and Lucy arrive at their workplace. It is here that Lucy and Gru learn that they have been relieved of their special agent duties with the Anti-Villain League (AVL).

Gru is subsequently reunited with his brother, Dru. Williams' song 'Fun, Fun, Fun' underscores the family's travel to Dru's location, Freedonia (00:23:32). The use of the song here provides a cohesive link to the earlier films and to the expand-

Figure 4: Screenshots of scenes underscored by the song 'Happy' (Williams, 2013)

ing family. Together, Gru and Dru enact a plan to steal a diamond. Gru, under his former villain guise, recovers the diamond in the hopes that he will be reinstated with the AVL. In contrast, Dru commits to the life of being a villain. Throughout the film, the subversive villainous elements are contrasted by the innocence of Gru's children and the unswerving loyalty of Lucy. For example, the song, 'There's Something Special' (Williams, 2017), underscores two scenes in which the daughters are sleeping (00:16:26–00:16:52; 01:15:36–01:16:10).[20] A light timbral quality is primarily used and there is extensive use of higher range singing. The phrasing of the verses is legato, which is coupled with a reflective delivery. There is an influence of doo-wop and soul, with call and response elements; some intricate vocal harmonies surround the main vocal line. Here, Williams' vocality is used to underscore the themes of innocence and family as it is sung from a collective perspective of Gru and Lucy in relation to their precious daughters. Interestingly, and although not purposefully written for the film, the inclusion of 'Freedom' (Pharrell Williams, Vincent Brown, Anthony Criss and Keir Lamont Gee, 2015) is used to underscore a scene in which the jailed minions are seen to embrace villainy and manipulation (00:44:07–00:44:57). It is another example of diegetic rhythmic elements as the minions click in time to the music (00:44:20–00:44:25). As the narrative continues, 'Doowit' (Williams, 2017) provides a song that promotes empowerment and motivation to rise and take action. During the song segment, the minions are seen to be escaping from jail (00:56:49–00:58:14). The song title corresponds to the words of the song's hook. The lyrics reflect the minions' limited options in their quest to break free. Williams' vocal delivery intentionally includes a mix of melodic and rhythmic singing and some "yelling" in the hook's response segments. The vocal lines are prominent in the resultant aesthetic.

Conclusion

Williams described the process of writing songs to complement animated characters and themes as a "curated experience"[21] that required the music to be of a certain mood.[22] Unlike writing purely through the lens of personal experience, Williams explained that the process was different because "there are already pillars of intention... the writer, the screenplay, what the writer of the script intended".[23] Williams' animated vocality as heard in the *Despicable Me* films is therefore collaboratively mediated to align with the created 'pillars' of intent. As our research identifies, his typical vocality is at times partially adapted ('Happy'; 'Prettiest Girls') and even modified ('Despicable Me'). If stories convey characters, then arguably vocality offers the narrative another layer of emotive expression through sung vocal sound.

Animated films such as the *Despicable Me* film series are a form of children's entertainment where themes are explored through plot, imagery, scenery, characters, actors and music/songs. In exploring the animated vocality of singer-songwriter, Pharrell Williams, we identify that his singing voice in the *Despicable Me* films moves from nuances and vocal registration that are low, seemingly villainous and ambivalent, to nuances that are upbeat, high, bright and cheerful. As the narrative progresses, Williams' purposeful atypical dark and heavy vocal tone segues to his more typical light and brighter tonality. Both tonalities are relatable for child audiences, with the lighter tonality being non-threatening and the darker tone representing villainous qualities. For the analyses, we have specifically selected Williams' songs and performance from the *Despicable Me* series that highlight these contrasting tonalities. While Williams does not sing with Gru's spoken accent, the changes in his tone and rhythm choices reflect both mood and circumstance. His vocality therefore reinforces the evolution, and seeming regression in *Despicable Me 3*, of Gru's character. Indeed, Meledandri credits Williams' contribution through his songs 'Despicable Me' and 'Happy' as having a significant role "in establishing Gru's character and defining the tone for the movie [*Despicable Me 2*]".[24] Perhaps the significance of this is best offered by film executive, Tom MacDougall[25] who reportedly stated that in animation broadly: "You don't have a lot of time to have characters talk about their emotion... Songs are a way to fast-forward. Tonally, we can establish what a character is feeling".[26]

The discussion and analyses above identify the ways in which a singer-songwriter vocality may be used in animated film. It is evident that the linking of a particular sung vocality to character and plot heightens the potential for expression and aids in its effective communication. It serves a multiplicity of functions that provide insight into character traits, emotional states and narrative elements.

About the Authors

Dr Veronica Stewart is a singer, teacher and researcher, with a keen interest in the singing voice, songwriting and associated creative processes. Her PhD investigated the creativity of Australian singer-songwriters (2019). Veronica is also the director and principal voice teacher of the Sydney Voice Studio. She has worked with singers for over 15 years and now frequently works with contemporary singer-songwriters, fellow singing teachers and artists with a focus on sustainable vocal, musical and entrepreneurial creative practices.

Diane Hughes is an Associate Professor in Vocal Studies and Music at Macquarie University. Vocal health and wellbeing are a focus of her work; her research interests include singing contexts such as industries and recording, vocal artistry, emotion in song, the singer-songwriter and vocal pedagogy. She co-authored *The New Music Industries: Disruption and Discovery* (2016) with Evans, Morrow and Keith, published by Palgrave Macmillan. She is an advocate for music education and for multidisciplinary voice studies more broadly.

Notes

1. Vocalization refers to the embodied production of vocal sound.
2. Popular culture musics, or PCM (Hughes, 2010: 245), include pop, rock, soul or electronic styles of music. It also includes sub-genres and fusions of these styles. Without reference to the definition of "popular", the term is used in this chapter as a way of referring to musical style. The commerciality and consumption of songs created within these styles is not necessarily considered.
3. Vocal registers refer to different areas of the voice that correspond to specific anatomical/physiological configurations and vocal range.
4. Our research offers an analytical view of animated singer-songwriter vocality in ways that contribute to the development of Gru's characterization. The research therefore provides a distinct perspective that differs from other discussions on Gru's character development and/or traits (see Tabentane and Suprajitno, 2015; Ortega and Feagin, 2017: 25–27).
5. Meledandri's quotation is featured in "Bonus: Gru's Accent" [Additional DVD Content], in the 2010 DVD release of *Despicable Me* [Motion Picture], United States: Universal Pictures & Illumination Entertainment.
6. This information is from an article by Eric Eisenberg (2017), "How Steve Carell Found the Voice of Gru's Twin in *Despicable Me 3*", *Cinemablend*, https://www.cinemablend.com/news/1674980/how-steve-carell-found-the-voice-of-grus-twin-in-despicable-me-3 (accessed October 1, 2018).
7. Williams' creative process is discussed in an interview with Sheila Roberts (2013), "Pharrell Williams Talks DESPICABLE ME 2, What Inspired Him to Take the Music to a Happier Place, His Creative Process, and More", http://collider.com/pharrell-williams-despicable-me-2-interview/ (accessed December 5, 2018).
8. Williams also produces records and works with a range of artists.
9. Williams discusses his childhood exposure to music in an online interview with Jamaal Finkley (2010), "Pharrel Williams + Sound Check (Part 2)", *Black Tree TV*, https://www.youtube.com/watch?v=tZwDK2fh7-o (accessed January 14, 2014).
10. Ibid. Here, Williams extends his early exposure to different musics by discussing some of the musical sounds that he heard during his childhood.
11. Vocal ornamentation, also referred to as vocal riffs, vocal gymnastics, vocal licks or melisma, is often heard as a fast sequence of musical notes sung skillfully in succession. Contemporary melisma often features in pop, soul, gospel and R&B.
12. The filmic cue numbers in this section refer to the 2010 DVD release of *Despicable Me* [Motion Picture], United States: Universal Pictures & Illumination Entertainment.

13. Williams discussed this part of his creative process in an article by Brandon I. Brooks (2010), "Pharrell Williams Connects Music with Animation", *Los Angeles Sentinel*, https://lasentinel.net/pharrell-williams-connects-music-with-animation.html (accessed January 14, 2014).
14. The description is reported in an article by Josh Dickey (2013), "Pharrell and 'Despicable Me 2' – How a Song Can Change a Movie", *The Wrap Screening Series*, http://thewrap.com/thewrap-screening-series-pharrell-despicable-2-song-can-change-movie/ (accessed January 12, 2014).
15. Gru's negative childhood experiences are also referred to in an article about scoring for *Despicable Me* published in 2010, "Pharrell Williams Talks about Scoring 'Despicable Me'", *Theneptunes.org*, http://theneptunes.org/pharrell-williams-talks-about-scoring-despicable-me/#sthash.GEGKl1Yk.dpuf (accessed January 12, 2014).
16. This is a description of the villainous nature of Gru's characterization and was noted by Josh Dickey (2013), "Pharrell and 'Despicable Me 2' – How a Song Can Change a Movie", *The Wrap Screening Series*, http://thewrap.com/thewrap-screening-series-pharrell-despicable-2-song-can-change-movie/ (accessed January 12, 2014).
17. Meledandri's quotation is featured in an article by Josh Dickey (2013), "Pharrell and 'Despicable Me 2' – How a Song Can Change a Movie", *The Wrap Screening Series*, http://thewrap.com/thewrap-screening-series-pharrell-despicable-2-song-can-change-movie/ (accessed January 12, 2014).
18. In the *Despicable Me* series, Gru's minions are animated characters who act as his work assistants and house staff. These characters do not speak English, but a language of their own.
19. The filmic cue numbers in this section refer to the 2013 DVD release of *Despicable Me 2* [Motion Picture], United States: Universal Pictures & Illumination Entertainment.
20. The filmic cue numbers in this section refer to the 2017 release of *Despicable Me 3* [Motion Picture], United States: Universal Pictures & Illumination Entertainment. The film was viewed through the Kanopy on-demand streaming platform.
21. Williams includes this description in his discussion of his creative process in a 2013 interview and published by The Oral History of Hollywood, "DP/30: Pharrell Williams on his Music for *Despicable Me 2*", D/P30, http://www.youtube.com/watch?v=V9tJZ3d10sc (accessed January 14, 2014). However, Williams also reportedly describes the process as a "curated ride" in an article by Josh Dickey (2013), "Pharrell and 'Despicable Me 2' – How a Song Can Change a Movie", *The Wrap Screening Series*, http://thewrap.com/thewrap-screening-series-pharrell-despicable-2-song-can-change-movie/ (accessed January 12, 2014).
22. Williams' creative process is discussed in a 2013 interview and published by The Oral History of Hollywood, "DP/30: Pharrell Williams on his Music for *Despicable Me 2*", D/P30, http://www.youtube.com/watch?v=V9tJZ3d10sc (accessed January 14, 2014).
23. The quotation by Williams was located in an interview with David Greene (2013), "Pharrell Williams on Juxtaposition and Seeing Sounds", *NPR Radio*, http://www.npr.org/blogs/therecord/2013/12/31/258406317/pharrell-williams-on-juxtaposition-and-seeing-sounds (accessed January 12, 2014).
24. The quotation by Meledandri is from an article by Josh Dickey (2013), "Pharrell and 'Despicable Me 2' – How a Song Can Change a Movie", *The Wrap Screening Series*, http://thewrap.com/thewrap-screening-series-pharrell-despicable-2-song-can-change-movie/ (accessed January 12, 2014).

25. Tom MacDougall is the Senior Vice President of Music for Walt Disney Pictures and Pixar Animation as reported by Marc Graser (2013), "Disney ups Tom MacDougall to Senior VP of Music", https://variety.com/2013/film/news/disney-ups-tom-macdougall-to-senior-vp-of-music-1118064113/ (accessed July 30, 2019). While MacDougall is not connected to the *Despicable Me* series, his comments are included as they are relevant to the context of popular songwriting and vocality used for film.
26. This is discussed in an article by Marshall Heyman (2013), "Making the Cartoons Sing: A Minnesota Musician is the Go-to Composer for Animated Films", *Wall Street Journal Arts and Entertainment*, http://online.wsj.com/news/articles/SB10001424127887324323904578370821965519026 (accessed January 12, 2014).

References

Burnard, P. (2012) *Musical Creativities in Practice*. Oxford: Oxford University Press.
Chion, M. (1994) *Audio-Vision: Sound on Screen*. New York: Columbia University Press.
Coyle, R. (2004) "Pop Goes the Music Track: Scoring the Popular Song in the Contemporary Film Sound Track". *Metro Magazine* 140: 94–98.
Coyle, R. and J. Fitzgerald (2010) "Disney Does Broadway: Musical Storytelling in *The Little Mermaid* and *The Lion King*". In *Drawn to Sound: Animation Film Music and Sonicity*, edited by R. Coyle, 223–48. London: Equinox.
Feld, S., A. A. Fox, T. Porcello and D. Samuels (2004) "Vocal Anthropology: From the Music of Language to the Language of Song". In *A Companion to Linguistic Anthropology*, edited by A. Duranti, 321–45. Malden, MA: Blackwell.
Frith, S. (1998) *Performing Rites: Evaluating Popular Music*. Oxford: Oxford University Press.
Hughes, D. (2010) "Developing Vocal Artistry in Popular Culture Musics". In *Perspectives on Teaching Singing*, edited by S. Harrison, 244–58. Bowen Hills, QLD: Australian Academic Press.
Hughes, D. (2013) "An Encultured Identity: Individuality, Expressivity and the Singing-self". *Australian Voice* 15: 13–19.
Hughes, D. (2014). "Contemporary Vocal Artistry in Popular Culture Musics: Perceptions, Observations and Lived Experiences". In *Teaching Singing in the 21st Century,* Landscapes: The Arts, Aesthetics, and Education, 14, edited by S. Harrison and J. O'Bryan, 287–301. Dordrecht: Springer Netherlands.
Hughes, D. (2015) "Technologized and Autonomized Vocals in Contemporary Popular Musics". *Journal of Music, Technology and Education* 8/2: 163–82.
Hughes, D. and M. Evans (2018) "Communicating Artistic Integrity: Collaborative Production in Recording Processes". *Australian Voice* 19: 15–21.
Hughes, D., M. Evans, G. Morrow and S. Keith (2016) *The New Music Industries: Disruption and Discovery*. Cham, Switzerland: Palgrave Macmillan.
Meizel, K. (2011) "A Powerful Voice: Investigating Vocality and Identity". *Voice and Speech Review: A World of Voice* 7/1: 267–74.
Moore, A. F. (2001) *Rock: The Primary Text: Developing a Musicology of Rock*. Aldershot, UK: Ashgate.
Ortega, F. J. and J. R. Feagin (2017) "Framing: The Undying White Racial Frame". In *The Routledge Companion to Media and Race*, edited by C. P. Campbell, 19–30. London and New York: Routledge, Taylor & Francis Group.
Tabentane, R. and S. Suprajitno (2015) "Converted Villain: A Study on Gru's Changing Character Traits in *Despicable Me*." *Kata Kita Journal of Language, Literature, and Teaching* 3/1: 16–21,

http://katakita.petra.ac.id/index.php/sastra-inggris/article/view/3977 (accessed June, 7 2020).

Tongson, P. (2011) "Choral Vocality and Pop Fantasies of Collaboration". *Journal of Popular Music Studies* 23/2: 229–34.

Index

9 Muses of Star Empire 77
20 Feet from Stardom 124–6
200 Pounds Beauty 73, 82–6
'200 Years' 117

Abrahams, R. D. 57
acousmêtre 168
Adamson, L. 183
Adler, A. 6
After the Fox see Cassia Alla Volpe
'Afternoon Delight' 11
agency 7, 38, 40, 46–9, 94
Ago, Alessandro 24
Aguilera, Christina 139
Ahlert, Fred 183, 188
Akst, Harry 183, 188
Aladdin 157
Alba, Jessica 13
Alexander, Stevvi 125
Allen, Lily 115
Allen, R. 191
Allen, Tim 151–2
Allen, W. F. 59
Allers, Roger 153, 157
Alleyne, Ebony 13
Almost Famous 8
Altman, Rick 116–17
Altman, Robert 10, 112, 118
'Am I Blue' 188, 190
American Hustle 176–7, 180
American Idol see *Idol*
American Psycho 174–6, 180
Anchorman: The Legend of Ron Burgundy 11
Andersen, Hans Christian 38
Andersen, Janis F. 48
Andersen, Peter A. 48
Anderson, Dana 156
Anderson, Laurie Halse 46
'Angel' 202
animated vocality 198–200, **200**
Aniston, Jennifer 9
Antelyes, P. 190
Arcade Fire 142
Arie, India 122
articulation 6, 189

artless singing 4, 170–1
Ashman, Howard 199
At Long Last Love 3
Aune, R. Kelly 136
Auslander, Philip 27
Authentic Voice, The 40
authenticity 20, 27, 30, 35, 48, 77–8, 82, 84, 121, 127, 171
'Ave Maria' 143
Avengers, The 132

Bacharach, Burt 9
Bachman, Randy 11, 137
Bachman-Turner Overdrive 137
Bailey, Halle 49
Baillio, Maddie 9
Bainbridge, Caroline 34–5
Bakhtin, Mikhail 40–1
Balda, Kyle 196
Bale, Christian 174
Baliardo, Tonino 157
Bancroft, Tony 139
Bandirali, L. 52
Barratier, Christophe 17
Barrymore, Drew 119
Barthes, Roland 62, 80, 89–90, 170
Baskin, Richard 117
Battle: Los Angeles 142, 144
Baum, Vicki 46
Bauman, H. D. L. 40
Bayer, Samuel 140
Bayton, Mavis 48
Beam, Sam 13
Beaster-Jones, J. 93
Beatty, Ned 152
Beautiful Girls 8
Beauty and the Beast 157
Bedingfield, Natasha 11
Beethoven 173–4
Begin Again 120–1
Begley, Hillary 9
Belch, G. E. 135–6
Belch, M. A. 135–6
'Beneath Your Beautiful' 122
Bennett, Haley 118

Benson, Jodi 152
Berlin, I. 54
Berliner, T. 3
Berry, Christopher 54, 79
'Best Friend' 141
Best Movies About Singing, The 17
Beyoncé 47
Beyond the Lights 121–4
Bharathan, R. 91
Bhosle, Asha 93
Birds, The 177–8
Birdy 122
Birth of a Nation, The 44
Birtwhistle, A. 31
Biswas, Anil 93
Björk 20–23, 26–9, 32
Björkman, S. 23, 30, 34
Black, Jack 12
Black Hawk Down 142
"Black Vocality: Cultural Memory, Identities, and Practices of African-American Singing Styles" 67
'Blackbird' 122–3
Blakley, Ronee 116
Blue Velvet 171
Blunt, Emily 143
BoA 75
Bodyguard, The 11
Bogdanovich, Peter 3
'Bohemian Rhapsody' 8, 17
Bollywood 89
bonding, singing as *see* singing as bonding or healing
Borkowska, B. 136
Bowden, Darsie 40
Bowie, David 9
Boychoir 5–6
Bradshaw, P. 27
Brannon, Ash 150
Bray, Stephen 10
Breakfast at Tiffany's 138
Breaking the Waves 33
breath 6, 33, 62
breathy 12–13, 83, 93, 105, 115, 123, 154, 159, 172
breathing 6, 24, 33
Breakthrough 8
Bresson, R. 67
Brisebois, Danielle 11
Broeck, Sabine 68
Brooks, Brandon L. 210
Brophy, P. 185
Brown, Clarence 43

Brown, Nacio Herb 174
Brown, Vincent 207
Brune, George 139
Bryant, Joy 13
Buller, David B. 136
Buric, Zlatko 7
Burke, Tarana 128
Burnard, P. 198
Burnett, T Bone 12
Butler, Judith 67–8, 109
Byeong-Ki, Ahn 78

Cagle, R. L. 79
Cain, Christopher 39
Caley, M. 168
Campaign, The 137
Campion, Jane 43
'Can't Fight The Moonlight' 12
Cardullo, R. J. 116–17
Carell, Steve 201
Carmen 42
Carney, John 112
Carradine, Keith 116–17
Carter, Shawn 202
Cassia Alla Volpe 93
Cavarero, Adriana 64
Cera, Michael 11
Chan-wook, Park 77
Chaplin, Geraldine 116
Chapman, Topsy 56
character revelation, singing as *see* singing as character revelation, motivation and/or realization
Charles, Larry 140
Charles, Ray 125
Chaser, The 77
Chattopadhyay, A. 136
Chauhan, Sunidhi 90, 101, 105–6, *106*
chemistry, singing as manifestation of *see* singing as manifestation of chemistry or romance
cheonyeo gwishin 79
Chic 161
Chion, Michel 2, 35–6, 42, 58, 60, 90–1, 136–8, 150, 165, 168, 198
Cho, Y. 75
Choe, S. 84
Choi, J. 75, 82
Chopra, Priyanka 10
Chorus, The 17
Chung, A. Y. 41
Chung, S. 79
Citizen Kane 171

Clarke, Grant 183, 188
Clayton, Merry 124
Clements, Ron 38, 157, 184, 199
Clinton, Hillary 49
Clockwork Orange, A 173–4
Cloudy with a Chance of Meatballs 136
Coffin, Pierre 196
Cohan, S. 169
Cohen, Ethan 11
Cohen, Joel 11
Cohen, Sacha Baron 140
Coles, A. 114
Coll, F. 44
Collins, Phil 140, 143
'Colors of the Wind' 139
comedic components, singing as *see* singing as uplifting and comedic components
Con Air 136
Condon, Bill 47
Conrich, I. 77
Cook, Barry 139
Cooke, M. 183
Cooper, Bradley 11
Cooper, D. 2
Cooper, R. 114
Coppola, Sofia 9, 49
Coslow, Sam 183, 188
Coulthard, L. 172
Countdown 76
Courtship of Eddie's Father, The 141
Cowell, Simon 47
Coyle, R. 150, 153, 183, 185, 198–9, 204
Coyote Ugly 12
Cox, Ida 106
Crane, Frank 42
Creed, Linda 175
Criss, Anthony 207
Crocker, Matt 8
Croft, Romy Anna Madley 122
Cromarty, George 12
Crosland, Alan 1
Crow, Sheryl 124
Crowe, Cameron 8
Cruise, Tom 143
Crystals, The 125
Cukor, George 2
Cumberbatch, Benedict 54
Cummings, Burton 11
Cusack, Joan 151
Cusack, John 12
Cusic, D. 183
Cutler, Scott 50
'Cvalda' 25–6, 30–1, 32

'Daddy Won't You Please Come Home' 188–9
Dadlani, Vishal 89, 109
Dale, James Badge 61
Dance of the Wind 43
Danielsen, A. 30
Dano, Paul 54
Danoff, Bill 11
Dargis, M. 52
Dark Knight Rises, The 142
Datta, Sangeeta 92
David, Hal 9
Davies, Dave 41
Dawson, Roxann 8
De Sica, Vittorio 93
Deaville, J. 132, 140
Debdy, D. 52
Debussy 177
Del Rey, Lana 139
delivery *see* vocal delivery
DeMille, Cecil B. 42
Demme, Ted 8
Demy, Jacques 24
Deneuve, Catherine 24
'Despicable Me' (song) 203–4, *204*
Despicable Me 196, 200–1, 203–5
Despicable Me 2 196, 201, 205–6
Despicable Me 3 196, 201, 206–7
Destri, Jimmy 83
'Deux Arabesques' 177
DeVine, Adam 10
Dialogic Imagination, The 40–1
Diamond, Neil 8
Diaz, Cameron 9
Dibben, N. 22, 24, 26–7, 29, 32
Dickey, Josh 210
Dictator, The 140
Dietz, Howard 188
Diffrient, D. S. 124
Dirty Harry 178–80
Dixon, Mort 183, 188
Do Rozario 183
Doane, M. A. 150
Docter, Pete 156
Dogma 95 movement 20
Doherty, Thomas 133
Domanick, Andrea 114
Donen, Stanley 43, 171
Donner, Clive 138
'Don't Let Me Down' 122
'Don't Tell Me' 30
'Doowit' 203, 207
Dorsey, Tommy 192
Dorsey Brothers 184

Doubleday, V. 103
Douglas, Hal 136
Douglass, Frederick 55, 63, 69
Douglass, J. 185–6
'Dream Weaver' 161
Dreamgirls 47
Dresser, Louise 44
Driscoll, C. 44
Driver, Adam 12
Driver, Minnie 122
du Maurier, George 42
dubbing 2
Duffett, M. 28
Dumplin' 9
Dunbar, R. I. M. 7–8
Dwyer, R. 91
Dyer, Richard 1–2, 4, 22, 26, 60–1, 139, 150, 152, 170–1

'Each Coming Night' 13
Eastman, S. T. 134
Eastwood, Clint 178
Easy A 11
Ebb, Fred 53
Ebert 183
Eco, Umberto 102
Edge of Tomorrow 141–5
Edwards, Bernard 161
Edwards, Blake 138
Eisenberg, Eric 209
Ejiofor, Chiwetel 54
Elam, Katrina 45
Elfving-Hwang, J. 84
embodied 4, 8, 13, 27, 33, 44, 48, 80, 85–6, 105, 113, 126, 171, 197
Emma 12
enka ballads 74
Epstein, Stephen J. 77
Erivo, Cynthia 122
Eurich-Rascoe, Barbara L. 41
Evans, M. 197
Everyone Says I Love You 26
'Express Yourself' 10

Fain, Sammy 139
falsetto 11, 64, 186, 206
Fanning, Elle 6
Farrar, Geraldine 42
Fassbender, Michael 54, 61
Feld, S. A. 197
Felder, Warren 122
Felman, Shoshana 67–8
Femininity and Shame: Women, Men, and Giving Voice to the Feminine 41

Ferrell, Will 11
Feuer, Jane 25
film trailer 132–45
Finkley, Jamaal 209
Finney, Nikky 67
Finsterwalder, J. 134
Fischer, Lisa 124
Fisher, A. 114
Fisher, M. M. 59
Fitch, W. T. 5
Fitzgerald, J. 153, 165, 198–9
Flanagan, Mike 135
Fleeger, Jennifer 43, 50
Fletcher, Anne 9
Florence Foster Jenkins 6
Floyd, Samuel A., Jr 67
'Fly Before You Fall' 122
Franklin, Sidney 43
Frears, Stephen 5–6, 12
Freed, Arthur 174
'Freedom' 207
Freeman, Cheryl 184
Frith, S. 16, 20, 29, 34–5, 76, 170, 185, 198
Frizell, S. 49
Frock Rock 48
'Frontin'' 202
Fryer, P. 42
Fuhr, M. 76
'Fun, Fun, Fun' 203–5, *205*, 206–7
Furia, P. 3

Gabriel, Mike 139, 153
Gallaga, Peque 43
Gallup, G. G. Jr 136
Ganti, T. 89
Garfield, Allen 116
Garrett, Brad 118
Garrison, John P. 48
Gates, Henry Louis, Jr 52, 66, 68
Gates, J. Terry 48
Gaye, Marvin 12
Gazal 43
Gee, Keir Lamont 207
Gélinas-Chebat, C. 136
Genette, Gérard 133
Gettell, O. 49
Giagni, Riccardo 67
Giamatti, Paul 57
Gibson, Henry 116–17
Gibson, Laurieann 123–4
Gick, M. L. 177
Giedd, J. 5
Gilligan, Carol 46

Gipsy Kings 156–7
Girard, François 5
Girl of the Golden West, The 42
Girl of Yesterday, A 44
Gleiberman, O. 22–3
Glenn, Scott 116
Glover, Danny 122
Gluck, Will 11
Goldberg, Eric 139, 153
Golden, A. 112
Goldmark, D. 1, 153
Goodman, Benny 184
Goose Woman, The 43–5
Gorbman, C. 4, 169–71
Gordon, E. E. 114, 120
Gordon, Tina 10
Gorney, Jay 188
'Gospel Truth, The' 186–7
Goulet, Robert 157–8
Gounod 143
Graduate, The 138
Grahame, Gloria 46
Grammer, Kelsey 151
Grant, Hugh 118
Gray, D. E. 123
Gray, J. 134
'Greatest Love of All' 175
Green, Lacy 113
Greene, David 210
Greene, Fred 133–4
Greene, L. 171
Greene, Susaye 125
Grimley, D. M. 28
Grochowska, Agnieszka 6
Gross, S. A. 114, 126–7

Hackley, C. 47
'Hakuna Matata' **155**
Half Slave, Half Free 57
Halfyard, J. 184
Hall, Rebecca 7
Hall, Regina 10
Hallyu 74–5
Hammerstein, Oscar 24
Hammerstein, Oscar II 183, 188
Handel, George Frideric 18
Hangover, The 140, 143
Hanks, Tom 151, 157–8
Hanna-Osbourne, S. 114
Hansel & Gretel: Witch Hunters 49
Hanshaw, Annette 184–5, 192
'Happy' 203, 205–6, *207*
Harburg, E. Y. 188

Hark-Joon, Lee 77
Harnden, G. 185–6
Harris, Barbara 117
Harris, James III 83
Harrison, Nigel 12
Harrison, S. 6
Harron, Mary 174
Harry, Debbie 12, 83
Harry Potter and the Half Blood Prince 142
Hayward, P. 165
healing, singing as *see* singing as bonding or healing
health 78, 80, 113–14, 116, 122
Heart Full of Soul: An Inspirational Memoir about Finding Your Voice and Finding Your Way 41
Heavy, The 141
Helberg, Simon 6
Hepburn, Audrey 2, 169
Hercules 183–8
'Here We Are' 188
'He's a Rebel' 125
'He's Sure the Boy I Love' 125
Heyman, Marshall 211
Hicks, Taylor 41
Higginson, Thomas Wentworth 61
High Fidelity 12
Hill, Judith 124, 126
Hill, M. 153
Hills, Matt 141
'Hip to be Square' 175
Hitchcock, Alfred 169, 177
Hjejle, Iben 12
Ho-yang, Lee 78
Hogan, M. 47
Hogan, P. J. 9
Holliday, Billie 106
Holliday, R. 84
Honey 13
Hong-jin, Na 77
Hooper, Tom 2
Hounddog 39
Houston, Joel 8
Houston, Whitney 11, 176
How The West Was Sung: Music in the Westerns of John Ford 171–2
'How You Like Me Now' 141
Howard, K. 74–5
Howard, Ron 43
Hughes, D. 2, 4–5, 77, 112, 114, 125–6, 173, 196–7
Hugo, Chad 202
Hunger 67

Hunter, Evan 177
Hurley, John 172
Hurt Locker, The 142
Huston, Jack 176
Hutchinson, Ron 16
Hutton, Timothy 8
Hwan-kee, Min 77

'I am Light' 122
'I Just Don't Know What To Do With Myself' 9
'I Wanna Dance with Somebody' 10
'I Will Go Sailing No More' **155**, 159
'I Won't Say I'm In Love' 186–7
I.AM 77
identity 9, 38, 40–41, 45, 47–9, 56, 59, 62, 76–7, 79–80, 83, 85–6, 101–2, 173, 197
Idiots, The 20
Idol 46–7
'If I Didn't Have You' 156
'If You Want The Rainbow, You Must Have The Rain' 188
"Ikettes" 125
Ik-hwan, Choi 87
'I'm Easy' 116
'I'm Going Down' 11
'In the Air Tonight' 140, 143
'In the Musicals' 32
In the Space of a Song: The Uses of Son in Film 139
Incendies 142
Inside Llewyn Davis 11–12
interiority, singing as *see* singing as interiority
Iron & Wine *see* Beam, Sam
Isaac, Oscar 12
Isn't It Romantic 10
'It Don't Worry Me' 117
item number 89
'I've Got a Feelin' I'm Fallin'' 188, 191
'I've Seen it All' 31–2
Izardi, Elahe 17

Jackman, Hugh 2
Jackson, Janet 83
Jackson, Mick 11
Jackson, Peter 142
Jae-Yong, Kwak 82
Jagger, Mick 124
Jailhouse Rock 43
Jay-Z 143
Jazz Singer, The 1
Jean, Gloria 45
Jean-Jacques, India 123

Jin-seong, Choi 77
Jodorowsky, Adan 43
Johannsson, Johann 142, 144
Johansson, Scarlett 9
John, Elton 8
Johnson, B. 192
Johnston, Keith M. 133
Jolson, Al 1, 43
Jones, C. 2
Jonze, Spike 142
Jung, S. 86
'Just a Cloud Away' 203, 205–6

Kaif, Katrina 90, 94, *104*, 105
Kalinak, K. M. 171–2
Kampmeier, Deborah 39
Kander, John 53
Kanna's Big Success! 82
Keaton, Michael 152
Keighley, William 43
Kelly, Gene 171
Kelly, Machine Gun 122
Kenny, D. T. 177
Kerins, Mark 20, 31
Kernan, L. 132–3
Kerr, Deborah 2
Kesha 115
Khan, Farah 89, 101–2
Khan, Gus 188
Khosa, Rajan 43
Ki-hyeong, Park 78
Kim, C. N. 84
Kim, D. 74–6, 79
Kim, Gok 73
Kim, M. 41
Kim, Sun 73, 79
Kim, Yong-hwa 73
Kim, Youngmoo E. 135
King, Barry 22
King and I, The 2
Kingdom, The 142
Kinnear, Greg 13
Kiser, S. L. 75
Kloman, H. 118
Knight, Wayne 151
Knightley, Keira 120
'Know Your Way' 13
Koizumi, K. 157
Koo, J. 75
Kooijman, J. 175
Koplan, J. P. 41
Korean Wave *see* Hallyu
Koszarski, R. 16

Krieger, Henry 50
Kubrick, Stanley 173
Kumar, Akshay 93
Kyeong-hyeong, Kim 82

Labrinth 122
LaChanze 184
Lady Gaga 11
Lady's Morals, A 43
Laine, T. 175
Lal, M. 188
Lang, Eddie 184
Lang, Fritz 168–9
Lang, Walter 2
Lannin, S. 168
Larrieux, Amel 122
Larrieux, Laru 122
Lasseter, John 150, 152
Last Song, The 13
Launay, J. 7–8
Lawrence, Jack 139
Lawrence, Jennifer 176
Lawrence, Marc 112
Le Blanc, M. 77
'Le Freak' 161
Leap of Faith 186
Leeuwen, Theo Van 136
Legend, John 68
Legg, Andrew 68–9
Leigh-Post, K. 4
Lennear, Claudia 124
Les Choristes see Chorus, The
Les Misérables 2, 26
'Let's Get It On' 12
Levant, Oscar 183, 188
Levine, Adam 120
Levine, Lawrence W. 58
Lewis, Huey 175
Lewis, Terry 83
Li, Yipeng 135
Liebesman, Jonathan 142
Ligthelm, Salomon 8
Link, Harry 188
Lion King, The 153, 157
'Listen' 50
Lister, Michael 122
Little 10–11
Little Bit of Heaven, A 43, 45
Little Mermaid, The 38, 198–9
'Live and Let Die' 176–7, 180
Lord of the Rings: The Two Towers, The 142
Lost In Translation 9
Lost Voice, The 43–4
Love, Darlene 124–5

'Lover Come Back To Me' 188, 190–1
Lovett, Lyle 154, 157–8
Lynch, David 171

M 168–9
Maasø, A. 24, 30
Mabry, Lynn 125
Macdonald, Danielle 9
MacDougal, Tom 208
MacFarlane, Seth 141
Macksey, R. 133
Madonna 10, 30
Magnificent Ambersons, The 169
Majumdar, Ranjani 89, 91–3
Maleficent 49, 138–9, 142
Malkinson, A. 132, 140
Mamma Mia 26
Mancini, Henry 138
Manfredi, Isabella 114
Mangeshkar, Lata 93
Mann, Barry 125
Manuel, Peter 102, 109
'Maria' 83
Marich, R. 134
Marshall, Rob 49
Martin, Marsai 10
Marton, Andrew 43
Masser, Michael 175
Masters, Kim 3
Mattola, Greg 11
Maxwell, Bill 125–6
Mbatha-Raw, Gugu 121, 123–4
McCartney, Linda 176
McCartney, Paul 176
McCoy, S. 150
McDaid, Johnny 141–2, 144
McDowell, Malcolm 173
McGee, K. A. 106–7
McGrath, Douglas 12
McGregor, Ewan 12
McKay, Adam 11
McKim Garrison, L. 59
McLachlan, Sarah 160
McLean, A. 171
McLean, T. J. 153
McNally, David 12
McNamara, Sean 39
McQueen, Steve 52
'Mean To Me' 188, 190
Meizel, K. 5, 41, 47, 80, 197–8, 200
Meledandri, Chris 203
Men in Black 136
Menken, Alan 139, 183, 186–7, 199

Mercer, Johnny 138
Mercury, Freddy 8
Merrill, George 10
Mey, J. 41
Michael, R. 189
Michaels, L. 118
Michaelson, Todd 184
Midler, Bette 11, 124
Minaj, Nicki 122
Minghella, Max 5
Minkoff, Rob 153, 157
Mir, Ezra 89
mise en abyme 150, 157–61
Mishra 93
Mismatched Women: The Siren's Song through the Machine 43, 50
'Miss You Much' 83
'Moanin' Low' 188
Mole, Miff 184
'Molly Malone' 173
Monsters Inc. 156
'Moon River' 138
Moore, A. 186, 198
Morris, John 151
Mortgage on Life 46
Moulin Rouge 26
Movie Trailers 101 133–4
Moylan, W. 168
'Mrs. Robinson' 138
Mulan 139
Mulholland Drive 171
Mulligan, Carey 53, 61
Mulroney, Dermot 9
multivocality 40–1, 65
Mundy, J. 172
Murray, Bill 9
Musgrave, G. 114, 126–7
Music and Lyrics 118–20
musicality 6, 11, 62, 136, 197
Musker, John 38, 157, 184, 199
My Best Friend's Wedding 9
My Fair Lady 2, 169
'My Favourite Things' 24
My Sassy Girl 82
My Tutor Friend 82

narrative, singing as *see* singing as narrative
Nashville 10, 115–18
Neville, Morgan 112, 124–5
'New York, New York' 53, 61
Newman, Randy 150–1, 154–60
Nichols, Mike 138
Nichols, Red 184

Nicol, Lisa 17
Nightmare on Elm Street 141
Nijhawan, Amita 91
Nilsson, Harry 141
Nixon, Marni 2, 169
Nixon, R. 117
Nolan, Christopher 142
'Non lo dirò col labbro' 18
Northup, Solomon 52–7, 65–6
Nyong'o, Lupita 54

'Oceans (Where Feet May Fail)' 8
Odell, C. 77
Oduye, Adepero 56
Oh, I. 84
O'Hara, Maureen 46
Oja, Carol 191
'Old Macdonald Had a Farm' 178
Oldboy 77
Oliver, P. 190
Olmsted, Frederick Law 63
Olney, J. 68
'Once Upon a Dream' 139
'One Way Or Another' 12
Ong, W. J. 58
Ortega, V. R. 133
O'Steen, B. 150
Our Nation: A Korean Punk Rock Community 77

Paik, K. 152, 156–7, 160
Paley, Nina 184
Palmer, T. 189
Paltrow, Gwyneth 12
Park, G. 84
Park, S. H. 77
Park, S. U. 85
Parker, Nate 122
Parks, Gordon 57
'Part of Your World' 199
Pascale, L. M. 7
Paul, Riccha 106
Paulson, Sarah 54
Pavarotti, Luciano 43
Pawlowski, B. 136
Payne, A. 64
Pearce, E. 7–8
Pendavaris, Janice 124
performance, singing as *see* singing as performance
performance 1, 6, 9, 10–12, 20–3, 25, 27, 29–30, 33–4, 45, 56–9, 63–4, 74, 76, 78, 103, 119–21, 126, 140, 143, **163**, 168, 171–2, 174–80, 186, 191, 201, 206, 208

Pharrell *see* Williams, Pharrell
Phone 78
Piano, The 43
Picard, R. G. 135–6
Pickford, Mary 44
Pinto, J. 92
Pipher, Mary 46
Pipitone, R. N. 136
Pitney, Gene 125
Pitt, Brad 54
Pixar films 150
'Please Mr Kennedy' 12
Plum 6
Pocahontas 139, 153
'Pocketful of Sunshine' 11
Posner, Mike 122
Potter, Dennis 172
Powers, Ann 59–60
Presley, Elvis 43
'Prettiest Girls' 203–4
Preven, Anne 50
Price, Zachary 55
Prince-Bythewood, Gina 112, 122–3
production *see* vocal production
"Proxemics of the Mediated Voice" 24
Psycho 169
Pulp Fiction 172
Pure Country 2: The Gift 39, 45

Quinlivan, Davina 33

Radano, Ronald 64
Rae, Issa 11
"Raelettes" 125
Raise Your Voice 39
Ramsey, G. P., Jr 56, 68
range *see* vocal range
Ranger, Ralph 188
Ratzenberger, John 151
Rave iBand 106–7, *107*
Ravjiani, Shekhar 89
Ray, Nicholas 43, 46
Redmayne, Eddie 2
register *see* vocal register
'Reflection' 139
Reid, Whitelaw 63
Renaud, Chris 196
Reservoir Dogs 172
Resnicoff, M. 41
resonance *see* vocal resonance
Reviving Ophelia 46
Reyes, Angelita 52
Reyes, Lore 43

Reyes, Nicolas 157
Rich, Ruby 52
Rickles, Don 151
Riders in the Sky 160–1
Ridley, John 54
Rihanna 143
Rimes, LeAnn 12–13
Rischar, R. 185
'Risseldy Rosseldy' 177
Robbins, Jerome 2
Roberts, J. Storm 190
Roberts, Sheila 209
Robinson, Andy 178
Robinson, Julie Anne 13
Robinson-Martin, T. 186
Rodgers, Nile 161
Rodgers, Richard 24
Role of the Reader, The 102
'Roll Jordan Roll' 53, 56, 60–2
Rollini, Adrian 184
romance, singing as manifestation of *see* singing as manifestation of chemistry or romance
Romberg, Sigmund 183, 188
Rooh 107–8, *108*
Rose, Billy 183, 188
Rose, The 11
Ross, D. 183
"Row, row, row your boat" 179
Rubicam, Shannon 10
Ruffalo, Mark 120
Ruiz, Marcel 8
'Run Nigger Run' 53, 59
Rush, Ed 12
Rush, J. 115–16, 118
Russell, David O. 176
Russell, M. J. 74
Ryan, Roz 184
Rydell, Mark 11

Sacker, Herbert 122–3
Sandé, Emeli 122
Sanders, Rupert 49
'Save Me' 122
Scarborough, Dorothy 59
'Scarborough Fair' 138
'Scatterheart' 31
Schaffner, Franklin J. 43
Scharf, Z. 35
Schepelern, Peter 22, 24–5
Scherer, K. R. 1, 136
Schifrin, Lalo 178
Schlaug, G. 47–8

Schlesinger, Adam 120
Schwartz, Stephen 139
Schwarzbaum, L. 22–3
Secret Life of Walter Mitty, The 9–10
Sell, Mike 62–3
Sellers, C. 187
Selmasongs 28, 32
Serra, Carlo 65–6
Shada, A. L. 135–6
Shame 53, 61
Shanks, John 11
Shaw, Wallace 151
'Sheila Ki Jawani' 89–90, 93–110
'Shelter' 122
Shope, Bradley 107
Shore, Kalie 113
Siefert, M 91, 169
Siegel, Don 178
'Silent Worship' 12
Silver Linings Playbook 176
Silverman, David 156
Silverman, K. 43, 61, 90
Sim, Oliver David 122
Simon and Garfunkel 138
Simon, Paul 138
Simone, Nina 122–3
Simons, Seymour 188
Singin' In The Rain 43, 171
singing
    as bonding or healing 7–8
    as character revelation, motivation and/or realization 9–10
    as interiority 13
    as manifestation of chemistry or romance 9
    as narrative 5–7
    as performance 11–12
    as uplifting and comedic components 10–11
'Singin' in the Rain' 174
Singing Kid, The 43
Sita Sings the Blues 183–5, 188–91
Slave Songs of the United States 59
Sleeping Beauty 138–9
Smith, Bessie 106
Smith, Jacob 27–8
Smith, James Thomas 122
Smith, Jeff 137–8
Smith, K. 18
Smith, Murray 137, 142
Snow Patrol 144
Snow White and the Huntsman 49
Sogyumo Acacia Band's Story 77
Somervell, Arthur 12
Sonata 43
'Son of a Preacher Man' 172
Song Suffragettes 113–14
Sonn, C. 114
Sonnenschein, D. 168, 178
sound *see* vocal sound
Sound of Music, The 23–4
'Sound of Silence, The' 138
Sounds of Commerce: Marketing Popular Film Music, The 137
South by Southwest 113
'Space Oddity' 9
Speak 46
Spector, Phil 125
Spheeris, Penelope 8
Spice Girls 46
Splash 43
Springfield, Dusty 172
Springsteen, Bruce 124
Star is Born, A 11, 39
'Star Is Born, A' 186–7
Stevenson, J. 20–1, 24, 35
Stewart, Donald 40
Stewart, E. L. 68
Stiller, Ben 9
Stilwell, R. J. 143
Stolen Voice, The 43
Stone, Emma 11
story-within-a-story *see* mise en abyme
Stover, Cassandra 46
Strait, George 45
'Strange Things' **155**, 159
Straus, J. N. 44–5
Strauss-Schulson, Todd 10
Streep, Meryl 6
Stroman, S. 189
Stromberg, Robert 49, 138–9
Sundar, Pavitra 92–3
'Sun's Gone Dim, The' 142, 144
Sunshine on Leith 26
Superbad 11
Suzuki, Yumiko 82
'Sweet Caroline' 8
SXSW *see* South by Southwest

'Taking Care of Business' 137
Tangherlini, Timothy R. 77
Tanner, L. 183
Tarantino, Quentin 172–3
Taupin, Bernie 8
Taylor, Charles 41
Taylor, J. 1

Taylor, Richard 13
Tchaikovsky, Pyotor Ilyich 139
Teague, Jessica 27
technique *see* vocal technique
technology/ies 1, 3, 27, 29, 34, 43, 91, 116, 127, 184, 193, 196–7, **200**
Ted 141
Teen Spirit 6–7
Tees Maar Khan 89, 93
Testament of Dr Mabuse, The 169
Thèberge, Paul 32–3
'There's Something Special' 203, 207
'These Eyes' 11
'This Is Not the End' 144
Thomas, Vaneese 184
Thompson, Katrina Dionne 57–8
Thorpe, Richard 43
Thurman, Uma 172
Tillet, Salamishah 55
Timberlake, Justin 12
timbre 2, 93, 109, 118, 125, 144, 157, **200**
'Time's Up' 113–14
'Tiny Dancer' 8
Titze, I. R. 136
Tohoshinki 75
Tolomeo 18
Tomlin, Lily 117
tone *see* vocal tone
Tongson, P. 5, 197
Top of the Pops 76
Top 10 Unexpected Singing Moments in Non-Musical Movies 17
Tourneur, Maurice 42
Towbin, A. 183
Townsend, Ed 12
Toy Story 150–9
Toy Story 2 150–60
Toy Story 3 150–1, 156, 161
Toynbee, J. 185, 192
trailer *see* film trailer
Travers, P. 24
Travolta, John 172
Trilby 42, 44
Tripathi, S. 183
Trousdale, Gary 157
Turino, T. 104
Turk, Roy 183, 188, 192
Turner, Ike 125
Turner, Tina 125
Tyson, Mike 140, 143

Umbrellas of Cherbourg, The 24
'Unison' 22

Unkrich, Lee 150, 156–7
Unwin, M. M. 177

van den Eynde, J. 114
van Leeuwen, J. 152
Van Syckle, K. 67
Vande Kemp, Hendrika 41
Varney, Jim 151
Vasse, Denis 58
Ved-Maden 43
Vega, Táta 124
Veits, C. 133
Ventura, D. S. 43
Venuti, Joe 184
Vespertine 21–2, 32
Vitaphone 16
vocal cords or folds 4, 6
vocal
    delivery 5, 156, 160, 165, 198–9, 207
    dubbing *see* dubbing
    production 3–5, 90, 135, 140, 192
    range 80, 117, **202**, 206
    register 11, 22, 27, 32, 117, 137, **200**, 203, 206
    resonance 12
    sound 4–5, 13, 63, 65, 122, 206, 208
    technique 4, 6–7, 119
    tone 2, 6, 12–13, 27, 115, 154, 159–60, 188, **200**, 208
vocality 5, 52–3, 64–6, 80, 90, 158–61, 196–8
Voice in Cinema, The 90–1
Voice Thief, The 43
von Detten, Erik 152
von Trier, Lars 20–21, 25, 35
Von Trier's 100 Eyes 35

'Wake Up' 142
Wald, G. 186
Walker, Polly 12
Waller, Fats 188
Wang, DeLiang 135
Wansel, Andrew 122
Ward, A. R. 154
Ware, C. P. 59
Wareing, Garrett 6
Warren, Diane 12
Warren, Harry 188
Warwick, J. 75–6
Watson, Emily 33
'Way Back Into Love' 118, 120
Wayne's World 8
'We Belong Together' **164**

Weidman, A. 92–3, 104
Weil, Cynthia 125
Weinstock, Marc 132
Weith, John A. 59
Welch, Graham F. 6, 76, 79–80, 135
Welles, Gwen 10, 116
Welles, Orson 169, 171
Wellman, William A. 39
Wells, P. 154, 185
Werner, J. 192
West, Kanye 143
West Side Story 2
What Women Want 136
'What Wouldn't I Do For That Man' 188
What's New Pussycat? 138
'When She Loved Me' 160, **162**
Where the Wild Things Are 142
Whispering Corridors 78–9
Whispering Corridors 4: Voice 87
'White' 78
White: The Melody of the Curse 73, 77–82
White, Armond 52, 66
White, Graham 63–4
White, Lillias 184
White, Shane 63–4
Whitman, Brian 135
Whitfield, Norman 11
'Who's That Knockin' At My Door' 188–9
Wicked 49
Wide Open Sky: Little Voice, Big Dreams 17
Wiersma, B. A. 183
Wierzbicki, J. 177
Wiig, Kristen 9
Wilder, Matthew 139
Wilkins, Ronnie 172
Williams, Pharrell 196, 201–8, **202**

Williams, Vanessa 139
Wilson, David 68
Wilson, Rebel 10
Winkler, P. 156
Winter Sonata 75
Wirkola, Tommy 49
Wise, Kirk 157
Wise, Robert 2, 186
Wizard of Oz, The 49
Wolfe, C. 28
Wolfmother 143
Woman's Secret, A 43, 46
Wonder, Stevie 124–5
Woo, K. J. 85
Wood, G. 169
Wood, Natalie 2
Woodruff, Bille 13
'Woody's Roundup' **162, 163**
Woollen, Mark 134–5
Wright, Darlene *see* Love, Darlene
Wright, Gary 161

X Factor 47

Yassin, Bavi 43–4
Yates, David 142
Yes, Giorgio 43
'You've Got a Friend in Me' 150–60, **155, 163, 164**
yuhaengga 74

Zanes, Warren 125
Zarate, J. M. 4
Zarina 89
Zippel, David 139, 186

www.ingramcontent.com/pod-product-compliance
Lightning Source LLC
Chambersburg PA
CBHW051057230426
43667CB00013B/2333